SUFFLED HOW IT GUSH

A NORTH AMERICAN ANARCHIST IN THE BALKANS

by Shon

AUSTRIA
HUNGARY
Ljubljana
SLOVENIA
Zagreb
Trieste
CROATIA
Osijek
Subotica
Ada
Timisoara
Sisak
Vukovar
Sighisoara
Brasov
ROMANIA
Pula
Mrkonic
Grad
BOSNIA
AND
HERZEGOVINA
Belgrade
Bucare
Sarajevo
SERBIA
Mostar
ITALY
Adriatic
Sea
MONTE-
NEGRO
Pristina
Sofia
Kosovo
Prizren
BULGARIA
Kukes
Shkoder
Tetovo
Skopje
Kruje
MACEDONIA
rrhenian
Sea
Tirane
Ohrid
ALBANIA
Thessaloniki
Sarande
IE BALKANS
DOTTED LINE INDICATES
BORDER OF FORMER YUGOSLAVIA
GREECE
Aegean Sea
Ionian
Sea
Athens

MAP ILLUSTRATION ©2005 ANNEKA I.

Suffled How it Gush: A North American Anarchist in the Balkans

by Shon Meckfessel © 2009
This edition © 2009 AK Press (Oakland, Edinburgh, Baltimore)
Orignially published and printed by Eberhardt Press, 2006.
Special thanks to the folks at Eberhardt Press for their cooperation in the 2009 edition.

ISBN-13: 978-1-904859-85-7

Library of Congress Control Number: 2008927319

AK Press   AK Press
674-A 23rd Street   PO Box 12766
Oakland, CA 94612   Edinburgh, EH8 9YE
USA   Scotland
www.akpress.org   www.akuk.com
akpress@akpress.org   ak@akedin.demon.co.uk

The above addresses would be delighted to provide you with the latest AK Press distribution catalog, which features the several thousand books, pamphlets, zines, audio and video
products, and stylish apparel published and/or distributed by AK Press. Alternatively, visit
our web site for the complete catalog, latest news, and secure ordering. Visit us at www.
akpress.org *and* www.revolutionbythebook.akpress.org.

Printed in Canada on acid free, recycled paper with union labor.

Cover by John Yates (stealworks.com)

CONTENTS

Arad, Romania.

fOREWORD

REBECCA WEST, IN HER GARGANTUAN CLASSIC
Black Lamb and Grey Falcon,[1] observes that every Western
traveler in the Balkans eventually picks their favorite ethnic
group and proceeds to view the situation in sympathy with them.
She goes on to dismiss the Croats for their base Catholicism
and the Bosnian Muslims for betraying their racial heritage
of Eastern Orthodox Christianity. Like many Western authors
writing on the Balkans, West may have been swayed by domestic concerns. As a British diplomat writing on the eve of
WWII, her vision of the Serbs as an inherently heroic people
may have had something to do with her program to strengthen
Britain's ties to Serbia.

Hundreds of books about former Yugoslavia have been published in the US since the outbreak of the war in 1991. Most of
them fall under what the locals call "social porn," a nonfiction
thriller/horror genre full of tragedy and passionate appeal.
Consequently, the sagely explanations offered as background
to the drama tend to offer inherited wisdom, stock ideological
and historical packages taken off the shelves of imperial condescension and nationalist reductionism. As Maria Todorova
observes in *Imagining the Balkans*, the Carnegie Commission
chose to reprint their 1913 analysis on the causes of the original
Balkan Wars rather than commissioning a new study.[2] Didn't
anything important happen during those 80 intervening years,
or is imperial wisdom so eternal?

As in Rebecca West's case, these books seek to define and
defend state interests in the countries where they were written.
Former president Bill Clinton quotes Kaplan's *Balkan Ghosts* to
explain why intervening in such a primitive land of ancient

ethnic hatreds would be useless and dangerous.[3] Then suddenly Elie Wiesel is writing about the new Holocaust to explain why the Pentagon changed its mind.[4] Alongside valuable essays such as Ruth Seifert's in *Mass Rape: The War Against Women in Bosnia-Herzegovina*, one example by American academic Catharine MacKinnon presents a suspiciously imbalanced view, without bothering to cite any sources for her claim:

> The saturation of what was Yugoslavia with pornography upon the dissolution of communism—pornography that was largely controlled by Serbs, who had the power—has created a population of men prepared to experience sexual pleasure in torturing and killing women.[5]

The claim was not only silly, but dangerous: Croatian feminists warned that the nationalist government was citing MacKinnon's paper as justification of its own atrocities.

Nationalist politicians from the area and their mouthpieces monopolize the "native" voice, their rhetoric interpenetrated with US and Western European state discourses, Stjepan Meštrović, a Croatian-American professor from Texas, explains in his book *The Balkanization of the West* that the World was hesitant to accept Croatian war crimes only because "the stain of Nazism and German war guilt in general was thrown on Croatia... Why would postmodern intellectuals single out Croatia as the scapegoat for all of Europe's guilt about Nazism?"[6] Meštrović is published by Routledge Press, about as respectable as American publishing gets. Croatian author Slavenka Drakulic serves not even her own state, but the encroaching ones. In her series of popular *Vanity Fair* articles and pop-politics books, her only consistent position seems to be the pitiable backwardness of her own people, and their inherent desire for Western attention.

On the other end, American leftist author Michael Parenti gets through half of *To Kill A Nation* before hinting that any single Serb could be guilty of ill intent.[7] Kate Hudson, despite much research and analysis on the role of international financial institutions, still cannot resist stating, "the real danger lay with the development of an exclusive ethnic nationalism in Croatia."[8] She apparently dismisses the dinosauric Yugoslav army, increasingly under Milošević's influence and a great factor in Croatia's move towards defensive-minority politics, as an unreal danger. Diane Johnstone, in her *Fool's Crusade*,[9]

reproduces the Left's love affair with Serb nationalism as well. Apparently Milošević is now a moderate, while Tudjman (of Croatia) and Izetbegović (of Bosnia and Herzegovina) are extreme nationalists, whose equivalent in Serbia is Vojislav Šešelj. Šešelj, created by Milošević as a false opposition candidate to make himself look moderate, is different from the opportunist politicians of the other republics. The leader of one of the most infamous paramilitaries in the Croatia, Bosnia, and Kosov@ wars, he is known for pulling rusty forks and guns on his opponents in Parliament.[10]

I began this book with hopes of suggesting, by means of a very subjective travel journal, a different vantage point. Many conversations are paraphrased, anecdotes are not necessarily in chronological order, and characters—especially my travel companions—come and go without formality. Motifs may gather into themes, which may or may not gather into something like a position, depending on the reader. I focus on the opinions of anarchists because they let me sleep on their floors, because theirs is the only political tendency I found in the area that consistently rejects the false dichotomy of neoliberalism and nationalism, and because I, being one, often agree with them.

Thankfully, in the time since I started this book in what seemed a void between pro-Western neoliberalist/Croatian-Bosniak-nationalist and authoritarian-left/Serb-nationalist narratives, I found a few books outside this false dichotomy. Though written before the NATO bombing of Yugoslavia in 1999, *Burn This House*, an anthology of anti-nationalist writers from former

Yugoslavia,[11] is perhaps still the best introduction in English to recent events. Croatian exile Dubravka Ugresic's *The Culture of Lies* presents a brilliant, beautifully written analysis of the mechanisms of nationalism, particularly the political uses of victimhood.[12] Having read it in August, 2001, I felt like I'd already read the script during the events in the United States that began the following month. Maria Todorova's *Imagining the Balkans* is the quintessential analysis of imperial Western constructs of the Balkans as European Other, and the way these constructs have played in the exercise of imperial power. Catherine Samary's *Yugoslavia Dismembered* is an excellent, concise anti-nationalist summary of Yugoslavia's recent history.[13] *The Social Construction of Man, the State, and War* by Franke Wilmer examines how much of the conflict lies in dominant categories of political thought, not at all particular to the Balkans.[14]

Outside ex-Yugoslavia, most contemporary books about Albania, Bulgaria, and Romania were released immediately after the disintegration of the communist bloc in 1989. The books share a brash optimism—Jesus Jones' "Right Here, Right Now," and the Scorpions' "Winds of Change" were the obvious soundtrack—in the West's promise of freedom and prosperity to lands cursed by totalitarianism and protectionism. Undoubtedly, the popular revolutions which overthrew the old totalitarian regimes have won a measure of freedom. But fifteen years have shown, as in Russia and the rest of the former Soviet bloc, that such optimism was at best naive, especially in the economic sphere.

The authors cited above contend that what have often been posited as the causes of the wars and collapses have been more often their effects. All the countries of the Balkan peninsula—Albania, Bulgaria, Romania, the former Yugoslav states, even Greece—now share common curses and perhaps a common fate; shared struggle whispers rumors of hope for overcoming these effects, for new possibilities within the Balkans and within the world. This book, informally, is an attempt to demonstrate these shared crises and this shared culture—born from long resistance, the basis of such a possibility of shared struggle—while acknowledging differences.

I also could not help but write a book of the beauty of an area too renowned for ugliness.

s.m., San Francisco, June 2005

INTRODUCTION

Marko, who lived here in Sarajevo during the war, points out the tram window. This area has been hit over and over until the miles of apartment blocks are now splattered architectures of concrete crumbs and rebar. Dan and I gape. Marko beams at us. "Interesting, huh?" he laughs.

As the clock and the world map separated and normalized time and space, and thus tamed the world for the last great empire, so does any explanation of cultural difference now become a standardizing of human distance, of internal time, in the service of Empire. Understanding a foreign moment in one's own terms conquers its strangeness, invades it, incorporates it—the imperialist motive of social science. But changing oneself to resemble a foreignity, only accepting it by making oneself strange, different, and difficult for oneself to understand—this is the personalized struggle for interdependent plurality. As a Californian, I am colonized by the world's daydreams, and my liberation lies in dreaming them backwards. To travel or read not as a scientist but as a pervert, not to collect knowledge, but to get fucked-up, is to struggle for global survival: to bring the "Clash of Civilizations" inside yourself.[15]

In 1998, I stumbled into an anarchist cultural center called Attack! in Zagreb, Croatia. Dan and I were on our way to Vis, an island that once housed submarines for the Yugoslav army, on the recommendation of two Croatian friends we'd met backpacking through Prague. We had only intended to spend a single day in Zagreb, and only heard of the anarchist center when a record store employee spent an hour searching through old magazines for the address he thought we'd be interested in. When we walked in, everyone stared, then asked us questions in Croatian. They couldn't believe us when we said we were from the US. Six hours later, we still hadn't left our table.

Three months later, Dan and I were sitting in a bar in Timisoara, Romania, just across the border from Serbia, the last remaining republic still called Yugoslavia. A very drunk woman, an ethnic Serb from Timisoara, sat down at our table and began to angrily lecture us on how our government had brainwashed us. Less than a hundred miles away, NATO jets had just that day started saturating Yugoslavia with bombs. When the woman finally paused for a breath, I slammed my bottle down on the table and yelled: "The American State is my enemy too!" She paused, then roared for the bartender to bring me a beer.

One of her friends approached Dan with a knife and tried to cut off the patch from his shirt, which read, "No war between nations, no peace between classes." On the patch, a dove carried a molotov in its talons. Dan quickly took off his shirt and gave it to the man as a gift.

"*Balkanishche*!" The woman yelled. Balkanism.

I AM SITTING ON A HILL OVERLOOKING THE ATTACK! center with Oliver, the first friend I'd made there in 1999. We are drunk. I meant to come here for just one day, but since we've met, I've spent almost two years in the Balkans, over several trips, traveling with many different friends from here, from the States and elsewhere. I still haven't been to Bulgaria. *Balkanishche*. I admit to Oliver that I am writing a book, since my video documentary failed.

Oliver stares at me gravely. "If you're going to write a book about here, it has to be about madness."

IN 1986, IN THE NAME OF NATIONAL LIBERATION FROM the yoke of oppressive Yugoslav communist federalism, a group of Serbian intellectuals proclaimed the Serbian nation's right to self-determination in the Memorandum of the Serbian Academy of Sciences.[16] In the neighboring semi-autonomous province of Kosov@, masses of Serbs, who had once been a majority there, roared in approval, convinced that their perceived persecution by Albanians in the province would soon end. Slobodan Milošević soon made his career by promising them, "No one is going to beat you," although some claim he was talking to the nervous guards near the stage, and was accidentally too close to the microphone. The appeal of national liberation spread to the other republics within Yugoslavia, as they grew nervous with Milošević's domination of the country. Soon Croatian politicians unearthed a "thousand-year-old dream" of independence, and declared Croatia a state for Croats, and the Yugoslav army invaded Croatia to prevent it from breaking away.

Serbs within Croatia responded by breaking away from break-away Croatia itself, citing their right to national self-determination, and declared their own Krajina Republic. Alija Izetbegović—jailed in the 1980s for authoring a book that advocated turning Bosnia into an Islamic theocracy[17]—declared the independence of Bosnia and Herzegovina, and troops from both Serbia and Croatia invaded to aid their respective constituencies in their struggles for self-determination. Bosnian Muslims, suffering under a genocidal lack of guns and delineated identity, belatedly began to define themselves with the nationalistic name Bosniaks, in place of the previous official category of Muslims. Macedonia broke away peacefully, only to suffer international sanctions, since Greece was worried (on questionable grounds) that the Macedonians might seek to nationally liberate Greece's northern area, also known as Macedonia. Slovenia also broke away with little trouble. Now Slovenia prides itself on catching Asian and African immigrants on their way into the European Union, and shudders at its own vast numbers of refugees from the war, while showing little interest in incorporating anyone new into their liberated nation.

In Kosov@, the Albanians responded to the Serbs' claims of national liberation with their own. Protests in 1981 in Pristina for increased autonomy within Yugoslavia were met by fierce repression. The movement grew and adapted non-violent tactics of resistance to the state, forming an entire parallel economy in which they lived largely outside the Yugoslav state.[18] As they watched the war unfold in Bosnia, many Kosovars lost faith in non-violent economic methods, and the Kosova Liberation Army formed. After four years of increasing persecution by the Serbian military, the KLA—with the aid of one of the most intensive bombing campaigns in history, conducted by NATO—largely succeeded in liberating Kosov@ from Serbs, as well as Roma (Gypsies)[19] Jews, and other unwelcome nationalities. They then moved into neighboring Macedonia and are still attempting to liberate their national constituency there, while some local Macedonian militants respond in turn, reluctant to become a minority in a "greater Albania."

Though Albanian Kosovars hope that Kosov@ might join Albania, Albania itself fears the possibility. Kosovars are of the Gheg ethnicity, along with the northern half of Albania, while the capital is dominated by Tosks. An armed movement for Gheg national liberation would greatly threaten the Tosks, many of whom remember dislocation from the Florina area in what is now northern Greece.

In Romania, the majority nationality remembers with pride its liberation after WWI, when Transylvania was liberated from Hungary, and continues to persecute Hungarians there. Roma are regularly killed with impunity, their villages burned down with open approval of the State.

Besides some finger-wagging about exceptionally effective actions and some greedy readings of potential borders, this logic has been impatiently validated by the international forces' ideas of peace and reconciliation. The necessity of the nation-state as political unit was never questioned, of course; many shrugged, scientifically demonstrating that the region inevitably had to resolve its borders in such conflict. "Ancient ethnic hatreds" had to play themselves out sooner or later. In 1995, Western forces aided Croatia in driving hundreds of thousands of Serbs out of its borders, destroying tens of thousands of homes and bombing a column of refugees in the process. The same year, Clinton's diplomats divided Bosnia, where one in three marriages had been across ethnic lines, into a smattering of ethnic "cantons," on a video game screen no less.[20] The international messiahs responded with bombs and fences and called it peace.

The Serbs in Bosnia, meanwhile, were fighting all along for the most conservative of political claims: one state for their people, of unbroken continuous shape, which simply required a few transfers and removals of populations to aid in mapping their national liberation. Now that the facts are on the ground, and essentially accepted by the international community, how long will the people of the Serbian Republic in Bosnia continue to accept separation from Serbia? Following the same logic, will Croatia forget its claims to not-so-homogenous Herzegovina? Will Muslim leaders feel secure at the notion of a state made of discontinuous cantons? Does peace ultimately admit of such shortcuts?

Westerners decrying "primitive ancient ethnic conflicts" should remember that it is the application of their own "modern" political ideas—ethnic political community and the nation-state not the least among them—which has inspired these conflicts. Is ethnic conflict really foreign in the US, Western Europe, and their colonies, as these commentators smugly assume?

WHEN NATIONAL LIBERATION IS THE ONLY REALISTIC means to freedom, when universal compulsory mass murder is the only realistic means of self-determination, what do you do with reality? When poverty and servitude are the basis of rational economic order, how can a reasonable person be rational?

Absurdity as hope; life battling necessity.

> *"Anarchy is the mother of order."*
> —KROPOTKIN
>
> (Written on the walls of a few anarchist dwellings
> in southeastern Europe.)

"Tell Us Your Secret Name," Belgrade, Serbia.

TRIESTE, ITALY

*"When the real world is transformed into mere images,
mere images become real beings... The spectacle is not merely
a matter of images, nor even of images plus sounds. It is
whatever escapes people's activity, whatever eludes their practical
reconsideration and correction. It is the opposite of dialogue.
Wherever representation becomes independent,
the spectacle regenerates itself. ...
In a world that is really upside down,
the true is a moment of the false."*

—GUY DEBORD, *THE SOCIETY OF THE SPECTACLE*[21]

SCRAPING MY BODY ALONG THE PAVEMENT AFTER GETTING OFF ANOTHER ALL NIGHT BUS, I PASS A YOUNG MAN SITTING ON THE OLD MARBLE EDGE OF A CANAL. HIS FACE IS BURIED IN A JAPANESE GUIDEBOOK. A FEW BLOCKS LATER, THE IMAGE OF HIS T-SHIRT SURFACES IN MY MIND: A CHINTZY COMPUTERIZED MAP OF THE WORLD, BEHIND THE WORDS "LA SOCIÉTÉ DU SPECTACLE, GUY DEBORD, PARIS, 1967" IN VIDEO-GAME FONT. TEN BLOCKS PAST, I FORCE MYSELF TO TURN AROUND.

"That is the most amazing shirt I have ever seen in my entire life," I tell him. A bit startled, he charmingly nods. "Where did you get it?"

"Japan," he answers firmly.

"In a political bookstore or something?" I am stretching his English too far, clearly causing him anxiety. "Umm, do you like that book on your shirt?" I try slowly.

"Book?" he asks, strained.

At the same spot, ten blocks away, I again force myself to turn around. He looks up startled as I start, "This shirt I am wearing is made by my friend, an anarchist from Yugoslavia."

He smiles with difficulty, and asks, "Do you know a good hotel here?"

I tell him I also have just arrived, that maybe I will sleep outside. He stares as I take off my shirt. As I approach him, he shakes his head and tries to dissuade me. "But my shirt is too small for you." I hold out the shirt insistently. He takes off his shirt, tries on mine, spreads his shoulders in the morning sun. I put on my new shirt. We shake hands like old friends and wish each other good travel.

If the Spectacle is suddenly so boldly "independent" in its "reproduction," to the point of farce, perhaps it is a sign that this is where its power ends, that I've reached the outer edge of the Spectacular World.

STUMBLING OFF AN OVERNIGHT BUS, I'M NOT SURE WHERE to start. Where can I change money at 6 a.m.? How do you say "phone book" in Italian? Do the phones even take change, or do I need some card or something? What time does the Yugoslav embassy open? Does it even exist?

I hope I have better luck than I did when I called the Yugoslavian embassy in Ottawa from California. Every time I started to ask a question, the person on the other end of the line said "CLOSED!" and hung up on me. Serbia hadn't been giving visas to American tourists since the US bombed them.

Dan had once tried to enter Yugoslavia without a visa, just before the NATO bombing. He was turned back to Sofia, Bulgaria, to obtain a transit visa. In the window of the Yugoslavian embassy hung a sign, "Transit Visa All Countries $25 US." The officer gazed at him through the glass. "Transit visa, $40." Dan pointed at the sign and the officer repeated the demand blankly.

After handing over the money, Dan waited, one hour, two hours, for a response, and finally left for a walk. He met a Turkish family facing a similar situation. They shared lunch, then a snack. After a full eight hours with no sign of activity in the embassy, a teenager from the family left to explore the embassy. He returned and motioned for Dan to follow him. Over the fence behind the embassy, four officials were giggling contentedly in the shade, surrounded by a number of empty *rakija* whiskey bottles. Dan waved over the fence, the guards looked surprised, and in five minutes he and the Turkish family were on their way.

I decided to come to Trieste for a visa after a friend in Zagreb told me that Milošević was about to be overthrown, and that I could follow her home to Belgrade to watch the revolution up close. My friend from Belgrade told me that I could probably just bribe the border guards to gain entry, but since it was listed in US passports as forbidden to enter Serbia, I wasn't sure I wanted to break both countries' laws at once.

Finally, I have the right currency and the phone number to the embassy. I call repeatedly, until I am eventually put through to someone who speaks English.

"I would like a tourist visa to enter Yugoslavia."

"Yes, good, from which country is your passport?"

"From America."

"Impossible!" The phone disconnects. I call back to receive the same response. Now my phone card has expired.

Having an entire day to kill before a bus returns to Zagreb, I decide not to give in so easily. I write down the consulate's address from the phone book: 54 Strada del Friuli. After hours of searching, I decipher a bus map leading to the outskirts in which the street is located. Counting the stops, I get off and walk to Strada del Friuli. Several blocks up, the numbers approach the one I seek: 44, 46, 48. Around the corner, 50, 52, 56. I return, pace back and forth, but 54 does not appear. The numbers up the street tease 58, 60, 62. I pace again, and finally dive down a tiny alley on the other side of the street. The alley winds down a few hundred feet, opening into a mansion behind an iron gate, under a Yugoslav flag.

People chat in Serbian and swarm leisurely in front of the door, which I edge through. I stand in line for half an hour until I realize that everyone in front of me is purchasing bus tickets to Novi Sad or Belgrade, not official papers. Behind me, a few people shuffle in and out of an unmarked wooden door. I try the door, and find a large room filled with 50 or so people standing in a patient cloud around a scratchy little yellow window. After several minutes, the window slams open, and one person in the middle of the cloud jumps dutifully forward. A voice from behind the window chastises her, then the window slams shut. The woman returns, arms crossed, to her previous spot. Everyone stands quietly still. After another twenty minutes, the window again flies open, and one person across the room rushes forward to the front. The voice behind the window yells angrily, and he stands expressionless. After a few minutes, the window again slams shut. No numbers are counted, no forms signed, no money exchanged. After two hours of contemplating the Gogolian situation, I creep out of the building, back up the winding alley, defeated. I don't seek another visa for Yugoslavia for two years.

JUST AS EVENING FALLS AND I FIGURE I'M GOING TO SLEEP in the caves in the hills outside of town, I find the anarchist bookstore. Everyone is shuffling around busily preparing their newspaper, but they graciously pause long enough to shake my hand. Someone asks where I'm from, and I tell them that I'm writing a book on the Balkans. They continue working on the paper and chatting, but I make out a little of their Italian: "Do we have any reason to trust this guy? What if he's from the police, or the CIA?" "Well," says one, "if he is, he's not going to learn anything new, since they've already got all our houses bugged." Everyone chuckles and nods, and Ivan invites me to sleep at his house.

After they close the infoshop, Ivan takes me to his favorite bar. On the way, we pass graffiti that proclaims in proud, undefaced letters: *"Zona Fascista"* (Fascist Zone). Savo's bar sits farther down, under a back-lit sign that says "Bar." Ivan brings a round before I can object. His friend Francesca walks in the door and over to our table. I ask Ivan about his not-very-Italian name; his grandfather was Slovene, he says. Ivan doesn't speak much Slovenian, though he wants to learn. I admire the Moka coffee-maker button on his jacket, and notice he is sketching another on his napkin.

Francesca's perfect English is accented with Scottish and German tones; after traveling, she tells me, she even finds herself finishing

Italian sentences with English grammar. "I was half enjoying it, and half a bit in pain," she describes. After she calls home, her Sicilian accent returns for a few hours. She tells me of her job working in homes for those with mental disabilities, how she feels bad being paid because she is unsure whether she is any more sane than any of them. She speaks of her grandmother from Tunisia, and her grandfather who taught Esperanto. I think the Balkans must start somewhere around here.

I ask them about the graffiti we passed on the way here, and the poster of Mussolini I saw today in a magazine store. Are there still fascists in Italy? Ivan nods. "There are many of them in the country's ruling coalition, and in Trieste, they are a majority. They even have the same name and symbol as Mussolini's party. The politics of Berlusconi, the infamous current Prime Minister, certainly do not contradict the presence of fascism—his ownership and control of 90 percent of the media, his massive business interests worth billions, and his manipulation of the courts to change laws under which he is currently facing piles of corruption charges. It's back to Mussolini's Corporatism. The police, especially, have many ties with the fascist organizations. That was pretty obvious in the anti-G8 [Group of Eight] protests in Genoa, where they forced protesters to salute Il Duce's poster, among, well, other things."

"Have you had problems with the police?" I ask.

"A little over a year ago," Ivan starts, "we were having a meeting in the infoshop, and outside there was a loud sound, like a 'pop!' We walked out to see what it was. Police had already gathered down the street and had blocked off the area. We walked up and asked them what had happened, and they told us a small bomb had exploded and shattered the window of a storefront, an office of some agency regulating trade with eastern Europe. Francesca had shown up to drive us home after the meeting. As we approached her car, the police stopped us and told us to come to the station. We were wanted as suspects for the 'terrorist bombing.'

"After a week or two, we each received a notice in the mail that we were under investigation. Our phones started making a lot of funny crackling sounds. One night, after many months, I checked behind the light switches in my kitchen, since they were acting strangely, and I found a microphone behind one in the kitchen, then two more in my bedroom."

Francesca breaks in: "They were the cheap kind that gets power from house current, not the more expensive battery-operated kind. I was kind of offended we weren't worth the better model."

Ivan goes on. "They dropped everything just before we went to trial, since they had no evidence, and they don't have to admit using taps or bugs until they go to court. Probably they just wanted to intimidate us, to get us to stop our organizing."

Francesca says, "I'm not even an activist. I don't know what they want me to stop doing."

Later, back at Francesca's house, she pulls out a ziplock bag with the collection of microphones. They look like some Radio Shack kit assembled without the proper tools, far too much electrical tape and messy clumps of solder. You'd think the Italian police would have enough practice to get it right.

Ivan continues after ordering another round. A few weeks ago, he and his girlfriend, Gina, were arrested again. The police showed up at a late-night party, perhaps because the neighbors had complained, and ran everyone's IDs. When they saw Ivan and Gina's "criminal" records, they took them to the station. After they dumped out their bags, they picked up Ivan's swiss army knife with a sinister "Aha!" and seized it as incriminating evidence. Ivan expects the 500 euro fine for possession of an illegal knife, though the blade length was well within the legal limit. The cops then poured out Gina's bag, left, returned and fiddled with her items for some time, then with a sudden, "Ooh!" one of the police picked up two unwrapped chunks of hash, which Gina had never seen before. Even if she would be dumb enough to carry it around, who puts hash in their bag without wrapping it first? The police didn't charge them with anything. "Probably they were trying to provoke us into doing something they could arrest us for, or just to scare us again."

Francesca pauses. "After Genoa, they have the right to do anything. We told them we were going to complain, and they laughed, 'Go ahead, I'm sure they'll start an investigation!' Even after so many testimonies of abuses, medical records of smashed bones, so many photographs of pools of blood and videos of what the police were doing in Genoa, nothing's happened. The investigation hasn't led to a single conviction, of police or officials, despite a mass movement across the country asking for resignations. The Minister of Interior Policy, the official responsible for the police forces

in Genoa, is still in office."

Back at Ivan's house, listening to the Cramps, Ivan draws another Moka coffee maker on a napkin. I admire his collection of Moka coffee cooker drawings on the walls, the refrigerator, the stove, the bottom of a cast iron pan. "You know," he says after a pause, "my industrial design teacher saw that I always draw this, and he told me that the Futurists designed it." At least the Fascists can design a mean coffee cooker.

ON THE WAY TO SAVO'S BAR, I AM IMPRESSED WITH THE sophistication of the graffiti. Neatly painted slogans: *"Intifada! Palestina Libre! Basta Sionismo!"* dot the walls between spray-painted White Power signs. I tear down an anti-immigration poster as I pass, and a waiter at a cafe on the street shoots me a hard glare. Farther down the road, a clean-cut man with a professional haircut guffaws with friends out front of a closing cafe, flaming Celtic Cross on his ironed T-shirt. I wish the Kung Fu instructor that I hitched a ride from, his car covered in anti-fascist soccer stickers, was here.

Stepping in directly from the *Zona*, the variety of people in Savo's bar is almost blinding, not at all like a *Zona Fascista*. Savo pours me a drink before I can ask. I tell him where I'm traveling, and he proudly informs me that both his parents were Yugoslavs: one Slovenian, one Serbian, and his uncle is Palestinian. He interrupts a conversation at the end of the bar to introduce me. The younger guy is from Sarajevo, the older from a small town in Serbia. The most popular pizzeria in Trieste, Savo tells me, is actually owned and run by Serbs. "The real Triestino has a French father and Croatian mother, or whatever. Trieste was made up of Austrians, Italians, Slovenes, Croats, Greeks. You can still see by the churches. It was a port city, cosmopolitan. But now, you can see it's Italy."

After a few beers, I can't let Savo rush by without asking him another question about Trieste, about the Balkans, about Yugoslavian history. He shoos me off, insisting that his English isn't good enough to say what he means. But in between thumping down shot glasses along the bar, he can't resist answering. "You know, Louis Armstrong once went to the folk festival in Guča, Serbia. They tried to give him an award, but he handed it back, because he said they were much better trumpet players than he was!" Then Savo curses me again for distracting him and vows not to answer another question. I realize he is holding conversations up and down the bar in four languages.

Dino from Sarajevo, dressed in a leather jacket, has a broad, young face that ages as he speaks. As the first Clash album plays, Dino tells me about growing up in Sarajevo, about its great jazz scene. He usually plays classical guitar, but sometimes lapses into *sevdah*, traditional Turkish-influenced Bosnian soul music. Other times, he prefers blues and rock. His father is Bosniak, or Bosnian Muslim, and his mother is Serbian. During the war, they split up, and his mother took him and his brother to Serbia. He talks much of how special and dangerous Belgrade is, though it's been a few years since he was there. In Yugoslavia before the breakup, he says, "we were one culture, very Muslim and Bosnian," and speaks of how many different kinds of music there are in ex-Yugoslavia. Dino says, "Everywhere are good people, all my best friends are Serbians; but also there are nationalists." Dino is a poet who has no faith in the power of words alone in our era, and worships the admixture of words into music. He makes me promise to send him tapes of Robert Johnson and Lightnin' Hopkins, and we say good night.

Somebody screams outside the bar. I run out with several others to intervene and see one woman trying to smash another's head in with a chained-down bench. I stop when I realize the woman being attacked is hurling racist epithets, and the woman grabbing the bench is African. Savo pulls me back inside and draws down the metal store covering. He shakes his head; they're obviously regulars.

AGAIN SITTING AT SAVO'S, AS I TRY TO WRESTLE A DRUNK rock-singer off my shoulder, a kinetic woman in neo-flapper attire sitting on my other side asks me, in Italian, where I am from. When I tell her California, she grabs me, introduces herself as Christina, and goes on in elated Spanish. I smile apologetically and shrug, *"No comprendo, lo siento."* She can't believe that I don't understand. I try again, but only Serbian/Croatian words come out after a rusty Spanish beginning. She starts to yell, staring at me as Francesca translates: "How can you *not* speak Spanish? I was born in California. I lived there speaking only Spanish for years, in many different cities. Where do you live, where do you work, who are your friends, if you only speak English? Is it in the same California I grew up in?"

I try again to respond with the most basic words, but when I try to respond in Foreign Language, my mouth only knows Serbian/Croatian. Francesca explains to Christina that when she'd lived in Germany, she forgot how to speak anything but English, though her German had been good. When you are busy learning a new language, she says, you sometimes have to forget all the other ones. Christina resumes talking to her friends; I sip my beer.

The next night, I run into Christina again. Without the drunk rock-star on my shoulder, we have a better chance to speak. Between my faulty Serbo-Spanish and help from our friends, she tells me about growing up in California, as well as Colombia, before moving to Trieste. "I want to go back and visit my friends in Los Angeles, I haven't been there for years. Or to Colombia. I feel like I have three nationalities, I'm not sure if I'm supposed to be an Italian, an American, or a Colombian..."

"Pero, eso es muy dobro, no?" I answer in Serbo-Spanish, and everyone laughs. *"Muy dobro,"* she affirms.

DAN AND I LAY OUR BACKPACKS ON THE BUNK BED.
On the other side of the train compartment sit two youths.
One of them wears a black shirt emblazoned with a skull and
grenades, and the words "Death Death Death." They are star-
ing up at us. "Rome?" I ask as I sit down on the edge of the bed.
They nod. "Vacation?"

The one in the shirt shakes his head, "work." What work? I
gesticulate.

"*Carabineri!*" beating his chest and his friend's: the notorious
Italian conscript military/police force.

"Aha, is there a protest in Rome? You are going to work at a
protest?"

"No, this time no, just normal, patrol," he says. "But before—Yes!"
His eyes seem to look behind me, then return to mine. "BLACK
BLOC!" he yells, proudly, punching his fist into his palm with
each word.

Dan and I, dressed head to toe in black, anarchist buttons
on our bags, nod sternly—yes, we have heard of this infamous
Black Bloc.

"Pepsi?" he offers.

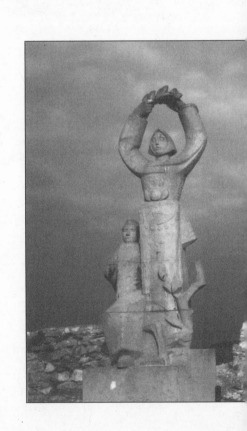

PART ONE:
EX-YUGOSLAVIA

Kale fortress in Skopje, Macedonia.

Tea in Ljubljana, Slovenia.

OLD MEN
WITHOUT SOCKS

IN MANY KITCHENS IN THE LAND THAT USED TO BE A COUNTRY CALLED YUGOSLAVIA, THE STOVES ARE NEITHER GAS NOR ELECTRIC. THEY ARE HALF GAS, HALF ELECTRIC. THEY HAVE NAMES LIKE "SLOBODNA" (FREEDOM), "RED STYLE," AND "MOJ PRIJATELJ TOM" (MY FRIEND TOM). THOUGH MASS PRODUCED IN THE MOST PROSPEROUS AND PEACEFUL TIME KNOWN FOR MANY GENERATIONS, SOME ANONYMOUS PROPHET OF PESSIMISM GUESSED THAT SOMETIME IN THE LIFE OF THE APPLIANCES HE WAS DESIGNING, THERE WOULD BE SHORTAGES AGAIN, EITHER OF GAS OR OF ELECTRICITY. THE CONSUMER COMMUNIST PUBLIC AGREED, AND THE DESIGN WAS A FAVORITE IN THE STATE-RUN SHOPPING CENTERS.

The designer and the public were right, and the stoves' design have since been convenient for wartime survival. But the gas and electric question, if answered, only raises more questions. Did the stoves convince their owners to put them to use? And who else created the conditions for their design? Who holds the gas and electric patent? Can pessimistic stoves precipitate war?

BEFORE THE GENOA PROTESTS, THE ONLY TIME ERIK HAD been in a crowd was at soccer matches. He doesn't say, but I assume he was a hooligan. The professor who brought him marched with Tutti Bianche, the Italian group who pad themselves like huge marshmallows for dynamic self-defense. Soon, though, Erik started following the black bloc. Twenty minutes before Carlo Giuliani was shot in the head and run over twice by a *carabinieri* van, Erik took a tear gas canister to the head at the same location and left to get stitches. "Did you notice in the pictures," Erik asks me, "how Giuliani was wearing a white shirt when he was killed, but after the cops surrounded him he was wearing all black?"

That protest changed Erik's life. Now he is a staff reporter for Ljubljana's long-lived *Radio Student*, and for the legendary student magazine *Mladina,* which helped touch off the Yugoslav crisis with its frank criticism of the Yugoslav army. Erik is working on a book about the global anti-capitalist movement. He expounds on the global crisis of capitalism like a sports reporter, and he knows his team stats. Today his subject is the struggle in Slovenia over its place in the global Empire. My pencil tries to keep up.

"What is happening now in the world, I just can't believe. I mean, I guess I can, it happened here, in Croatia, Bosnia, Kosovo, Serbia." He shakes his head. "You know, my three best friends in high school were a Croat, a Muslim, and a Serb. It's a cliche about how deeply diverse Yugoslavia was, but it was really like that. But people here are getting so racist now, sometimes the very same people who were married to or had best friends of different ethnicities. Sixty percent of people polled in Slovenia say they 'have prejudices,' but say they're not racist. Out of 2,000 Bosnian refugees here, the government's only granted 44 of them refugee status. Many of them are still living in barracks, after ten years. Ten thousand people who used to be citizens of the Republic of Slovenia in Yugoslavia, who were even born here, are stateless now, *sans papier*. They're denied citizenship just because they're not ethnic Slovenes.

"When I grew up, we were the same people. These 'European' Slovenes are really snobs, trying to distance themselves from everything Balkan. Most young people can't even speak Serbo-Croatian anymore. I mean, look at what's happening with minorities in this 'Europe'—I guess Slovenia is just trying to catch up.

"Even if Slovenia gets into the European Union, we'll be second class citizens. A Slovenian peasant is promised one-fifth the subsidies that a French peasant gets, and we'll have four representatives in the EU Parliament, out of 672. And the worst is this whole move for Slovenia to join NATO. They don't even have a reason. The government is like, 'Slovenia must join NATO, because if Slovenia doesn't join NATO, it would be like if Slovenia wasn't in NATO.' Of course, there's always: 'Slovenia could be a target for terrorists, so we have to be on the winning side.' There's not even promise of EU membership if we join—not that I think either is a good idea.[22] It's just the sheer ego of the politicians, they want to feel important.

"NATO is nothing but an institutionalized arms dealer. Lockheed Martin already has contracts with prospective NATO members. And it also has people sitting on NATO's expansion board, which decides who gets in! Slovenia has already bought up a bunch of Hummers, which are good for tundra and desert, but not really the Alps. I mean, did you notice at the Slovenian Ministry of Defense, there's a US flag right underneath the Slovenian one?!

"But have you heard about the anti-NATO campaign here?" he continues excitedly. "It's only been going seven months, but once they put up 170 banners on freeway overpasses and such, each banner five meters (15 feet) long. Another time they put up 5,000 posters! My favorite said: 'The only difference between NATO and terrorism is that NATO uses its planes more often.' Another poster pointed out how many new houses each Slovenian could have, for the cost of NATO membership. They have put up posters on military jeeps in the Department of Defense, and on statues of Slovenian heroes. Before the editor of the *NATO Review*, Christopher Bennet, came to speak, they dropped three massive banners at the University of Social Sciences, and graf-fitied 30 slogans. They're an anonymous group, but, you know, that's what my sources say."

Metelkova, a former army base bulldozed by city and reclaimed by squatters, Ljubljana, Slovenia.

"Is it making any difference?" I ask.

"Some media coverage has been on their side, so I think it's working. At first polls showed that the public strongly supported joining NATO, but now some polls show more than half are opposed to membership. Slovenia is the only candidate for membership with a strong protest movement. Even if the government ends up joining, it's a start for the future.

"You've heard about the struggles here to defend the squats—the empty buildings occupied as social centers? Metelkova, where squatting artists and anarchists took over the Yugoslav army's base when they pulled out, is still going, but Molotov is in trouble. It's amazing, letters come in from all over the world to stop an eviction in Ljubljana.[23] For two hours, this is the center of world struggle, and as soon as you look it moves. Have you read Negri and Hardt's book *Empire*?[24] It's really like that, the Empire doesn't have a center: financial transactions between the EU, the US, and Japan are in the billions. Where's the center of that? So the resistance has to be the same way, from Seattle to Prague to Genoa to Buenos Aires. As the revolution comes, Empire faces Pascal's theory of infinity—the center is everywhere, but there is no perimeter."

TEA AND I ARE WALKING BACK TO THE DORMS LATE ONE night when a bearded, sober old man passing on the street turns to us and says: "I found everything, I even found 5,000 Tolars, but I couldn't find my socks. Not even in the closet." We wait, curious. "I have a friend," he continues, "he was going everywhere this one night, a very crazy night, and anyway he ended up going back home without his socks. 'Where the hell did you leave your socks?' his wife asked him, but he didn't know. So she divorced him." He waits to see if we understand. Tea thanks him and the man starts to walk away, then stops and says, "Oh, I forgot to tell you the point. I know where my socks are, in a drawer next to my wife, but if I woke her up I wouldn't be here going to the bar to meet my friend."

Tea tells me, "Slovenia is in the Balkans so long as it insists that it's not." Perhaps it's good that the EU has now swallowed Slovenia, and is trying to incorporate the rest of the Balkans. The old man without socks alone cannot destroy capitalist society, but I cannot imagine 70 million of such old men without socks becoming rationalized in the manner required to sustain it. Max Weber claimed that capitalism would have never caught on without the strange secularized-Protestant drive to accumulate wealth without enjoying it.[25] Will the Good Ship Capitalism, cobbled together in salty Britain, run upon its final reefs in the craggy Balkans?

"When people from the South see themselves as people of the North, the first thing they ban is a relaxed and casual street encounter. Somehow North is equated with restriction in their minds," I later read in Tea's zine about her travels in Italy. In Rome she writes, "I laughed too, thinking it's funny how places only become cozy and yours once you leave them—be it for the exile of your heart or of your wallet. To be unnecessary but not redundant is an interesting position. The Pakistani street vendors of sunglasses in sunny weather, and umbrellas in rain, are in that position."

> *"Terror by remembering is a parallel process to terror by forgetting. Both processes have the function of building a new state, a new truth."*
> —DUBRAVKA UGRESIC[26]

IBRAHIM PICKS UP DALIA AND ME AS WE HITCHHIKE. HE doesn't speak English. "Do you speak Croatian?" I ask.

"Yes, I speak Bosnian," he replies. He is driving back home to Germany. When I realize how jumpy he is, I want to get out, but Dalia has already dozed off in the back.

"Tony Blair is Bush's dog," he says to start the conversation, "but Bin Laden is also Bush's dog." We each relax a little bit. "September 11th was such a stupid waste of lives," he says. "How have things changed?" I tell him that despite the panicked fear and outbreak of nationalism, perhaps now Americans are feeling vulnerable, more like a part of the world, and maybe will be slower to start so many wars.

"Why does America give Israel so much money to kill Palestinians?" he inquires.

I call Sharon the Milošević of Israel and Palestine, aggravating conflict to make his own career.

"Sharon is worse than Milošević, he's killed more people," Ibrahim asserts. I decide not to correct him.

I tell Ibrahim about hopes for the protest movement, that within America many people, especially young people, are trying to change things. "Were you at the protests in Seattle?" he asks. I tell him that protests and other acts of resistance are continuing, but that the government has been cracking down, and many people are maybe becoming too scared to act.

"The whole world is scared," he answers.

I ask Ibrahim if he thinks the Bosnian army could have ended the war without the NATO intervention. Would there even have been a war without the UN arms embargo, if the Yugoslav army hadn't had such a tempting advantage to start with?

He pauses, and delivers his verdict. "It's all about money."

He lets us out with a polite handshake in Ljubljana and speeds off. In a couple of hours of conversation, he hasn't mentioned what his job is, if he has a family, where in Germany he lives, or where he comes from. I consider the millions of hours of official mourning over September 11, how every suicide bombing in Tel Aviv is a national tragedy, how the questionable story of a Serb peasant with a bottle up his ass sparked the Serbian fury in Kosov@. Ibrahim told me how sad he was about the Palestinians, the Iraqis, about the Congolese, the Kurds, about September 11, but he forgot to mention the 200,000 killed in Bosnia, or the two million refugees,[27] including, probably, himself.

"What did you guys talk about?" asks Dalia.

NATASHA ORDERS ANOTHER ROUND FOR US IN NOSTALGIA, a bar nestled alongside the river. Tito, the benevolent dictator of old communist Yugoslavia, strikes dashing poses between posters of partisan war movies and slick Yugo-rock bands. "There used to be just one kind of flips." She lifts the bag of peanut-crusted cheeto-snacks from the table. "Now there's all these different kinds of flips, like Agri-Snacks, and Grizzlies, made in each new independent country or even imported from Germany or Austria, but none of them are as good as old Yugoslavia's Smoki Flips." I tell Natasha that the other day in Croatia, I heard a lady say, "Give me a bag of Smoki Flips,"

Bowling Salt X-treme flavored chips, Slovenia.

though Smokis haven't been available there since Croatia seceded in 1991. Yugoslavia, though unstable economically, was certainly rich in flips. Yugoslavs, those who refuse to adopt an ethnicity, may not have an official identity or a state anymore, but at least they still have their own snack.

I CATCH A RIDE HITCHHIKING IN SLOVENIA WITH A GUITARIST of Slovenia's, and perhaps Yugoslavia's, most famous band, "Laibach." During the 80's, Laibach was part of an avant-guard art movement named Neue Slovenische Kunst, New Slovenian Art, provocatively titled (like the band's name) in German rather than Slovenian. During Communism, espousing Satanism, as many metal bands have done in the West, would have seemed a quirky anachronism; Fascism, instead, was the ultimate taboo. Laibach rode the line between ironic kitsch and horror by unapologetically conjuring these images from Yugoslavia's ugly past.

The group once covered the entirety of the Beatles' "Let It Be," such as it might have sounded had Hitler Youth made it with synthesizers, and later gave the same treatment to "Jesus Christ Superstar." They recorded dark-dance albums with names like "NATO" and "Kapital." In Yugoslavia every year, athletic youth would run a marathon relay carrying a torch across all of Yugoslavia to commemorate Tito's birthday, and each year, artists would submit posters to represent the event. Laibach one year submitted an image, which won the contest, only to then reveal that it had been taken from a Nazi sporting design. In another scandal, one of the members penned an essay proclaiming love of the State as a progressive sublimation of love of one's own father. In the time after Tito's death when the Yugoslav state still attempted to vouchsafe the lives of its citizens like a Great Father, Laibach poetically revealed the commonalities of totalitarian statehood, without ever quite making their real allegiances clear.

Since the war, fascism has lost its taboo for many, to the extent of becoming somewhat mainstream. Laibach has failed to change its gimmick, and as a result draws a large number of Nazi Skinheads to its shows in the area, who may or may not be in on the kitschy joke. I am, regardless, happy for the ride, and my driver seems a likeable enough fellow. He is curious to meet an American as fascinated with former Yugoslavia as he was, and we compare impressions on the areas he has traveled with the band. Finally, he asks if I have ever been to Kosovo, and I tell him I haven't yet, but plan to soon. He pauses, choosing his words carefully. "Kosovo, you will see, demands a... can I say, a very strong sense of humor."

FRANCISCO TELLS ME THAT IN **1991,** MANY YUGOSLAV ARMY troops were told that Italy had invaded Slovenia, and that they were going to liberate Slovenia from Italy, not to attack it for breaking from Yugoslavia.

"Ironically, the first casualty of the war, which at the time was constructed as Belgrade-as-FRY using the force of the 'Yugoslav' state to put down an illegal and militarized succession in Slovenia, was a Slovenian soldier in a FRY [Federal Republic of Yugoslavia] uniform flying an FRY helicopter with supplies into the FRY bases in Slovenia. He was shot by a Slovenian soldier fighting for the 'independence' of Slovenia, to which his government claimed it was legally entitled."[28]

"IN AMERICA," ASKS SASHA, "DOES EVERYBODY REALLY have their own number, what do you call it, a 'Social Security' number? Is it true that people keep it a secret from each other? If you find out someone else's number, can you harm them?" Sasha, Tea, and I are walking along, looking for a place to sit and enjoy our beer in the autumn air. Tea motions to a statue across from the train station.

Sasha tells me about her generation's confusion: growing up under Socialism with ideas of brotherhood and unity among all peoples, the equality of humanity, going on camping trips and road-building retreats with the Young Pioneers. Then, just as Sasha hit her teens, everything shifted. This had all been a lie, said the new rhetoric. The different nationalities had never been friends. She visited Bleiburg, where Tito's partisans killed perhaps 20,000 people just after the Second World War, both local fascist forces as well as many of their innocent hostages. Suddenly, Tito had been a criminal, the idealism had been a cover for oppression and exploitation. Sasha says her generation is schizophrenic. Everything turned on its head just as they were coming of age, so they don't know if there even is a right-way-up.

"Oh, you speakee English?!" Someone shouts from behind us. We turn around, and two young men leer at us. They dangle bottles of "Smile," a light beer with a happy-face sun on the label.

"Pa, možemo da pričamo srpski, ako hoćes, bre," we can speak Serbian if you'd rather, Tea growls. We turn back around and resume our conversation.

One of the guys rubs his hand across Tea's short hair and sneers, "Are you a boy or a girl?" She pulls away and shoos him off. They sit down behind us. "What are you doing tonight?" the same guy yells.

I try to diffuse the situation by chatting with them. "Just having a beer, man," I say.

"Chee jaw chaw jaw chaw!" he shouts an inch from my face, suddenly next to me. The "Smile" bottle is stiff in his fist. I turn away and try to keep my cool.

"Maybe we should go?" Sasha suggests. The kid's finger is wrapped through a hole in my shirt; he holds firm and stands up with me, eyes hard. "You deserve a bullet in your fucking head," he mumbles.

"Čekaj," hold on, I manage in Serbian. He looks confused.

"Čekaj what?" He looks indecisive. I watch his hand, imagining it going for a knife, but he just pulls up his pants.

"Hey man, I'm hungry," I shrug at him. "We're going to get dinner. See you later." He looks at me hard, tipsy. "All right? We're getting dinner. Have a good night." We walk away.

A few blocks away, I ask, "So, what was up with those guys?"

"Fucking assholes," says Tea.

"No, I know, but I mean, were they Serb refugees or something, maybe mad about the US bombing?"

"No, they were definitely Slovenes," says Sasha.

It takes me a minute. "But, then why did you offer to speak in Serbian? Weren't they speaking Serbian?"

"They were trying, but they don't know it, mostly they were speaking Slovenian." My forehead wrinkles questioningly, until she continues. "There's a lot of kids that don't feel like being Slovene is manly enough, so they act like tough Serbs. Well, what they think Serbs are like. We call them 'čapci.'"

I consider her words. "I guess in America, most gangster rap fans are suburban white kids, some of them dress and talk like they think Black people dress and talk. But I didn't meet Black people who acted like that when I lived in Oakland, or in Philadelphia, or Brooklyn, the people the white kids think they're imitating."

Tea and Sasha agree, yeah, something like that. We stop at a souvlaki restaurant.

PUMPING MY LEGS AS MY BIKE EDGES UP THE HILL, I WONDER how long it takes for a body to decide to digest one's own muscle mass. Slovenia's reputation for mountains is apparently not an overstatement, and today, my third day biking alone across a country that's not as small as it looks on the map, I forgot to stop for lunch. As I switch on the LED headlight on my heaving handlebars, it doesn't seem like I'll be eating any day soon. This may not be the most devout of Catholic countries, but no Slovenian villager is going to open their store or restaurant on a Sunday night. More seriously, I also forgot to fill up my water bottle.

Just as I've about decided to give in to panic, lights stream out from between trees ahead of me. I pull my bike up into a village and park alongside a wide field. Middle-school kids in team shirts lunge for the soccer ball while the rest of the village sits lazy on the bleachers. I grab my water bottle and walk up to the first group on the edge of the bleachers. "*Voda?*" I ask weakly.

After a moment of disbelief, my new hosts hurry to sit me down on an empty spot. A plastic cup of water is shoved in my hand, and within moments, a giant plate packed with fresh baked bread, under a greasy pile of ribs from the day's spit pig. In another moment, miraculously, a tall can of Slovenian "Union" beer is placed next to my knee. None of my neighbors in the stands speak English, but they look over at me every few minutes and make sure I am healthy before looking back at the game.

After thanking my new friends as much as possible with no common language, I start towards my bike, explaining with my hands that I want to get in more miles that night before setting up camp. One younger man makes me promise to stay until his return, and comes back with a t-shirt advertising the nearest bicycle shop. I try not to question if I, huffing along on my disposable bike, am really the best sponsor choice. Before letting me leave, I am then passed along to a teenager who urges me into the village store and insists that I take several bottles of water and as many snacks as my pack can handle.

Back on the empty moonlit mountain road, my mind goes back to a moment in the anti-WTO protests in Seattle in November, 1999. My Slovenian friend and I step in from the procession on the street to gaze between the shards of a broken Starbucks window. Suddenly, she jumps back—"There's someone in there! Let's go!"

I start, then smile. "What are they gonna do, call the cops?" We peer around at the shelves of yuppie coffee gadgets, satisfied, and walk away.

Later that night, watching the coverage on national news in a neighborhood bar, she shakes her head. "You Americans are really insane about property, it's like your religion. Windows get broken all the time at protests in Europe, but it's not, like, news." Her sentence pauses as she sips her Amber. "But here, it's like it's a higher priority than people's lives."

Lit by stars and a nearly full moon, the road winds up to a mild summit. On the left, a house sits shrouded with scaffolding under tattered canvas. Construction seems to have left off for the season, if not the year. Scouting the shell, I find an unlocked door into the basement. Furniture sits napping, tucked in to the dusty corners. I also forgot to pack a tent. The dusty basement floor makes a fine mattress under my sleeping bag, and I drift off dreaming of pavement and potholes.

"Oh!" I poke my head out of my sleeping bag as a construction worker is staring down at me. In a moment, he is consoling. Sleep! Sleep! Very sorry!

I sit up, no, no problem, it's OK, I leave, you work! Embarrassed, he insists. Please, no wake! No work now, you sleep! And hurries out the door, shutting it softly behind him.

If the Slovenes are reputed to be cold hearted Westerners by Balkan standards, they're still a whole lot nicer than what I'm used to.

HERE, IN THE BUILDING OF FUN SHOPPING CENTER, ARE the fruits of progress. Interspar is a one room depot with everything: meat, bras, lawnmowers. This is what author Greg Palast would refer to as a "Storegasm."[29] At first, this store didn't carry any Slovenian goods at all, but under protest it put a few alongside its global riches, like its one variety of flips. Since citizens here were given partial ownership in industries when they were privatized, in a rare post-Socialist nod to wealth distribution,[30] Slovenes might be expected to prefer local goods. Perhaps these Bowling Salt X-treme flavored Chio chips are local. But there are more kinds of Tequila than of *rakija*, or of the regional wine. I pick up an EU-made Poco Loco Taco dinner kit and a bottle of Heinz Mexican ketchup made in Poland. A five dollar bottle of Tabasco tempts me despite myself. A woman in front of me sticks a piggy bank with a euro sign on it in her basket.

"The last breath of civilization expires on this coast where barbarism starts," Austro-Hungarian diplomat Chateaubriand wrote of this area in 1806.[31]

THE BUS IS DRUNK

WHEN HE CAN'T FIND ANYPLACE ELSE TO CRASH, NENO SLEEPS IN THE PASSENGER TRAINS THAT HAVE BEEN TAKEN OFF THE ACTIVE TRACKS FOR THE NIGHT. EVERYONE DRINKS AND SOCIALIZES OVER THE FOLD-OUT TABLES, THEN RETIRES TO A SLEEPER COMPARTMENT. WHEN SARAH AND I TOLD NENO THAT WE'D LOVE TO DROP BY, HE WAS SURPRISED, BUT OFFERED TO BE OUR HOST. SARAH AND I KICK BACK IN OUR FIRST-CLASS SEATS AND GREET OUR NEW TRAIN COHORTS. NENO AND HIS GIRLFRIEND IVA ARE FIGHTING AGAIN. EVERYONE ELSE IS WELL-DRESSED AND IN GOOD SPIRITS; WE TOAST EACH OTHER BY CANDLELIGHT. MOST OF THE OTHER RESIDENTS ARE OLDER, AND ALL ARE MEN. WE ASK ONE ABOUT IVA AND NENO'S FIGHT, AND HE SHRUGS: YOUNG PEOPLE IN LOVE.

Two men come in and are happy to see Neno. He and Iva interrupt their yelling to make introductions and catch up with the men. One of them talks at length, while the other seems tired and gazes at the floor. Finally, Iva explains: "This guy speaking is the brother of that guy, who had a very bad day. His ex-wife that he loved very much was cut in half by a tram today. He's on a lot of pills so he can't feel anything." We offer him our plastic bottle of *bambus*, a tasty concoction of one-third Coca-Cola and two-thirds wine. He thankfully accepts. The brothers converse in hushed tones, while Iva and Neno resume their discussion, which is getting louder. I think to myself that such a passionate conversation would be considered a fight in California, but I guess it's just the way people talk here.

Iva, we find out soon, is actually calling Neno a chauvinist pig who should be ashamed of himself, and that she is sick of his shit. Neno responds by lunging at her and grabbing her by the throat, which doesn't interrupt her reprimand. The rest of us jump up to pry Neno's fingers loose as Iva, still screaming, starts to turn blue. Slowly, we manage to separate them until the speaking brother pulls Neno into the hall. Iva sulks and doesn't want to talk about it.

Sarah and I turn to the man who has had a bad day, thankful for the help. He smiles a bit, weakly, and we pass the *bambus*.

"*Sprechen-sie Deutsch?*" he asks.

"*Kleine, kleine.*" Just a little, we answer.

"Have you ever been to Germany?" Sarah and I decipher. We both nod, gave a thumbs-up for Germany, and list off the towns we can remember visiting.

"*Da, da. Berlin, Hamburg, Heidelberg... Berlin, sehr dobro. Mnogo kunst.*" Berlin, very good, much art, we manage in mixed Croatian and German.

"Adolph Hitler?" he asks.

"*Nein, nein, ništa Adolf Hitler,*" we answer almost yelling, with emphatic thumbs-down.

"*Ludwig Wittgenstein,*" adds Sarah.

"*Da, da, Wittgenstein,*" he answers.

"*I Apfel-Struedel, sehr gut,*" Sarah says: Apple Strudel is also good. We all nod.

"*I također Goethe, I Beethoven,*" I add.

"*Da, da, sehr gut. Aber Adolf je Bog.*" Yes, very good, but Adolf is God.

"*Nije, nije! Immanuel Kant!*" No he's not, no he's not. Immanuel Kant.

"*Da, Kant. Aber Adolf je Bog.*"

Sarah and I consult one another. Obviously, it isn't the time to lambaste the man who has had a bad day. But it would be patronizing to allow his Nazism to go unchecked.

"In Germany, they don't like Hitler anymore," I manage. "Go there and ask."

"That's not true," he answers in German. "I lived there for ten years."

Then, not really believing he could be a real Nazi, I ask a stupid question. "*Šta misliš Juden?*" What do you think about Jews?

He makes a slicing motion across his throat.

"*Zašto?*" I ask. Why?

"Jesus Christ," he says solemnly, stretching out his arms on an imaginary crucifix.

"We've got to explain to him that the Romans killed Jesus, not the Jews," says Sarah. "How do you say 'Romans' in Croatian?"

If the plural of "Amerikan" is "*Amerikani*," I figure the plural of Roman is "*Romani.*"

"*Znate-li Romani?*" I ask him. You know the Romani?

"*Da, Romani, poznam, naravno.*" Of course I know Romani, he nods.

"The Romani killed Jesus, it wasn't the Jews!" I yell victoriously.

"*Nisu, nisu?!*" No they didn't, replies our Nazi friend, confused.

"*Da, da,*" I insist, the Romani, not the Jews. "*Poznate-li Pontius Pilate?*" You know Pontius Pilate?

"*Da, poznam.*"

"*Pontius Pilate je bio... Romani!*" Pontius Pilate was Romani, I yell like a prophet.

"*Nije!*" No he wasn't, protests the incredulous Nazi.

Yes, Pontius Pilate was Romani. I rest my case. We pass the *bambus* in silence until Neno, now calmed, returns.

As we drunkenly stagger from the train, Iva asks me why I tried to convince the man that Pontius Pilate was Romani. "I don't think the Gypsies were around back then," she says.

DICTIONARIES FOR THE FOLLOWING LANGUAGES STAND IN a row on my shelf: Serbo-Croatian, Croato-Serbian, Serbian, Croatian, and Bosnian. With the exception of one huge hardcover Croatian dictionary published in New York in the early 1970s, and one Croato-Serbian tome lingering nostalgically on a friend's shelf in Belgrade, most of the dictionaries published before the '80s are Serbo-Croatian. Yugoslavian publishers also made dictionaries for the related languages of Slovenian and Macedonian, as well as the totally different Romani, Hungarian, and Albanian tongues. Coursebooks for these and other minority languages like Romanian and Turkish doubtlessly gather mold in countless attics. But Serbo-Croatian dominated the land as the official tongue of Yugoslavia, spoken by nearly all of its 22 million inhabitants until the breakup in 1991. Now, the language has been officially banished.

One of my Serbian dictionaries is a copy of Morton Benson's classic Serbo-Croatian dictionary reprinted in 1982, with apparently nothing but the name changed. Those are our words now, you don't get them any more, the cover implies. I didn't want them anyway, its neighbors on the shelf sneer. The Croatian dictionaries have to be constantly reprinted, to perfect the process of cleansing the Croatian language of Serbian linguistic pollution. Suddenly, sports are to be called *shport*, not sport. Even foreign loan words, so common in the traditional language, are suspect—the new Croatian word for "helicopter" is *zrakomlat*, or "air-beater," not the "Serbian" word *helikopter* that everyone has always used here until now. But besides the Serbian "e" spelled as *"ije"* in Croatian, and a small number of dialectical differences for basic words like "bread" and "train," the great majority of the contents are identical. ·

One friend, whose parents are Serb and Croat, catches himself using a *novogovor*, or "newspeak," word as we walk and stops in frustration. "You try so hard not to let them slip in your ears," he says, "not to let them fall off your tongue, but they just become such a normal part of life, it's hard to fight them anymore." One student I meet in Zagreb, who moved here from Sarajevo during the war, found a traditional word, the one everyone always uses, crossed out on one of her essays at the university and replaced with its *novogovor* equivalent.

She refused to "correct" it. The professor flunked her.

The no-longer existent Serbo-Croatian language, as its unwieldy name reveals, was itself invented as a political contrivance. Its beginnings were first standardized by Vuk Karadić in the nineteenth century, who called the language "Serbian" and viewed the language of the neighboring peoples as dialects of Serbian. As the hold of the Austro-Hungarian Empire weakened, the Illyrian movement, made up of Croats, Serbs, and Slovenes within Croatia who often referred to themselves as "Illyrians" and referred to their language as "Illyrian" or "Yugoslavian" (South Slavic), sought to unify all the South Slav peoples in a state independent of the empires that divided them. Their Austrian rulers, threatened by the idea, pressured them to call the language "Croatian." After World War II, Tito's communist rule, with its doctrine of "brotherhood and unity," made the idea of a "Serbo-Croatian" language (or sometimes Croato-Serbian, each with or without the hyphen as political climate dictated) essential to Yugoslavian unity.

But what, really, do people here speak? The answer is relative to the scale of "here." Some people still proclaim themselves Serbo-Croatian speakers. As one professor at the University of California at Sacramento pointed out, the difference between Serbian and Croatian is greater than that between Swedish and Norwegian, though no one ever speaks of Swedo-Norwegian. Most people use the official terms "Bosnian," "Croatian," and "Serbian." But even these categories are deeply problematic. The variation within dialects of Croatian—for example, what is spoken in the southern coastal area of Dalmatia, on the various islands, in northwestern Istria, and in the capital—are far greater than the differences between standard Croatian and standard Serbian. People on some islands can't always understand the people on the next island over. Two official, exclusive Croatian grammars exist in a tongue-tied Cold War, indicating that the state is afraid to take sides in such a politically touchy issue. And the "*ije*" that distinguishes Croatian from Serbian is also spoken in Montenegro, the seat of Serbian folk culture. The newly-named Bosnian language is identified by its frequent Turkish vocabulary, its Serbian syntax, and its Croatian pronunciation.

Nationalist linguists even claimed that Serb and Muslim women in the same town spoke different, ethnic dialects,

Zagreb, Croatia.

that in general neighbors spoke not like each other, but like their own ethnic standard.[32] But neighbors spoke what each other understood, not what was assigned by the rulers of their imputed, politically constructed ethnicities.[33]

"Most of the inhabitants of the land of Rum [the Ottoman name for their European territory] are of mixed origin," wrote Mustafa Ali in the seventeenth century. "Amongst the more prominent there are few whose genealogies do not go back to a convert to Islam, or whose ethnic origins, either on their mother's or father's side, do not go back to a filthy infidel, despite the fact that they themselves have grown up as upright and outstanding Muslims."[34]

Olja from the Attack! center in Zagreb says, "My friends and I were talking, and everyone had Croatian, Serbian, Bosnian, Hungarian, Italian roots. We are all mixed here." She pauses. "We are all Borg!"

Klonko, the anarchist architecture student sitting next to her, states, "There *are* people with clear origins, but we don't associate with them."

Self-identified Yugoslavs after Yugoslavia, mixed ethnics and non-ethnics are goods for the bazaar; not for sale in the official stores of national identity, not name-brand lives.[35] Simple dictionaries and neat maps make refugees and genocides. Construction paper identities make cut-and-pasted lives.

BUT IS THIS CUTTING-AND-PASTING REALLY SO BALKAN, OR contrarily, is it the attempt to de-Balkanize the Balkans, and create states that live up to respectable Western standards?

> Given the complexities of social relations, however, any attempt to reconstruct political space in homogeneous terms can never be fully realized. Homogenization projects are always works in progress, always requiring some level of violence, overt or covert, explicit or implicit, to reinforce and reimpose an idealized sameness on the messy realities of society. Strategies of violence do not end with the ethnic cleansing, but rather are an integral part of the very process of thinking about political space in homogeneous ways.
>   Indeed, the pressure for homogeneous political space is ubiquitous. In some respects it is a requirement of the international state system itself, which divides the world up into geographical units that are, in terms of sovereignty and international law, considered to be internally homogeneous. This pressure is also seen in liberal political systems that display a tension between assumptions of a common community, that is, the equality and equivalence of all citizens, on the one hand, and the realities of social, economic, and cultural heterogeneity, on the other hand...[36]
>   It seems contradictory that the West has effectively come down on the side of those who have used violence to achieve the ethnification of territory and the territorialization of ethnicity—which, after all, is a long tradition among liberal states in the West—while, at the same time, portraying the Balkans as a pre-modern irrational field of violence, and demanding that the Balkan natives accept an ethos of multiculturalism.[37]

ONE DAY, I AM READING ALONE AT A TABLE. THOUGH most of Zagreb's restaurants now cater to the emerging bourgeoisie, a few Socialist Realism diners like this one survive. Decorations are sparse, the radio is loud, and the traditional fare is better than at the pretentious places, at a third of the price. When the tables are full, patrons stand at a counter in the middle of the room. An older but not elderly man walks over with his cane and sits with me quietly, and when I ask him about his beer, he tells me it is good. Listing off all the other beers, which are also good, he says the newspaper is all lies for ignorant people. It is good that I am young and need little and that the world is mine, he says, and he knows I have many girlfriends since I have no wife. Looking at the book in my hand, he tells me he has never heard of Joseph Conrad because he didn't finish school. Though people in the Balkans are open and warm, they are all people with deep roots. It is good to have a history, which America doesn't, but—his hands pause with gravity—we must remember that we are all children of Mother Earth. He too has seen many beauties of the world, the mountains of Colorado and the cathedrals of Paris. He tells me that he is an old man because he almost forgot his hat, but, with the same smile both deep and wide, and the same genteel stare into my eyes, that I should not forget to live well, and it was a pleasure to meet me but he has to go home now that his beer is finished.

IT'S PINK FLOYD NIGHT AT THE BIKER BAR IN OSIJEK, and my hosts won't let me buy my own drinks. Since Petra's son is working behind the bar, I can't refuse the offer. My two new friends, the only members of the Osijek Greens, catch me up on their activities. The group had once been larger, but had undergone several splits as the two became frustrated with other members' political ambitions and nationalism. On one national survey about ethnicity, which forced citizens to define themselves by narrow ethnic categories and thus implicitly support the emerging nationalist rhetoric, Petra proudly declared herself a "penguin."

With the rapid privatization of state services in Croatia, they've had plenty to keep them busy. Deutsch Telecom recently bought out the Croatian telephone company, and at the same time bought out the major telephone company in India. Soon afterwards, Deutsch Telecom was itself bought out by AT&T. Immediately, wages were cut and prices rose by identical percentages in India and Croatia. Unions in both countries protested the same issues at the same time. Sadly, the unions' ties to local politics and ambitions rendered them disinterested in contact with each other.

Osijek Greens had more success in their protest campaign against Croatia's monopoly power company. Hrvatska Elektroprivreda became independent from the Yugoslav power company in the early '90s and emerged with a monopoly on electricity in Croatia. It underwent a dubious privatization scheme under President Tudjman in '94, and the new government hasn't changed it at all. No one knows who the real investors are, though Enron was known to have had half a million dollars invested in the company. The company just announced a fee hike of twenty-five percent, the second in four months; some people are even paying double what they did before privatization. Osijek Greens have set up a box in the main center of town, in which around fifty people have dropped their electrical bills in protest, rather than sending them with payments to the company. "As you noticed, though," Petra says, "the box isn't there anymore, since earlier tonight someone stole it." Their campaign is coordinated with similar actions in two or three other cities in Croatia. I tell her that I recently read in a book that such utility sell-offs have been mandated by the IMF, at threat of loan cutoff if not obeyed.[38]

"Of course," she says.

Bruno, the younger of the two, urges Petra to tell me about Benneton. She waves him away, but he insists. She shakes her head, conceding. "It all started when one of our friends went to jail for a couple of days. He was surprised as he looked around in there. Nearly everyone in the small jail was from Romania, Bulgaria, or Turkey. In the morning, all of them left at the same time, though he was kept in his cell. Around 6 p.m., all of them reappeared and went back into their cells. We started investigating on our own and confirmed that the prisoners were working in the new Benneton factory during the daytime, before being quietly shuttled back to sleep in the jail. The workers were paid for their work, though we don't know how much. Perhaps they'd come to work in Croatia, but it seems more likely that they'd been trying to get into western Europe and were caught in Croatia, and were exploited by the factory instead of being sent back. We broke the story to the local press, who ran one short article about it. The local officials here declined to comment, but a month later there weren't any Benneton employees in the jail anymore."

Soon after, Osijek Greens discovered that the same Benneton dye factory was dumping unfiltered waste directly into the local river, Drava. The dumping was in violation of Croatian environmental law, but the city government, having paid nearly one million dollars to get the contract, was reluctant to prosecute. The factory also broke zoning laws, despite being in a "free trade zone." Petra notified the press and began to file grievances with the environmental board. Naomi Klein, the Canadian anti-global-capitalist author, heard about Petra's efforts and offered help, sending her information on Benneton's misconduct in Rijeka, another city in Croatia, and also in Turkey.

Anonymous callers started to phone Petra in the middle of the night. She stopped answering calls she didn't recognize on her caller ID. Police began to stop her on the street and ask for her identity papers, though she'd been born and raised in Osijek. The harassment increased, until one night she was stopped six different times during the five minute walk from her home to visit her son in the biker bar. She told the last cop to go to hell.

A few days later, an old friend, a water analyst, called her at six or seven in the morning to invite her to inspect the factory with him. He would arrive in five minutes. Petra persuaded him to give her half an hour. She phoned several friends to at least let them know where she was going, since he refused to let her bring anyone else. The "old friend" showed her around the factory, asking: "Isn't this machine clean? Does it look like it could pollute anything?" Despite being normal working hours for the plant, absolutely no one else was there; the only other person they saw was the Italian head of the factory, who cheerfully introduced himself as he was coincidentally riding his bicycle past them on the factory floor. After two hours of the "tour," he sat her down in the factory cafe and asked: "Are you happy now?" She assured him the tour had satisfied all her concerns.

Petra didn't stop agitating. "Maybe they will hit me by car, maybe they will beat me, but it will pass. What can they do? Nothing. I didn't know what would happen, and I wasn't afraid." Finally, an old friend who worked in City Hall called her in the middle of the night in a panic. She'd found a letter from Benneton headquarters in Italy asking: "Who is this woman?" Her friend begged, "Please stop, they will kill you." Petra decided to leave town for a vacation; even her son didn't know where she went. When she returned, she was called in for a meeting with the Ministry of the Environment; the regional Benneton boss shook her hand with a giant smile from across the table. Everyone signed what Petra called a "peace treaty," which assured that Benneton would be held fully accountable to all applicable laws. Nothing happened for six months, then the factory closed. The factory has since partially reopened as a "test plant," but it still hasn't resumed full production.

The next day, a bit hung over, I leaf through Osijek Greens pamphlets:

> When everything finished in chaos and self destruction, human will desire for nature and beauty, again—if survive. We must to make an end everyone who dissemble the Earth in big red-hot, bored and asphalted surface, on which coming generation will ask why we done that to them. Source of all pollutions is mental pollution. Drugaciji svijet je moguc. Altro mundo e possible Another world is possible.

AND WHO WAS "LEADING" THE COUNTRY IN THIS TIME OF WAR and transition? The Croatian Democratic Community party, or HDZ, claimed to be protecting Croatia and its interests when it came to power shortly before the war. As war was breaking out, the HDZ assassinated the Croatian chief of police in Osijek, Josip Reihl-Kir, who was successfully talking with the nervous local Serbs. One of the top leaders of the right-wing of HDZ, Gojko Susak, still nervous at the prospect of peace after having Reihl-Kir killed, fired missiles by his own hand into the Serb village of Borovo Selo to get things moving. An interview with Reihl-Kir's widow, and footage of the missile-firing can both be seen in the excellent BBC documentary *Yugoslavia: Death of a Nation*.[39] Croatian police, presumably on orders, went on to kill an entire Serb family in Zagreb, including a twelve-year-old girl.[40] Were these perhaps the cooperative actions that Tudjman and Milošević agreed on in their Karadjordjevo Meeting, which concluded the day before the standoff in Croatia began?[41] "The level of collusion between HDZ and SDS (Serb Democratic Party) hardliners from fall 1990 through spring 1991 was significant; both had an interest in constructing homogeneous political space; neither group was popular; and both faced pressure for fundamental change. For both, the response was to use fear and violence to change political space."[42]

Were such actions an expression of popular will? In 1990, the HDZ received only half of the Croatian votes. (In the same election, only 25% of Croatian Serbs voted for its Serb counterpart, the SDS.)[43] In 1992, only 29% of eligible Croatian voters chose

HDZ. University polls showed their approval rating at below 30% for most of their reign. While President Tudjman was busy defending the WWII Nazi-puppet NDH government as a legitimate "expression of the historical will" of the Croatian Nation, two-thirds of Croatians said they saw the NDH (Independent State of Croatia) as a criminal state, and expressed higher concern for justice and the economy than for right-wing issues.[44]

In polls in both 1995 and 1999, less than 13% of Croatians wanted Serbs to leave Croatia; 68% said they should be assured of their human rights within the state, and 14.6% more said they should be given cultural autonomy. In a poll in 1995, more Croatians said that they were dissatisfied with "abuse of power, privilege, and corruption" (13.6%) and "injustice and criminality in privatization" (13.8%) than Serb "occupation of parts of Croatia" (9.0%)—this while one-third of the proclaimed Croatian state was still under Serb control, shots were still being fired. In 1999, with the war raging in Kosovo, only twenty percent of Croatians agreed to the statement, "The best is for members of individual nations to live together in their own state," while more than three times as many people polled disagreed. In 1996, when the party tried to crack down on dissent station Radio 101, over 100,000 people took to the streets—according to one party official, "hard-liners in the HDZ felt so threatened by these street protests that they wanted to use force against the demonstrators."[45]

A *Washington Post* article entitled "Croats Find Treasury Plundered" details the extent of the war and post-war government's neo-liberal (deregulation, privatization, no social spending) plundering. The country's banks were plundered for $2.6 billion, and the government left $2 billion more in guarantees for fraudulent loans. Domestic and Foreign debt totaled over $15 billion, nearly the same amount of debt as all of pre-war Yugoslavia.[46]

When the government sold the telephone company to Deutsch Telecom, which Petra had told me resulted in wage cuts for employees and price hikes for customers, Tudjman and his party skimmed off $100 million for themselves, and as funds to aid in the next election. Tens of thousands of profitable companies were given as presents to friends of the party, milked, and left for dead. "It now appears that the officially sanctioned thievery in Croatia ... was greater on a per capita basis than in any other

East European nation undergoing this transition..." Officials in the post-Tudjman government are quoted as saying that "Corruption has reduced the Croatian economy to a shambles. Banks have collapsed, hundreds of companies are insolvent, and unemployment is at twenty-two percent and climbing."[47]

"Croatia's small privatization agency, established in 1992, was supposed to help oversee the nation's transformation from socialism to free enterprise. Instead, it became a headquarters for institutionalized looting, officials here now say."[48] I wonder as I read this, am I supposed to be surprised, again?

Eugen walks with me past the abandoned medical factory we are squatting together. "The nationalist card was all they had. They couldn't manage the complicated machinery of the state, so they played their one card while they took everything. And they're still the richest people in the country."

THE CROATIAN VIDEO FOR "I WANNA BE AMERICANO" blares over my head in the bus station. Yesterday in the car the radio played a Croatian song named, in English, "American Girls are American Girls." I suspect that people here, on the provincial outskirts of the Empire, are much more American than those of us within its formal borders. The set of images and hopes and ideals that they call America, with Hollywood's encouragement, plays a huge role in social life, a hard cultural currency against which the local suffers massive inflation by constant trading in and selling off. The dreams of prosperity and success, of openness and escape from tradition, of novelty and sexiness are defined as American, but created locally as an antithesis to frustration here. At home, I never think of it, and these ideas people have of America would be foreign if I saw them there. If power is exported from the US in the form of products, ads, and bombs, the American Dream is a global product, imported into the US, or manufactured overseas for domestic consumption.

OUT THE WINDOW DRIVING THROUGH KNIN, I STARE AT a peace sign joined with the Serbian nationalist symbol. Here in 1995, Croatian forces, with support from the US, drove out more than 200,000 Serb civilians in a week. I try to imagine the long line of peasants driving their tractors east on this road, their homes burning behind them. The symbol is painted on a wall standing incongruously in rubble. The rubble looks familiar from the news. News, the reality TV show that stays popular because it is, in Baudrillard's words, "hyper-real": more real than our daily lives.

Tvrtko described Vukovar to me in opposite terms: "People walk around and live their lives in the middle of all this rubble. You keep looking, but it's just not real." In Vukovar the ubiquitous shrapnel-pocked design reminds me of acne. "Change of bus in Vukovar," the woman in the station told Francisco and me.

"OK, fine," I said.

"You want to see Vukovar?" she asked us, glaring.

In 1992 in Vukovar, Serbian forces under the name of the Yugoslav army drove out thousands of Croatians for being part of a republic that had voted, legally by Yugoslavian law, for independence. Tellingly, *one third* of the forces defending Vukovar against the Yugoslav army and paramilitaries *were ethnically Serb*, according to a UN report.[49] Tens of thousands were killed in Croatia over the next six months. The exact numbers will probably never surface, since, according to Tvrtko from Zagreb, even the Croatian government wouldn't want to admit how many people died in order to achieve "national liberation." On the other side, Milošević claimed the war was necessary to keep Yugoslavia together, but its first victim was the trust that made Yugoslavia possible. Politicians in each republic were eager to trade this trust for new job openings in their own new little countries, and responded in the same rhetoric of fear.

Lara tells me: "You know, one thing people don't understand about the war... So many of the people in the paramilitaries were criminals let out of jail to fight in the war, and civilians kidnapped—either they had to join up or be killed, fighting along with 'normal' family guys. Sometimes, they didn't even know what 'side' they were on, just roaming gangs. It wasn't even about politics for them, just raping, killing, getting rich by looting and selling drugs and guns. The military police were the biggest heroin dealers in the area; it wasn't even a scandal when they were caught. Even with the official armies, this week in this village the Croatian army would be with the Bosniak army against the Serbian one, then the next week in the next village over, the Croatian and Serbian armies would cooperate against the Bosniak one. And of course everyone was on amphetamines and *rakija*. People can only pretend it all makes sense a long time after it happens."

Later, I remember Lara's words while reading anthropologist Carolyn Nordstrom's book *Shadows of War*, which attempts to trace the relation between wars and the global black market. She discovered in the course of her research that the myths that sustain war are neatly the exact opposite of its realities:

> I began to understand the images of war conveyed in the media and literature. They were variously devoid of priests and women, children and rogue troops, low-class altruists and high-class profiteers. Political violence is corralled as the province of rational militaries and mostly rational soldiers...
>
> Despite the fact that some 90 percent of all casualties today are civilians, that more children die in war than soldiers, and that the front lines run through average citizens' homes and livelihoods, texts on war, museums, military novels, art, and statues all help reinforce the idea and the ideal that war is about male soldiering...
>
> No matter who shoots whom, certain power elites make a profit... These acts take us through soldiers and civilians alike who run arms and run orphanages, who sell drugs or take them to forget the horrors of war, who black-market antibiotics and textbooks in acts that are simultaneously profiteering and altruistic... From the legal arms sales through the negotiated oil futures to the illegal diamond trade, war is good for business in the cosmopolitan production centers of the world... The casualties of war would find a tragic truth in Charles Tilly's characterization of "war making and state making as organized crime." The modern state is as dependent on war zone profits as it is on keeping these dependencies invisible to formal reckoning. Part of its power rests on the optics of deception: focusing attention on the need for violence while drawing attention away from

both the war-economy foundations of sovereign power and the price in human life this economy of power entails. This is the magician's trick: the production of invisible visibility.[50]

Or, the production of the State begins with consensual blindness.

SITTING UP LATE LIKE ALWAYS, WASHING MY FRIENDS' DISHES to do something besides smoke, listening to the anarchist pop band Chumbawamba, I remember all my ideals with a flush, how I couldn't wait to get out and do right, live my thoughts with passion, so easy to pick something to do out there with so many things wrong, an activist just waiting until I could be active. And now I'm trying to shake this fear that's had me hiding from the windows all day, seeing skinheads in every old lady on the sidewalk, seeing again the raised fists and shark eyes of the Archie Bunker horde amassing across the street to kill me and my friends as we hid behind the bored riot cops. We wondered what they'd done to Oliver before the police got there, trying not to say *hvala*—"thanks"—to the cops for saving our lives, trying to keep laughing when the skinheads threw tear gas into the rally, the first ever Gay Pride rally in Croatia. We fled the gas towards the smiling thugs who waved us towards them, my smiles and laughter in their faces, and in the march I couldn't understand why no one was chanting or singing as they threw eggs and rotten grapefruits and plums and lighters at us. Now I'm thinking of cutting off my green mop of hair since it showed clearly on both TV stations. Wasn't this what I wanted when I sang along, *"Enough is enough is enough, give the fascist man a gunshot?"* And now "The day the Nazi died," *"Tell them that the Nazis never really went away, and we'll never rest again until every Nazi dies."* Would Chumbawamba know how to finish them off, that crowd of a hundred or so that gathered after the rally on the other side of the seven cops who didn't seem to care either way? Would they possess the superpowers none of us had? I tried to comfort my friend who was shaking and crying, as I realized that if I was the skinhead mob, I'd rush the police and push them aside and kick in her and my face and ribs and skull and knees until all 100 of us got bored. *"Nothing ever burns down by itself, every fire needs a little bit of help,"* and I know we won because the whole country is apologizing and reassuring us that it's European and ready to join the EU, even if they smashed up the club that hosted the gay film festival and the subculture club for being "commies," even if they chanted WWII fascist slogans *"Za dom spremni,"* "Ready for our homeland," even if I can't think about leaving the house for the press release tonight. I was dumb enough to come all the way here for this march, telling the raver girl I met on the train that I was going to Zagreb so I could get beaten up by skinheads. Even if my friends, who live here every day, will be recognized. I guess they already get beat up now and then. They just wince and laugh at all these threats, like at a bad joke that's still funny. And that *sieg-heil*ing English woman at the march who got arrested for attacking people with her two-foot-tall plastic mother Mary, that was great.

I start the Chumbawamba tape over again. *"We don't go to God's house anymore, it's more fun in the doghouse. Everything will be all right."*

HOW DO I WRITE ABOUT WHY I LOVE BEING HERE MORE than anywhere, why I can't stand to be away, how can I describe the perfect pleasure of day after day politely scouring the corners of each others' minds as I sit with friends in kitchens, drinking too much Turkish coffee, smoking too many Walter Wolfs. Walter Wolf cigarettes, the essential mystery printed in English across every pack: "It is from passions that all of our pleasures are derived. Speed is one such passion!" Like Homer in *Wings of Desire* said: Why is war so much more interesting than peace? Eating too much mayonnaise and pasta salad, talking about the music and movies and books and adventures and loves and miseries that we share and that we don't, making stupid jokes with our limited common languages. Maybe the non-essential, though impossible to express, is finally the most important.

MY HANDS TREMBLE AS I HOLD THIS SACRED RELIC OF THE modern age, the crinkly blue plastic wrapper of a package of Vegeta. Once, not so long ago, Vegeta was the embodiment of dreams too sweet for hope. MSG and vegetable flakes seemed a luxury reserved for the more fortunate. After WWII, Yugoslavia was leveled, decimated, its population murdered. One in ten had perished on the frontlines, in their homes, or in the camps. Foreign powers had, as in previous cycles of conquest, exploited history to turn the locals against one another. Absolute poverty, starvation, and hatred ruled. Who could have guessed that within a generation, every home in miraculously reconciled and reconstructed Yugoslavia might boast a package of Vegeta?

Not just the consumers, but the producers of Vegeta marveled at their fortune. For here in the Podravka factory in Koprivnica, Republic of Croatia, Socialist Federal Republic of Yugoslavia, the great dream of the twentieth century had been finally been achieved. Many of the active founders of post-WWII Yugoslavia had fought in the Spanish Civil War, and brought the ideas implemented in Barcelona, Andalucia, and Aragon back to Yugoslavia. After Tito's split with Stalin, the Party was open to ideas to distinguish and legitimize Yugoslavia as its own entity, and the anarchist ideas of federalism and self-management found their way, in awkward company with single-party rule, into what became known as Titoism. *Samoupravljenje*, or self-management, was one of the great mottoes of Titoism. The catch was that the single-party State still made sure things didn't get out of hand. Some shouted that authoritarian political rule and state mediation of ownership made samo-upravljenje taste like MSG in a soup with no vegetables. But the Worker's Councils proved enduringly popular. One essay even argues that the recent war(s) were carried about mainly by those parts of the population not successfully organized along samo-upravljanje lines.[51] Political dictatorship or no, something was in the soup.

Vegeta was prized not only by the miraculously recovered Yugoslavs, but by all who tasted its charms. In Trieste, whole sacks of Vegeta were swapped in the black market for vacuum cleaners, TVs, and Italian scooters, which the Vege-smugglers brought back home. As the one country whose citizens had the right to travel freely both east and west, through nearly the entire world, the streams of the clandestine Vegeta market quietly sabotaged the Cold War. Visitors of business and pleasure brought Vegeta as gifts to their partners and friends in Egypt, India, and Ethiopia. Yugoslavia, together with these countries, stood proudly at the front of the Third World, set victoriously aside from the disastrously wasteful and dangerous war between the

First and Second Worlds. Vegeta was the first glimpse of globalization as hope.

The anarchist influence in the idea of self-management expressed themselves even in the possibilities considered as Yugoslavia's old system began to collapse. At the first Party Congress after Tito's death, in 1982, Rade Koncar, a member of the Party committee for Belgrade, proposed on the floor of Congress "that the republic-based federal organization of the party be scrapped and replaced with organization on the basis of lines of production." Soon after, "famed economist Branko Horvat, for example, suggested in 1984 that 'all political parties' (i.e., the Communist Party in its sundry regional organizations) be abolished and that Yugoslavia be reorganized as a 'partyless' socialist system operated through citizen's associations."[52] Had such anarchist approaches to organization won out, it is hard to imagine how different Yugoslavia's future might have been.

Ironically, only Croatia, where people rip the Y's off their Yugos, still has much Vegeta on its shelves. People in Serbia can only afford the lower-grade generic *Začin C*, Spice C. A giant Vegeta mural in the center of Ljubljana was recently replaced with a photo-ad for Nestle instant coffee. How many cooks are still searching for an adequate substitute? Was it truly a mix of vegetable flakes, or was it, as its detractors claim, just so much MSG?

THE NAZI SKINHEADS DON'T SEEM TO MIND THAT I AM tape recording our conversation. They teach Sarah and me another soccer chant, similar to the others—"Your mother can sit on my very extremely huge penis." We have another round of drinks. One of them explains into the recorder that if a Serb showed up at his doorstep, he would feed the Serb everything from his fridge, that he would give him beer and introduce him to his family, that he would even make him sleep in his bed as he slept on the floor. "But if you try to take my city away from me..." he stares, and I hope he can discern through the fog of drink that I'm not trying to take his city away from him. I don't remind him that this would not explain why he'd been fighting with Croatian paramilitaries in Bosnia.

He recounts to me how once, during a trip to Germany, he was overjoyed to run into a group of local Nazi skinheads. "My brothers!" he yelled as he approached. They asked where he was from. When he told them, one of them growled, "You're not my brother, fucking Slav."

"No, no, don't you understand?!" he yelled. "In the war, the Ustaše were your closest European allies! We even had concentration camps!"

The German Nazi skins were perplexed and discussed among themselves for some minutes. Finally, one of them said, "Slavs are sub-human, we would never be allies with them." The group beat him until he couldn't move. His voice stops in sorrow.

The other Nazi explains that when he was fourteen, his best friend was killed by Serb forces. "What would you do?" he asks. The paramilitary didn't want someone so young to have a gun, he claims, so he got to clean up, with the body bags and everything. He stops talking, then points for me to shut off the tape recorder. I wish I'd changed the subject a few minutes ago. If only my glass wasn't full, it would be a good time to order another round. Then the Nazi skinhead tells me to turn my tape recorder back on.

"Vietnam. Slavery. Native Americans... You don't talk to me about war. You don't talk to me about genocide."

Dalia and I are walking to a small tram stop in Zagreb in the middle of the night. After the Gay Pride march, I'd rather avoid the larger ones. We wait and wait, but no tram appears. A white unmarked bus pulls over just as Dalia's pack spills all over the street. We gather her things in our arms and jump on. I try to walk forward to ask the driver where the bus is going, but he is belting out songs with a couple of friends. I go back to sit next to Dalia, who is making faces with a middle-aged guy at the back of the bus. When he makes a breast-squeezing motion, she gives up. He comes up to sit with us. "Listen to this," he says as he puts headphones on me. Cheerful metal fills my head.

"Russian!" he says.

"Are you Russian?" asks Dalia.

"I am from Australia," he says in thick Slavic. The bus speeds through another red light, and passes a pair of taxis on our left. "But Zagreb is my town. If you want anything, if anyone bothers you, come to me."

I wander again up to the front now that the driver's song is done. The bus hasn't stopped since we boarded it 20 minutes ago. "Where is the string to stop the bus?" Dalia asked the Australian.

"The bus is drunk. You cannot stop the bus."

I claw my way to the front seat by seat. "*Slijedeči stajalište?*" Next stop? The driver looks up, surprised at my question.

"*Slijedeči?*" he repeats in mild disbelief. I nod. The bus skids to the curb, in front of our street, exactly where the tram would have stopped.

WE ARE IN ATTACK!, IN ZAGREB. A BAND IS PRACTICING "La Bamba" behind us for the upcoming Mexico night party, and we are drinking as usual. The video camera is rolling, since I still think I am making a documentary. I am interrogating Tvrtko, the anarchist friend whom everyone always points me with my questions.

"What about the bill passed by the US Congress at the beginning of '91 that abruptly stopped loans to Yugoslavia, while promising debt forgiveness with new loans to new 'democratic' governments?[53] And Germany's early recognition of Slovenia's and Croatia's independence... Did the US and Germany want to break up Yugoslavia?"

Y arriba, arriba.

Tvrtko shakes his head. "It didn't help. But really, I don't think you can say it was caused by international forces. People want a simple conspiracy to explain things. Western Europeans and Americans want to keep all the guilt for themselves. I think governments prefer one regional strongman they can deal with— just look at a map, would you want to deal with a map like we have now? They also didn't want to give Russia an excuse to step in. I mean, the international forces didn't do much to help, but I think in the end it was local causes."

I tell Tvrtko about one analysis I've read, that the different republics' political cultures within the Yugoslav Communist Party, like Serbia's circle-the-wagons centralism versus Slovenia's and Croatia's decentralism, created a sort of panicked feedback loop in response to the crises in the 80's, but that most Yugoslavs weren't even aware of the conflict, much less took it to heart. And that at the outbreak of the fighting, the US at least was so keen on keeping Yugoslavia together that they offered Milošević the services of the 82nd Airborne division, according to the respected Serbian independent paper *Vreme*.[54]

Yo no soy marinero, soy capitan.

Tvrtko smiles. "Did you know that once, I think in the early '70s, when Tito was particularly tight with Haile Selassie, Emporer of Ethiopia, they agreed during a terrible famine that every Yugoslav family would adopt one orphan from Africa? I mean, can you imagine? Of course, there would never have been the war. Like, would an African-Serb shoot at an African-Croat? But I mean, besides that, just think of the music... African polyphony with Turkish rhythms and Slavic frenzy. It would have been the best ever."

Para bailar la bamba.

I empty my bottle and say: "Another stupid question for the camera. What do you think of the NATO bombing of Serbia and Kosovo?"

"What do you mean what do I think?"

"I mean, do you think it brought peace or anything?"

"No."

Una poca de gracia.

"What about people who think Serbia and Kosovo are so messed up that we had to do something, that there was no better option?"

Por ti sere, por ti sere.

"Well, we're all so messed up, why don't you just bomb all of us?" grins Tvrtko widely.

Ah la bamba, ah la bamba.

> *"Dick is a weapon,*
> *Gun is gun,*
> *Gun is for fighting,*
> *Dick is for fun."*

35,000 WOMEN IN BOSNIA AND CROATIA, USED AS A CANVAS FOR men's messages to each other.[55] Michael Parenti, the American leftist who attributes the stories of mass rape to the American imperialist propaganda machine,[56] apparently never read this graffiti in front of me on a wall in Zagreb or the thousands of testimonies transcribed by international aid agencies. Like prisons, like napalm, suffering withheld the dignity of being. Where is *their* graffiti?

STANDING AT THE URINAL IN MOCVARA PUNK CLUB, A WOMAN pushes past me to get in a men's room stall. A guy standing

Clock dealer, Hrelic Market, Zagreb, Croatia.

next to me starts shouting, pounding on the door. What the hell do you think you're doing!?

"Why do you care?" I ask, buttoning my fly. "The line to the women's room is long and this stall was empty."

"Look! I don't know where you're from, but THIS is CROATIA!" His shoulders square off like patriarchy triumphant. The woman flushes and walks out, ignoring him. "THIS is CROATIA! We don't do those kind of things here!"

"I mean, apparently some people do, she just did." The guy stands, drunk, no response. Pissed.

THIS MUST BE THE MOST DEMOCRATIC USE OF TELEVISION, ever: *Nightmare Stage*, every Friday night on Croatian television, starting at midnight, lasting an indeterminate time, but always at least six hours. One live camera, a host named Zeljko Malnar, his *rakija* bottle, one table, and a handful of whatever guests he can get to sit down. Often, Johnny explains to me as we tune in, Zeljko goes from bar to bar beforehand, finds the most interesting clients, and promises them a drink from his bottle if they come into the studio. Perhaps for one night, they have all insomniac Croatia as an audience for their fallen dreams of youth, their intolerable marriage of 50 years, or the success of this year's paprika crop.

Tonight, the table is full. On the far end, a man holds a large brown jug labeled "XXX" in his sleeping fingers, drool peeking out of his snoring mouth. As the camera zooms in on his face, he sits up startled, estimates his surroundings, shoots a suddenly ecstatic thumbs-up into the camera, and settles back into his televised nap.

Beside the passed-out man, one of Croatia's most influential lawyers sits a bit tense in his tailored suit. Zeljko directs a question to him, which my friends beside me on the couch don't translate. The lawyer begins slowly, then with emphatic, precise gestures, begins to explain the faults of Croatia's legal system, the problems it faces, the importance of establishing consistent precedent with lessons from the experience of other countries but with attention to Croatia's own situation. As he continues for some time, the cameraman becomes a bit impatient and checks repeatedly on the state of the passed-out man and his XXX bottle. Zeljko interrupts the lawyer's presentation now and then with questions, and concentrates with casual attention on the lawyer's eloquent responses.

Between the lawyer and Zeljko, a thin, middle-aged man with spurious hair fidgets in his chair. Zeljko, finally satisfied with his immediate curiosity in Croatia's legal situation, asks this man to read from his work. The spurious-hair man eagerly opens the notebook in his lap and recites in low, emphatic tones. My friends beside me on the couch begin to groan and laugh, cover their faces with their hands, finally yelling at each other to drown out the man's voice. "This guy is infamous, some kind of erotic poet. You don't want the translation, really." I beg them until my friends hush their laughter. "OK, OK. He just said, 'I bury my face in the aromatic petals of your flesh flower.' Are you satisfied?" I encourage them to return to their conversation.

The host, at the other end of the table, retains a serious, concerned expression throughout the recitation. He pours himself another shot from the *rakija* bottle.

Behind him, on a chair removed from the table, sits a man eating Chinese food with an expression of bemused distance. Occasionally, he looks up as the camera approaches him, shrugs, and resumes his meal. His face looks familiar, but I can't remember from where. He interjects a word or two during the poet's recitation, then interrupts between poems with a sentence or two. The camera focuses on the styrofoam on his lap for a moment before returning to the passed-out man, who, awake again, waves his bottle with disconnected slurs.

"Who's the guy with the Chinese food?" I ask Johnny.

"Ah, you don't recognize him? That's Stipe Mesić, President of the Republic of Croatia."

EUGEN SAYS, "MESIĆ IS CUTTING LOOSE NOW THAT HIS OFFICE IS almost up. Every year, he gives a speech to Partisan veterans at the sight of the Jasenovac concentration camp. This year, he actually said, "Some bastards would have you believe that horrible things didn't happen here." Bastards, yes, that's the perfect translation. Of course, he's talking about his fellow politicians."

Cvijeta tells me, "I can't wait til Stipe is out of office. I mean, he's a good president, I just want him out of office so I can have a drink with him. It's kind of embarrassing to say as a second generation anarchist."

FOR NOW, TOMMY ISN'T HALLUCINATING—"SEEING MOVIES" as he calls it. For once, he isn't telling Dan and me that he's going to kill himself before he turns eighteen and they put him in the army, or that he's going to take trains without any money all the way to London. He's napping. I stare over his ruffled mohawk at the dry summer landscape as the train bumps its way toward Sisak. Hangover and sleep deprivation bring out the dirty window glare. A grumbling mechanical peace works its way into my spine through the seat.

That night in Sisak, the water bottle full of *bambus* pauses in disbelief in Adelita's hand. "Why would you ever want to move to Croatia?" she demands.

"Why wouldn't we? What more could you ask for?" I ask. She hands the bottle over.

"Not so many tourists come here," she explains.

"I can't understand why." I fumble to pass the bottle without dropping my veggie burger. Her entourage of young punkers stare at us mystified and ask her for translation.

Dan and I trip down the street toward a concert behind our hosts, screaming out a dedication. "The stars at night, are big and bright, deep in the heart of Sisak! The *bambus* flows, skinheads receive blows, deep in the heart of Sisak!" We try to explain that not everything about Texas is bad, though certainly Sisak has more punks than all of Texas. Adelita translates. Unlike Sisak, Texas hasn't had a recent mass violent expulsion of refugees, but not for lack of ethnic tension. The kids shake their heads and laugh at us.

"Under Tito, things were so much better," says Adelita. "People got along, we had money for whatever we wanted, we could travel anywhere in the world. Now, there's so much hatred, so much poverty. We can't even visit our relatives in Serbia. I guess I'm kind of a communist," she blushes in conclusion. We sip our beers quietly and wait for the show to start. Growing up in the Cold War, I never would have envisioned Adelita when I heard about Communism.

TOMMY KEEPS GRABBING ME OUT OF THE PIT TO GIVE updates. "I'm kissing this amazing girl, I think I'm really in love. Isn't she very beautiful?" As soon as I congratulate him and return to the pit for some more pummeling, he grabs me again. "She is mad at me, we are fighting, but I like her so much."

"Why are you fighting?" I ask.

"I was kissing her sister too, but I really love her, and she doesn't understand." Then he disappears, and I go back for new bruises.

These Sisak kids sure have a lot to get out of their system. A huge anti-racist SHARP skinhead slams me against the wall, chipping my tooth as my jaw slams under his elbow. My kind of town. Tommy tugs at my sleeve. "I am in love again, this time I'm sure, I will move here to be with her. She will hide me in her house from her parents."

"What about the sister you were kissing?" I ask.

"She hates me and won't talk to me, since I am in love with her best friend. But I cannot help how I feel." Tommy's new love walks up, glowing, and they disappear into a corner. Tommy isn't seeing movies after all, I guess.

DAN AND I ARE TRYING TO FIGURE OUT WHERE TO START with our elderly reprimands. The three of us shiver cramped under the blankets, piled nearly on top of each other in the basement storage unit of some friend's apartment complex. I shift around carefully, so as not to break any of the household items jabbing into my back. Tommy explains that people in Sisak spent much of their time in storage spaces like this during the war, relatively sheltered from shelling. Then Tommy remembers something: "Hey, I forgot. Everybody at the concert thought you were from the CIA," he says. "They decided to kill you, that's why they were beating you like that on the dance floor. But I told them you were my friends."

"Thanks, Tommy," say Dan and I.

"Pataphysics will be, above all, the science of the particular, despite the common opinion that the only science is that of the general. Pataphysics will examine the laws governing exceptions."

—ALFRED JARRY
EXPLOITS AND OPINIONS OF DR. FAUSTROLL, PATAPHYSICIAN[57]

"SEEKING THE ABSOLUTE WAS OF GREAT IMPORTANCE TO Jarry, for whom all relative truths were, at bottom, lies."[58] Before me on this table is the essential order, the logic. Pataphysics, the science that is to metaphysics as metaphysics is to physics. Here is the key to survival within impossible circumstance. This is the quiet secret to the continuance of the world beyond the imponderable threat of the future, hidden away in this place that the world has presumed to save from itself. It exists within this pile beside the dump that the more Western-gazing Croatians wave away with embarrassment. Around me, Hrelić, Zagreb's mighty outdoor black market, roars. Every ex-Yugoslav language, especially Romani, mixes in this hyper-density of space. Hrelić is far enough down the road that the thousands of merchants would have time to pack up and run off should the police ever appear.

Half drunk bottles of *rakija*, used socks, shiny sports cars with leather interiors, mouth-blown accordions, original Ottoman tea sets, immense piles of disco records, Soviet cameras, and Indonesian stamps. There, a woman in a neat booth selling only springs, thousands of them, somehow sorted. And this man, proud before a table of clocks. Before me on another table the secret is alchemically purified, revealed in a haiku of objects. Two boxing gloves. An air gun. Two '60s era vibrators, mint condition, within their original boxes. And a cage full of grown, squirming chinchillas.

> "The two conceptualizations of space continue to battle: on the one hand, the imagining of ethnically defined nation-states, with some arguing for ethnic exclusivity and even expulsions to create homogeneous space, while others argued for tolerance and liberal minority rights; and, on the other hand, the social realities of plural, multiethnic communities."
> —V. P., JR. GAGNON
> THE MYTH OF ETHNIC WAR: SERBIA AND CROATIA IN THE 1990s[59]

"FUCK YOUR MOTHER," THE BEACH GUY SAYS AS HE PASSES. I sit down with Saskia and Allie to finish our snacks. The beach guy glares hard and cold at us as he unfurls his beach blanket, a huge Croatian flag. "Guys," I mumble, "maybe we should get going." On the path out of the park, a bare-chested man in shorts shouts, "*Dodji*," come here, which we choose to ignore. He jumps up and flashes a badge. "We've left our passports at the squat, we are here in Pula for the music." He shoos us off disgustedly. On our way back, a moped slows so its rider can shout "Fucking punks!" We decide to take side roads. On one wall, graffiti advises: "Gypsies to the Camps."

Punks in Croatia have it hard, since to be punk is to be a Bad Croat, a refutation of the Good Croat image consecrated in the blood of "national liberation." Already, on the second day of the festival, several of my friends have been beaten up on the street by a disconcerting coalition of Nazi skinheads and Roma youth. Pula wasn't hit directly by the war, though many of the young people here doubtlessly went to fight in it. But why would the Roma want to beat us up? I guess small town life doesn't offer many entertainment opportunities. Or maybe some punks in the past have earned a bad reputation, like the one last year who decided he hated everyone who went fishing, and pushed an old man with a fishing pole held in his one arm into a lake.

I've already lost count of the days. Wake up, cook Turkish coffee on the beach, swim and dry off, and swim again all day in our underwear in the deep clear azure of the Adriatic. Night falls, we crowd into the store with the giant wine barrels, which does more business this week than the rest of the year combined, to refill our water bottles with red at a dollar-per-liter, and back to the squat for tonight's show. I run into a friend from Sacramento for the first time in four years. We chat and pass the bottle, somehow not surprised.

Mirna asks me for a cigarette in front of the squat. She tells me I'm lying when I say I learned Croatian, that I'm not from here. As the music starts inside, she grabs my hand. We sell patches for my friends from Belgrade as they go up front to dance. Someone says that their mother just called; she'd just seen ten carloads of skinheads load baseball bats into their trunks and drive towards the squat. I run around telling my friends in a panic, but everyone laughs.

"Crazy Nazis, there's 2,000 punks here, they're going to get hurt," Sanja says, chuckling.

Mirna pulls me up to the churning front. The Subhumans, the great political jazz-punk band, are playing in Croatia for the first time. The crowd tears at itself in joy. We smash each others' bones in, exchange the teary-eyed glares of loving maniacs, scream along in a torrential chorus, "Drink, sex, cigarettes; Ford Cortina, household pets. Bombs, war, famine, death? An apathetic public couldn't care less!" I have to crawl out after the show, I can't talk, just smile.

Somebody puts a giant stuffed-parrot-hat on their head, someone else turns up the stereo. My English travelmates' van doubles as a sound system in the dancehall parking lot; my stiff limbs start to jerk and twist. Devo shouts out: "We're through being cool!" Mirna throws me against the van, and we are lost in sloppy kisses. The dance party continues around us, everything is in order. We run off, stumbling over passed-out punks in front of their tents, in this direction and that, we roll off car hood after trunk, we maneuver through the meadow spotted with toilet-paper piles like it was a minefield and collapse onto a little hill beyond it, past the ears of the drunken parking lot.

Oregano shoots twist and crush under our weight, the richness of mint and sage smothers, hides our hushed touch in its shelter of smell.

The next day I am watching punks crawl over the walls of an ancient seaside castle a few miles outside of town. Everyone is stripped out of their black layers, swimming, jumping off the rocks, drinking, playing music from boom boxes. People show up after getting lost for hours in the tangling overgrown paths, as others dive into them to get lost. I dread some drunk punker falling off a cliff or into some giant castle hole, but it never quite happens. I am trying not to wonder if I'll see Mirna again. I sip my coffee as my friends exchange stories from the weekend. Šapo, singer of the veteran Croatian punk band Fak Of Bolan, "Fuck Off Hick," turns to me and says, "You see, this is the new ground. In the West, everything is already taken for granted, already expected."

Sarajevo, BiH.

NOBLE PATINA VS. BARROOM BANALISATION

THE DAY BEFORE WE'RE GOING TO LEAVE ZAGREB, EVERYONE IS GATHERED IN A QUIET PANIC IN THE ANARCHIST CENTER. THE MEETING HAS ALREADY STARTED WHEN I ENTER. ONE FRIENDLY PUNK TAKES TIME OUT OF THE TALK TO TRANSLATE. "WE MIGHT NOT GO, THE GATHERING MIGHT BE CANCELED. THE PRIME MINISTER OF VOJVODINA WAS ASSASSINATED, THERE'S RIOTS IN BELGRADE, THE POLICE ARE SWEEPING THE CITY... WE DON'T KNOW IF OUR FRIENDS IN SERBIA CAN MEET US IN BOSNIA. MAYBE IT'S NOT A GOOD TIME FOR TWO BUSES FULL OF ANARCHISTS TO CROSS THE BORDER." EVERYONE LOOKS WORRIED; THE DISCUSSION IS BRISK.

Someone's cell phone rings. The person nods, listens, OK, OK. "They don't care, they're coming anyway."

Roofless houses, bullet and shrapnel-ridden, line the road. We are in Krajina, where Croatian forces drove 200,000 Serb civilians from their homes within a single week in 1995, with US assistance.[60] We drive past the exit for Jasenovac, the WWII concentration camp for Serbs, Jews, and Roma.[61]

"Why are we going to Zelenkovac?" I ask my friend, a straight-edge vegan.

"We are going to eat meat and drink blood with the Serbs," he grins into the camera.

Everyone is excited. After talking for years with anarchists in other parts of ex-Yugoslavia, putting publications together, and maintaining friendships across the recently established borders, today everyone is going to meet in person for the first time.

At the border with Bosnia, we are all ordered off the bus. A few kilometers north, in the Muslim-Croat Federation of Bosnia, we would probably have little trouble, but here in the Serbian Republic of Bosnia, the other republic within the same country, a bus-load of Croatian punks is not a common sight. I am a bit worried about what the border guards will make of us, three Americans with a video camera and piles of empty videocassettes. Before me, the guards ask long questions of my Croatian friends, searching to the bottom of their bags. They do their best to explain. I cannot understand; are we being turned back? I step up and hand the guard my passport. He looks for a long second directly into my eyes. "OK, good trip," he smiles and pats my back without searching my bags. We pile onto the bus.

Out the window, I stare in wonder at the sole standing wall in a village that has been otherwise totally leveled. "Death. Violence. Destruction," attests the wall, in Iron Maiden heavy-metal lettering. I wonder if modern-thinking Westerners realize that the actors in this war, supposedly so stuck in ancient history, sometimes thought they were in a music video.

At our next stop, several kids gather around the snack stand in front of our rest stop. Everyone wonders at the packs of Smoki flips and Jaffa cakes. A couple look like they might have tears in their eyes. "I haven't seen these since I was 12," Danielle explains. "Smokis were always my favorite thing in my lunchbox."

The last bus drops us off a few kilometers from Zelenkovac in a small village. The entire bus stares out the window at us as it drives away. An old villager finds a coin in my ear and twirls it around in his fingers, talking continuously to me in Bosnian. Oliver points to me and says something to the old man, who laughs and walks away. "I told him you were a Blue Helmet, a United Nations soldier," says Oliver. I restrain myself from punching Oliver. Boro, the proprietor of Zelenkovac, arrives again to take another car-load to his "eco-village."

"You know Boro?" one friend asks me. In the Czech Republic, one man had heard I was heading for the Serbian Republic in Bosnia, and had said only, "Surely you will meet Boro." My friend tells me Boro's story as we wait for the car to come back for us. Boro had not gotten along well with his traditional family in small-town Bosnia. He asked for his inheritance early, in the sum of one donkey. With his donkey, many years, and finally the help from visitors from around the world, Boro built Zelenkovac into a giant complex of hewn log, complete with towering walkways to take drunk guests from the bar or kitchen up to their sleeping rooms, and stairways to the various campfire and picnic areas. A stream runs through the center, providing its own music when a radio or musicians aren't available. Locals gather around with roasting pigs and violins to celebrate traditional festivals. People from all over the world show up to escape city life for a week or two. In this area around Mrkonic Grad, where war was particularly vicious in part because of its isolation, Boro's eco-village retreat has brought the world to rural Bosnia on Bosnia's own terms.

In the village, everyone is exchanging hugs. Davor the juggler warns us not to wander off the paths, since the mines still haven't been cleared.

The Serbians finally arrive, waving away our concern about their trip here. They explain that Milošević's cronies are too busy attacking the popular student opposition group Otpor to worry about the marginal anarchists. The Serbians start arguing with each other about whether the opposition is exactly as bad as Milošević, or only nearly as bad. Nobody can believe me when I tell them that in America, I had to pledge allegiance to the flag every morning at school. "Serbia is a pretty nationalist place, but we never had to promise loyalty to a piece of cloth, my God."

Everyone gathers around the campfire, gulping down the same veggie mush young idealists conjure up everywhere. The beer bottles in the bottom of the fire have melted into a sort of party platter. A drunk Croatian punk lies on the ground singing Ustaša Nazi songs from WWII, but nobody takes him seriously. As I film him, someone is telling me, in English, "We don't want you to film this, OK? Why don't you turn the camera off?" But I don't understand his words until I watch the video later.

Tanja is spinning torches at the ends of chains, wrapping her pulsating body in a cage of hushed flames. Beside her, Davor juggles four fireballs in gloved hands. His face is lit with shifting shadows. A kid from Mostar very patiently explains to me how to distill *rakija* from human shit. Borba is running around, screaming about how disorganized everything is, how we have to be more organized to make revolution.

(Later, I attempt to explain anarchism to an Albanian-American friend in New York. At first, he waves his hand dismissively. But when I tell him about the Zelenkovac meeting, he says: "Together? And they were agreeing? But this is amazing!")

I don't understand at all what's going on, but I'm glad to be here. I open yet another beer. I notice the camera is in the mud, again. So much for the documentary.

THE NEXT NIGHT I TALK TO A KID FROM BELGRADE IN THE Swiss Family Robinson bar. A couple of other anarchists are here for the gathering, but it is mostly full of locals. "Tito ruined us," he explains. "For a few decades of prosperity, we will be slaves for hundreds of years. Life in Serbia is chaos. People have no faith in the system at all."

"Perfect for the anarchist revolution?" I ask.

"Serbia is the last place on earth that could happen," he insists, shaking his head. "Society is too divided, people are too disorganized. Everyone would rather see their neighbor's cow die than have another of their own." We talk about tanks in Palestine, about fuel-air bombs in Chechnya, about the curses of the world's order makers. He tells me with a hint of embarrassment about his job in Belgrade as a cat-burglar. He hopes he can stop soon, but he only robs rich people's houses.

"Robin Hood?" I ask him.

"No, he gave to the poor, I keep it for myself." He is seventeen-years-old.

"You know a lot about what happened here, about the war," he goes on.

"I know some facts," I yell, "but I have no idea about the experience." I am getting drunk, shouting over the bar's din. "I have no idea what it is like in Grozny, or what it was like in Sarajevo..."

He doesn't flinch, but I realize the entire bar is quiet, and everyone is staring at me. Perhaps I shouldn't be eulogizing the seige of a city in a bar crowded with its beseigers. "Or in Knin! Or Belgrade!" The others in the bar slowly resume their conversations. I decide to drink a little slower.

The next day, everyone meets in workshops around the campfire, in the dimly sunlit rooms, sitting along wooden beam walkways overlooking the camp. I can decipher only the subjects on the agenda: "Anarchism and Ecology," "Anarcha-Feminism," "Anarchist Revolution." If I was a real documentary maker, I would beg a friend to translate for me, or at least film a workshop and have someone translate it later. But I'm getting worried that people I don't know here think I'm a spy, lurking around with my broken camera, so I grab a beer by the fire instead.

That night, word gets around that everyone is nearing the last of their cigarettes. Finally, the word is passed along in drunken yells: "Last cigarette! Everybody in the bar!" The announcement patiently makes its away across the cut-log picnic tables, into the sleeping rooms, around the campfires, over the mud. We all gather in a great circle, exhausted but still joking and discussing. One by one, a hundred or so carefully grasp the cigarette, suck, pass it on, and hold the smoke deep. The cigarette survives two cycles, a miracle of loaves and fishes. Soon, we will enjoy a collective nic-fit, but now, we are satisfied.

The next morning as we are getting ready to leave, everyone interrupts their packing to gather in a circle. "I have some very bad news," someone says. "Late last night, someone broke the window into the bar and stole many, many bottles of beer. Either that person comes forward, or we're going to have to get up the money between all of us, to replace the beer, and the window." For a long minute, everyone was silent. "Well, I guess we're all paying." My hungover memory lurches here and there as we all pull out our wallets. Suddenly I remember, the night before on my way to bed, seeing the guy now standing to my left crawl out through the bar window. He'd looked at me startled, but I nodded at him without understanding. I grab Tvrtko's arm. "Can I talk to you for a second?" We stuff bills into the hat and step away from the group. "I saw it happen, I know who did it." Tvrtko stares hard at me for a second. "So? I don't want to know. I mean, we all know who did it. Anyway, it's all our responsibility, so we should all pay, right?"

Once the money is counted, the counter announces that the hat holds far too much money. Someone suggests putting the extra to defray the traveling costs of whoever needs it, and everyone yells in agreement. I pack my bag quietly, humbled.

ACCORDING TO THE BBC DOCUMENTARY *YUGOSLAVIA: DEATH OF a Nation*,[62] the first deaths of the war in Bosnia were not Bosniaks killed by Serbs, nor Serbs killed by Croats, but a population rising against its own "representatives" and against the war before it began. "The people of Sarajevo saw war looming and begged their leaders to prevent it." On April 5, 1992, a huge protest took the streets of Sarajevo, occupied the Parliament building and asked both governments—the pro-independence Izetbegović and pro-Milošević Radovan Karadjić—to step down. I pause the video to read signs like "Nema čekanja, dola vlada"—no waiting, down with government! "Our government has abandoned us, the people must take charge," yells one of the leaders. The protest moved on to try and take the Holiday Inn, where Karadjić was staying. Police opened fire on Karadjić's orders and killed six protesters. On the screen, Kadadjić boasts with a smile, "Our police took the necessary measures." Crowds run for cover in terrifying confusion.

Some of the people in the protest may have preferred for Bosnia and Herzegovina to remain a republic within Yugoslavia, while others preferred to become an independent state, but none accepted war as the means to achieve either. The leaders both explicitly acknowledged that war would result from their actions, and then chose it. Izetbegović said, "We would sooner give up peace for independence, than independence for peace." Karadjić quotes Milošević as saying, "Caligula proclaimed his horse a senator, but a horse never took its seat. Izetbegović will get recognition, but he will never have a state." Croatia's Stipe Mesić testifies that "I saw the Bosnian Croats and Serbs agree on a carve-up, along the Neretva river." A few minutes later in the documentary, Vojislav Seselj then goes on to say, "We had prepared this separation carefully for a long time. We didn't have to rush or anything like that. Everything went exactly as planned."

> For those elites who decide to protect the status quo, demobilization is a crucial goal, since the most serious immediate threat comes exactly from that part of the population being mobilized by challenger elites for fundamental change. One way to demonize the population is to reconceptualize political space, thereby fundamentally shifting the focus of political discourse away from issues around which challengers are mobilizing the populace, toward the question of who "owns" space; the right to make decisions about the space belongs to these "owners." Violence can play a crucial role in such a reconceptualization, eclipsing demands for change and redirecting the focus of politics toward a purported threat, as well as reshaping demographic realities on the ground in a way that reinforces the sense of threat. Such violence is thus targeted at least as much against the home-state population, those defined as "us," as it is against the direct victims of violence, since the major intended effects of the violence—demobilization and homogenization of politi-

cal space—are aimed at the home population; the impact on the direct victims may even be only a secondary effect.[63]

Were the Yugoslav wars not homogenous ethnic units over resources, as the all-knowing "Neo-Realist" [sic] voices of International Relations Theory assert, but wars of state elites against their own populations? A war fought through massive violence on the bodies and selves of the Other—violence to create an Other—in order to control the bodies at home?

> *"If you wish to understand what I have pointed to here,*
> *then 'take four birds and twist them to thee,'*
> *because Allah does not fly."*
> —HUSSAIN BIN MANSUR AL-HALLAH, *THE TAWASIN*[64]

IN BAŠČARŠIJA, THE CENTER OF THE CITY THAT IS THE center of this half of the country, there are no McDonald's or shiny office blocks. The wooden chessboards and *burek* stands are gathered like folds in a dervish's robes around the old Turkish fountain in the center, and like dust motes in a sunbeam pigeons cover everything. The steep bricks lead up past woodworkers and blacksmiths who labor on the sidewalk in front of their shops; I remind myself that Sarajevo also has steel factories outside the ancient center. Book stands lay at the foot of each of the mosque towers, selling Sufi books—Sufism has always dominated Bosnian Islam, Bosnia lying far from the Islamic orthodox centers of Baghdad and Cairo—outlining the "systematic ambiguity of being" of sixteenth century Islamic existentialist Sadra,[65] the gathering of birds of consciousness of Farid ud-Din Attar's *Conference of the Birds*.[66] Islam, the expression of the harsh passion of Arab genius, heretically inseminated with Zoroastrian and Buddhist whispers in the fruit and flower of Persian luxury, brought by the imperious Turk, translated into provincial Slavic. Yet through these wafting fragrances of influence lies the hardest of sciences: "The fervent practice of worship engenders in the soul graces (*fawaid*), immaterial and intelligible realities, and that the 'science of hearts' (*ilm al kulub*) will procure the soul an experimental wisdom (*ma'rifa*)."[67]

Some say Bosnians accepted Islam so they could continue in the popular Bogomil heresy, in its puritanical anti-authoritarianism, before Rome could arrive with its Inquisitions. Once under

Baščaršija, Sarajevo, BiH.

Ottoman rule, conversion was essential to distinguish oneself as urban middle class: Christianity was the mark of the *raya*, the peasantry. Today, traditionally dressed peasants sit on crates selling corn and barley to passers-by. This is how the density of pigeons has persisted through modernity: the reification of Sufic bird love. Urban design at the hands of every citizen—a quarter for a bag of birdseed—a living statue to flittering heresy, the East within the West. Even if five or six centuries ago some Islamicized Slavs were just opportunistic Bogomils or bourgeoisie, their love of the pigeon is by now sincere enough to deserve their central square.

The main crisis of *Mary Poppins* revolves around this exact conflict of capitalism versus bird feeding. Mary sings to the banker's children: "Early each day to the steps of St. Paul's, the little old bird woman comes. In her special way to the people she calls, come buy my bags full of crumbs. Feed the birds, that's what she cries, while overhead her birds fill the skies. Though her words are simple and few, listen, listen, she's calling to you, feed the

Poster distributed by the Organization for Security and Cooperation in Europe:
"If this is somebody's idea of peace in Bosnia and Herzegovina,
maybe you should listen to somebody else."

birds, tuppence a bag." When young Michael tries to spend his tuppence accordingly, the boss of his father's bank responds: "Fiddlesticks my boy. Feed the birds and what've you got? Fat birds." Michael refuses to invest his tuppence, the boss grabs them from his hand, the bank collapses, and everyone happily ends up flying kites. Pamela Travers,[68] author of the Mary Poppins books, was close friends with the Armenian scientific-mystic Gurdjieff, who was intimately connected with Sufism. Pamela Travers and Gurdjieff, much like Bosnia, have had no end of problems with fundamentalism interfering in their mystical explorations.

I spill my body over the bricks and stare up through pigeon clouds. An old man hobbles over and pulls me from the ground, visibly upset. He motions his hands in mysterious swirls and yells at me; I don't understand a word. An older peasant woman yells over her table of birdseed, "He tells you the ground is too dirty, there is too much bird shit." He bows deeply with his hand on his heart, and stares through my eyes with a jarring softness, uttering a phrase over and over. I shrug and try to smile. "He says he is a Muslim," says the peasant woman. I give him a thumbs up, Muslim good, Muslim good, I am from

America. He grabs me and embraces me. He will not release me from his embrace.

Staring up at the fountain, I sing a Rambo Amadeus song to myself. Rambo Amadeus is perhaps the Montenegrin rock version of the crazy old idiot-prophet Mullah Nasruddin. Rambo is such a perfect fool that it took some years for anyone to recognize his music as satire. At the beginning of one concert, he entered the stage to the audience's cheers only to ask if he could watch a football game first; he laid on a couch, on stage, watching the game on TV for an entire hour before getting up to play for them. At another, his backup band consisted of seven vacuum cleaners. He coined the term "Turbo-Folk" to describe the massively popular nationalist-oriented neo-folk-pop genre. Somehow the mocking undertones of the name were lost, and it became the standard term.

"One night I was walking home from the bar, and I found myself in Baščaršija square," goes the song. "Suddenly, bright lights came down from the sky. A little green man descended from the great glowing disk. 'Do not be afraid,' said the small green man. 'Do not be afraid. Our heart was broken by the same woman. Do not be afraid. Our heart was broken by the same woman.'"

ON OUR WAY TO THE TUNNEL MUSEUM, IN THE MIDDLE OF Sarajevo, the tram stops to wait for traffic. Directly overhead, a massive military helicopter hovers low. Dalia and I stop talking, and cannot remember what we were saying under the sound of its rotors. Out the window, I can read "SFOR"—the UN security forces—painted in huge white letters across its side. Across the street from our tram, the barrel of a giant handgun points at me from a billboard, with words spelled out in Bosnian, "By the time you see this it's already too late. Hand over all illegal weapons now!—SFOR." I remember seeing a poster distributed by international forces that reads, in Cyrillic letters surrounding a photo of an impromptu graveyard, "If this is someone's idea of peace in Bosnia and Herzegovina, maybe you should listen to somebody else." It has been eight years since the active fighting stopped.

The sign reminds me of something one anarchist, from Banja Luka in the Serbian Republic in Bosnia, wrote for the June 2004 issue of the American punk magazine *Maximum Rock N' Roll*. While opposed to all standing armies, he remarked how scary it is that the West is reducing Bosnia's army, while heavily funding its police forces—a classic colonial formula. In addition, UN officials recently shut down a local news station. Although he was relieved to be spared its stream of nationalistic propaganda, he was worried that the supervisory officials could simply close down a station they didn't like. With imminent privatization of public services—eighty percent of businesses had been publicly owned in Yugoslavia—and sudden massive foreign direct investment from the very countries supervising Bosnia's "recovery," he wrote, the "real dark days" aren't over, but lie ahead: "The current abolishment of human services—free education, pension funds, free health care—is just the beginning of the real nightmare that will come."

I stop for a much-needed shot of espresso with a shot of *rakija* before we take a cab to the tunnel museum. Edis Kolar shakes our hands as we enter the basement of his house. During the four year siege of Sarajevo, the half-mile long tunnel, starting from this basement and running underneath the airport runway, allowed the only passage from within the encircled city to the friendly neighboring area in Bosnia. Hundreds passed through it on some days. I stare at a photo of a newlywed bride lifting her gown over two feet of water on her way out. In another photograph, Edis and his father stand proudly in uniform beside Alija Izetbegović, founder of Yugoslavia's first explicitly nationalist party and the president of Bosnia during the war. The Kolar family hasn't lived upstairs since the house was shelled, but Edis runs the museum in the basement.

After walking down the remaining stretch of the tunnel and back, we enter a small room filled with camouflage militaria and shells. A coal cart once used to run supplies along tracks through the tunnel now holds weapons that the Bosnian army was not able to obtain during the war. Dalia and I sit down in the next room. Edis starts a video and leaves. Bodies litter the ground around burning cars in the streets where we were just walking. Jets unleash a salvo of missiles straight into towering office skyscrapers, now the looming burnt shells we passed on our ride here. Panicked reporters scream through tears as bodies are dragged away behind them. Background music of synthesized cellos lament as horror is edited down to death-kitsch. Edin walks back in and turns it off. "Do you have anything you would like to ask me?"

I'm not sure where to start. "I was just reading about the woman hired by DynCorp to investigate prostitution here in Sarajevo, who was fired when she found it was largely organized by a certain private contractor for the US military—named DynCorp. She found that as many as 20,000 women had been kidnapped into sex slavery in Bosnia; eighty percent of their clientele are international 'humanitarian intervention' troops.[69] My friend Marko, who lived here during the war, told me that he hates the UN blue helmets, how they treat people here, and that everyone knows that the international forces are only here for interests that don't have much to do with the interests of Bosnians. But then, he said he's glad they're here because there's no more war. Another friend in Zagreb said he would like to ask those who deny any local responsibility if they actually want the international troops to withdraw, and whose fault it would be then if war started."

Edis shakes his head. "You didn't need to intervene. The war might have never even started if the UN hadn't passed the arms embargo. The Četniks—I don't say Serbs, since of course all Serbs aren't Četniks—the Četniks had all the weapons from the Yugoslav military, which was the third largest in Europe. The UN tried to make peace by not letting us buy any guns as the Četniks were using theirs to genocide us. As soon as it was lifted, in the middle of '95, we started kicking ass. You know, NATO had to stop us at the end around Bihać, because we were taking back too much from the Četniks? We probably could have won the whole country, but they made us stop, even retreat, just before Dayton was signed. All we needed was one more week! We could have got Bihać, and so much more..." he says, pounding his hand and laughing, like he'd almost won the lotto.

I ask if there would have been actions like Operation Storm, or "Oluja," in Croatia, with massive population cleansings. He pauses. "Of course. So what?"

I am offended, but can't respond. If the action is seen as ethnic cleansing, I hate him. If it is seen as conquering more land for a multi-ethnic political order, taking land away from an ethno-nationalist one, I admire him. Either way, the question remains: can I agree with making civilians into refugees for having the wrong politics, for being under the rule of the wrong side? Is disagreeing with such realpolitik just hiding in my privilege of distance, or were there other real options?

Many people in the Bosnian army fought for a multi-ethnic, pluralist Bosnia. As the war worsened, some embittered soldiers fought in the same army at the same time for an ethnically pure state. Mujahideen mercenaries from the Islamic fundamentalist diaspora were certainly present at least in small numbers, protecting their fellow Muslims and nurturing territorial ambitions of their own, as other extremist volunteers had already come to the aid of Serbia and Croatia. The presence of such forces in Bosnia must have legitimized the fears of those soldiers in the opposing forces, who felt they were fighting to keep a large, multi-ethnic Yugoslavia against disintegration into ethnically pure countries—with Serbs as the threatened minority. The CIA may have been among the Bosnian forces too, alongside the multi-ethnicists and the mujahideen, establishing control of the emerging "sanitizing corridor" between East and West, which local politicians speak of openly in negotiations. All in the same army, beside the many normal people fighting for the right to live next to their neighbors in rich diversity. Am I offended or not? Are these the good guys or just another kind of bad guys? I change the subject.

"Are you worried about what they are doing here now? Like dependency on foreign investment, neo-liberalism, capitalism, austerity measures, all that?"

"Yes, I'm worried, everyone is. But we need factories, jobs. We can't build our own factories now, and nobody's going to donate 200 billion dollars to help us out. Donations are nice, but 200 billion?"

I tell Edis that Šešelj, a Serbian politician from Bosnia known for his war crimes here, who likes to threaten people with rusty forks in parliament, might win the presidency in Serbia. "It tells you something about that country. You know, we just had the first football match between Serbia and Bosnia, here in Bosnia. The fans from Serbia were chanting: 'This is Serbia! This is Serbia!' Imagine, you could hear them yelling from the neighboring stadium, which is filled now with thousands of graves from the war. The police had to escort the fans out of town. By the way, our team is horrible, everybody beats us. Even Malta."

I ask him if there are any Serbs on the team of the supposedly multi-ethnic federation. "No," he says.

"Why did the Serbs who lived in Sarajevo during the war leave after? Did people force them out?"

"There were 20,000, maybe 25,000 in Sarajevo during the war, but most left after. Nobody forced them out. Bosnian Serb politicians scared them into moving away, but nobody drove them out." I tell him Dalia and I arrived in the newly created Serbian Sarajevo, across the road in the Serb Republic in Bosnia. "Right," he says. "The 'city' of Srpsko Sarajevo. We say here that it's the 'city' with the largest park in the world." He laughs. He's right, it had a lot of trees and hills for a city, and not many houses. Why would the Sarajevo Serbs have believed politicians who'd just bombed them for four years, and move into such a strange little park/city, away from beautiful Sarajevo? Why would the non-Serbs drive out people who'd suffered the same bombing as them, especially if they were protecting a multi-ethnic Bosnia?

We climb into Edis' car. "You don't understand me," sings Roxette from the tape deck.

"What do you think about the story that Bosnian President Izetbegović ordered the bombing of the Markale marketplace in Sarajevo that killed 38 of his own population the day before the UN voted on intervention, and ended up getting NATO in on his side?"

Edis politely restrains himself: "Radovan Karadžić, leader of the Bosnian Serbs, made that up. It was a retaliation for our advances on Banja Luka and Bijac. They'd done it a year before and nobody claimed it was our side that time, when 67 died at the same place. Some Serbian tourist in the museum kept telling me they heard my president killed his own people to get pity and support, I couldn't stand it. It made me pretty mad to hear that."

We drive past a campaign poster that says, "Let's get back to the spirit and energy of Sarajevo 1984!" I'm depressed that the best Bosnian politicians can do is Olympic nostalgia. Posters next to it say, in Bosnian, "For Bosnia!" and various hopeful slogans about getting "into Europe."

"Who are you voting for, Edis?"

He laughs again. "I don't know. Doesn't matter. I'll see who the paper tells me to vote for. Elections are tomorrow, that's why you see all these ugly faces everywhere." I ask him about the current president. He considers.

"I don't know. I forgot his name. Doesn't matter. The EU makes all the decisions here. Anything decided by a Bosnian politician, or Bosnian voters, can be overrun by the EU supervisors. I probably won't even vote tomorrow, it's not worth closing the museum."

The Roxette tape croons "It's a little bit dangerous" as we step out of the car and thank Edis profusely. He shakes our hands warmly, wishes us a good stay, and zooms away.

IN AN ISLAMIC BOOKSTORE IN PHILADELPHIA, I PICK UP a videotape titled *The Martyrs of Bosnia*.[70] On the back, I read:

> The 1990s saw the genocide of the Muslims in Bosnia under the guidance of the International Community in scenes reminiscent of Muslim slaughter in the Crusades, Baghdad and the First World War. Volunteer Muslim fighters from all parts of the globe flocked to Bosnia to defend Muslim blood, property and honour. Many were injured, some were captured but a handful managed to obtain the ultimate prize of martyrdom in the Path of Allah.
>
> This unique video by Azzam Publications, the first of its kind in the English language with real-life combat footage and the first of a four part series, narrates the biographies of some of these magnificent individuals, who sacrificed their own lives in order to bring life to those around them.

I am grimly amused to read that the International Community guided the genocide of Muslims in Bosnia; Serb nationalists and many American leftists seem convinced that the International Community guided the genocide of Serbs, instead. One Croatian military official, a friend's father, once whispered to me as we shared a drink, "We never would have tried to take on the JNA (Yugoslavian National Army) if we hadn't had promises of help." He didn't imply that such negligent promises were intentionally malevolent, but surely some interpret the facts in this light. Maybe all of them are right. After all, I think Hannah Arendt did say somewhere in *The Origins of Totalitarianism* that the thesis of the modern state is: "Everyone should die."

When, at the beginning of the war, Bosnian Muslims were massively in need of guns and friends, such sacrifices from the international mujahideen "to bring life to those around them" must have been a blessing. But the influence "to defend Muslim blood, property, and honour" might not ultimately make the ideal guardians of Bosnia's multi-ethnic, secular tradition.

In a collection of essays by Croatian-American Josip Novakovich called *Plum Brandy*, I read:

We visited the housing under-secretary in Sarajevo ... He claimed that the fate of Bosnia lay in the distribution of houses and apartments: it was basically a real-estate issue. Recently a law was introduced to allow the refugees who stayed in vacated apartments to live there until they found better arrangements. Now, what that meant in Sarajevo was that the Muslim refugees who recently came from Srebrenica and many other places could stay in the apartments previously owned by Serbs and Croats for as long as they liked. Sarajevo had become basically a mono-ethnic city, Muslim, in a backlash against Serbian ethnic cleansing.[71]

I FIND THE SAME REAL-ESTATE PROCESS, ETHNIC MONIKERS swapped, in the southern city of Mostar, in Svetlana Broz's amazing *Good People in an Evil Time*, in an interview with a local Croat leader Jole Musa:

"When we read today what the politicians are writing we get the impression that everyone was fighting some kind of war of liberation and defense. ... The Croatian Defense Council in Mostar was a classical aggressive force, far more serious, with more serious consequences, than the Serbian troops had been.

"I made a statement that there were 5,000 [Croat] soldiers living in western Mostar who had occupied 5,000 apartments, and that it was time for them to go home, because there had been no combat in their home towns. Their homes were undamaged there, their chickens, cows, goats were being cared for by their mothers and fathers, while someone else's apartment in Mostar was like a second home to them. After that statement they tried to assassinate me, throwing a shell into my office, which I had left, thank goodness, a half hour earlier.

"Earlier this year while he was mayor of Mostar, Safet Orucević, a Muslim, got me involved in building Croatian homes in eastern Mostar. Then I will move on to work on building Muslim and Serbian homes in the western part of town. That is a job that no one dares or wants to do, because it is obstructed, particularly in western Mostar, by the Croatian authorities. It is also clear why. They need refugees to fight the war for them, and after the war to vote for them in elections."[72]

Perhaps the clearest example from the whole war happened in the village of Stupni Do and neighboring Vareš, where outside

Croatian forces locked thirty-eight Muslims in a church and burned it down, framing the event in a way that made local Croats—who, well into the war, were still living intimately with their Muslim neighbors—look as if they'd done the massacre themselves. Says Hamdo Fatić, interviewed in Broz's book:

> There was a terrible tragedy for Muslims on 23 October 1993 when Croatian troops known as the Maturice, brought in from Kiseljak, committed a massacre in the village of Stupni Do. They murdered thirty-eight innocent people and destroyed the entire village. As a rule it is always someone from somewhere else who comes in and commits the foulest evil in order to achieve a certain goal. Part of the plan was to burden the Vareš Croats with a sense of collective responsibility and the fear of Muslim retaliation for the massacre. That way the Croats would be forced to move out of town. The Croatian forces needed them as manpower elsewhere and the Croatian leaders also knew they didn't have military forces strong enough to hold Vareš.[73]

What Western pedants, parroting the words local tyrants used as justification for their atrocities, cite as the causes of the war, are revealed instead as its intended effects. Had such divisions existed before, it wouldn't have taken such unthinkably massive violence to impose them.

INSIDE A COPPER CARNATION THE ETERNAL FLAME BURNS in front of a meticulously maintained partisan monument to the 1945 liberation, the big red star still newly painted and polished. Across the street, the Iranian Cultural Embassy provides lessons in Arabic, though these descendants of Persians don't speak Arabic any more than people here do. On the other side of the street is another cultural embassy, many times more massive, with the letters "United Colors of Benneton" lit over its double doors. The placement of buildings seems coincidental. They nod at each other, perhaps muttering "tsk tsk tsk" within their walls, yet absurdly civil in their public proximity. Should politics risk such intimate diversity? Is it wrong, in the way it was wrong for Franco to bury fascists with their victims, to reconcile all in the mass grave of Spanishness? But the city, this city, is not a grave. These are not its dead. Up the street, teenagers make out next to tombstones in the park.

DERTUM IS A GREAT FOLK BAND OF BOSNIAN REFUGEES IN Slovenia. I include their liner notes here for their eloquent summation of the essential aesthetic of humanistic dignity, the noble patina which is the opposite of nationalist ethno-kitsch:

The lack of outlook to the future of time standing still in refugee centres for the wrong citizens of the wrong parts of Bosnia and Herzegovina has thrust into passivity and apathy the large majority of these invisible reservation dwellers. Among the living, the most noticeable and the loudest is certainly the group of refugee students, sheltered in the refugee camps in Ljubljana, whose rhythm is provided by a student of south Slavic languages, a Slovenian citizen of less appreciated ancestry.

Dertum creatively latched onto social life with the help of acoustic guitars, percussion and vocals. It revived archival examples of traditional Bosnian singing poetry, the sevdah, and related Macedonian songs. They have been covered uncountably many times and can nowadays be heard mainly on late night programs of the national broadcast centers of BiH and Macedonia, in academically lavish performances, overarranged in a state-building spirit.

The youths extracted the cores of these foundations of national indoctrination and translated them, with love and carefully measured vital pragmatism, originating in rock 'n' roll, into the language of three guitars, percussion, and modestly ornamented, unaffected polyphonies. They distributed the roles of the instruments very democratically and purposefully, perfected the solo parts, which they don't exaggerate, and very carefully pierced the hermeticallity of the traditional melos with miniature jazz and rock modes.

The cherished national heritage almost calls for barroom banalisation, which Dertum resists with a seriousness and respect at times befitting a reading-room, and on the other hand with the moderate discipline of individual members and the mature interpretation of the female vocalists.

The self-evident and automatic way in which the audience assigns them the role of cultural ambassadors of an endangered race became apparent to the timely mature youths at the right moment, and they immediately began to act responsibly and earnestly. A repertoire without unnecessary vulgarities and the absence of conceit in the virtuosity and joyfulness of concert music prove that the musicians can appreciate and foster the noble patina of their expression.[74]

WHILE YOUTH IN EXILE PLAYED TRADITIONAL SONGS TO fight against armed forgetting, youth in Sarajevo embraced modernist underground rock in rebellion against those trying to drown them in history. Forty bands played in the besieged city of around 200,000. Kids would run across sniper alleys and dodge raining shells to rock out with their friends. Hundreds made it to most of the shows, sometimes twice a week. "Would you want to die in a shelter with your parents, or at a show with your friends?" Marko asks me. His band, Pessimistic Lines, influenced by Sonic Youth and Bad Religion, is one of the few to have continued playing after the war. "It's hard to explain, but the whole atmosphere, it was great. No school or anything. Now people just go to their jobs, have their routines... You can't understand this, but I really miss it."

GRAFFITI ON THE MAIN POST OFFICE IN BANJA LUKA, the entire dialectic in perfect summary:

Ovo je Srbija!
This is Serbia!

(Just beneath, in different paint):

Glupače! Ova je Pošta!
Moron! This is the Post Office!

I'M RANTING AGAIN, TO MY FRIEND GUNDULA, A GERMAN journalist who spent years in the US as well as traveling through the Balkans. "This great book I read, *Sarajevo: Exodus of a City*, says that Sarajevo embodies a diversity far advanced of the multicultural diversity of the US. In the US, liberal multiculturalists advocate tolerance, a sterile relation of difference. Sarajevo, and Bosnia in general, and even all Yugoslavia, was and maybe is still defined as home to dramatic diversity. I'm a Sephardic Jew because you're a Muslim. I can only be Catholic if my neighbor is an atheist. The difference is demonstrative, not parallel."[75]

Gundula laughs at me. "But this is the same as what Huntington says in *The Clash of Civilizations*,[76] what you said you are writing to disprove! Civilizations are defined by their differences from each other."

She's shut me up. I look out the window for a bit. Finally, I punch my own knee in epiphany. "OK, OK. Both Sarajevo and Huntington are demonstrative, but Huntington is discrete while Sarajevo has always been intimate. Huntington's civilizations don't miscegenate, whereas here they can't help getting sensual."

In front of the bus station in Mostar, where everyone stares at each other without making eye contact, a very drunk man sits down with us. He does not look happy. "I was living in Norway, seven years," he explains with his hands, and in fragments of several languages. "Norway is very beautiful. I have a girlfriend there, a job, a life. They told me it's time to go home. Today I go home. Not home. No more home. Destroyed, smash, fire. They send me home. Norway is very beautiful."

I remember the dictionary in my pocket, and ask him to wait as I pull it out to help him make himself understood. He slaps his finger against the cover as soon as I get it out. "NO!" He points to the word "Serbo-Croatian." "Not Serb! Not Croat! I am not! Not!" He gets up and wanders off, disgusted.

I'm Surrounded by friends in a punk-rock animal shelter commune, a Serbian village outside Mostar. Some of the other residents are just beginning to return, judging. Next door an empty house is still painted with a crescent, and the words, "Ne Pali"—don't burn. Friends from different parts of Bosnia and international visitors take turns cooking different courses.

Over dinner, Jelena tells me of a recent football riot in the center of town. Croatia and Brazil were playing, and the Croats of Mostar were supporting Croatia, while the Bosniaks supported Brazil. Not only did Brazil's team have Ronaldo, they also weren't Croatia. The Croatia fans started smashing in shop windows, the Brazil fans attacked them, and the cops came in with tear gas. One person was shot, six police and many of the hooligans injured. "My brother had his jaw broken by a cop. Dumb kids."

I ask Jelena about the "miraculous" appearance of Mother Mary in nearby Medugorje. "Ha, Medjugorje, we just made our pilgrimage there a few months ago!" as she laughs with her fellow co-communalists. "No, I mean, we were just drunk and wanted to see how long it took to walk. We left after dinner and made it by morning. We fell asleep in the morning service but I don't think anyone noticed."

I pull Sabrina Ramet's *Balkan Babel* out of my pack and look up her entry on Medjugorje. In the early 80's, Pavao Zanic, the Catholic Bishop of Mostar, in the south-east of the republic of Bosnia and Herzegovina, still at that time within the Socialist Federation of Yugoslavia, suspended two young monks in an effort to curtail Franciscan influence in his diocese. Soon after, "six youngsters whom these two Franciscans had been counseling began to report apparitions of the Madonna, who, they said, was endorsing the Franciscans and blaming the bishop of Mostar for his 'severity.'" The Franciscan order assumed responsibility for ministering to the floods of those who soon made pilgrimages to the site, and the threat to their power in the region was curtailed.[77]

I ask Jelena how many pilgrims have visited Medjugorje, and she flips on their official site, evidently a bit pained. Apparently, the floods of pilgrims did not cease with the reinstatement of the two Franciscans in their positions. In the words of the site, "Since the apparitions began in 1981, millions of people of all faiths, from all over the world, have visited Medjugorje [10 million by '88] and have left spiritually strengthened and renewed. Many bring back stories of miracles in the form of healings (of mind, body and soul), supernatural visual events, and deep conversions back to God. You owe it to yourself and your loved ones, to investigate with an open mind and heart the messages which are given to us by Our Lady of Medjugorje."

After finishing my dish-washing shift, I settle down on the couch and read the following in *The Fortress*, by perhaps Bosnia's greatest 20th century author, a sort of Sufi Dostoyevsky named Mesa Selimovic. The book was published in Yugoslavia in 1970, and widely received. The narrator [who is struggling to resume life after returning from war to find his home destroyed] describes Ramiz, who has just returned from studies in Egypt to his native Sarajevo in the 18th century, and has brought with him some ideas that sound familiar in my current setting:

> Never from anyone had I heard so many cutting words, so much contempt for people in power, so much mad free-thinking, as I did listening to that passionate student of Al-Azhar University, who didn't know what fear was, or, rather, didn't know what authority was. He said—I remember even now my astonishment—that there were three great passions: alcohol, gambling, and power. People could be cured of the first two,

but of the third never. Power was the worst vice. For its sake, people killed, people perished. For its sake, people lost all human resemblance. It was irresistible, like the magic stone, for it gave might. It was the genie in Aladdin's lamp, who served every fool that owned it. On their own, these three passions represented nothing; together, they were the fate of the world. There was no such thing as honest and wise government, for the lust for power was limitless. A man in power was encouraged by cowards, backed by flatterers, upheld by rogues, and his idea of himself was always better than the reality. He considered all people stupid, because they hid their true opinions from him, and he took to himself the right to be all-knowing, and people accepted it. No one in power was wise, for the wise quickly lost their reason, and no one was tolerant, for they hated change. They immediately created eternal laws, eternal principles, an eternal order, and by linking their power to God thus affirmed their might. And no one would overthrow them did they not become a hindrance and threat to others in power. They were always overthrown in the same way, accused of oppression of the people, yet all of them were oppressors, and of treason to the ruler, but nobody ever thought of this. And no one had learned from it; they all flew headlong to power like moths to a candle flame. Weren't all the Bosnian governors imprisoned, exiled, or killed? And all their followers. And always came new ones, bringing their own followers and repeating the stupidities of their predecessors, since they couldn't do otherwise. And so it went on, in a circle, forever. The people could live without bread, but not without power. The powerful were a disease on the body of the people, like boils. When one burst another grew, perhaps still worse. You couldn't do without us, they told us, robbers would increase, the enemy would attack us, there'd be chaos in the country. Yet who made this country, who fed it, who defended it? The people. Yet they fined us, punished us, imprisoned us, killed us. And, moreover, they forced our sons to do so. They couldn't do without you. You must do without them. There are few of them, there are many of us. Were we only to lift a finger, so many are we, this filth would no longer be. And this we will do, my downtrodden brothers, the moment we have real people who will not allow vampires to sit on their necks.[78]

A few pages later, the narrator meets Ramiz, who explains where he came upon these ideas:

This had all been made clear to him by a dervish from the Hamzevian order. Authorities were unnecessary, neither ruler nor state, all that was oppression. It was sufficient to have people make all decisions by common agreement, ordinary people who went about their business without desiring to rule others and without allowing anyone to rule them. And sufficient was God's mercy that would aid them. The dervish had been killed, but his words had remained. All of them, save those regarding God's mercy. People could arrange whatever they needed among themselves.[79]

HERE IT IS, HERE IS THE GRAFFITI, SCRIBBLED ON POSTCARDS sent from the Hague to their old friends in Prijedor, in the documentary *Calling the Ghosts*, directed by Mandy Jacobson and Karmen Jelincić.[80] Sent by women—Jadranka Cigelj and Nusreta Sivac, to be precise—who suffered in the Omarska camp, who were raped in the camp, who survived and fled, and organized torture survivors from Bosnia to record their testimonies. And who successfully pressured the International Criminal Tribunal for the former Yugoslavia to get rape recognized, for the first time in international law, as a form of torture. Who, as veteran lawyers, helped indict their former torturers and set a historical precedent. Then they sent postcards back home, to those who drove them out, inviting them to see the inside of a war criminal prison. "Very nicely, just to say hello to them." *It's nice here, you should come visit.*

During the war, Catherine MacKinnon wrote as though (in the words of Dubravka Žarkov) "in her account, raped Muslim women had no existence beyond their fractured bodies," and, along with many other Western feminists, that Muslim women *a priori* must be incapable of speaking out about such things.[81] Mute victims are much easier to appropriate than whole, real human beings who have made it out alive. These would-be benefactors speak similarly to the camp guards that Jadranka describes: "The next morning, they took us ... at seven in the morning and told us that we no longer had names."

Croat survivors were usually not mentioned in international or Croatian press, and Serb women were barred from counting by all sides—not the least because few agencies thought to gather testimonies in Serb refugee centers. Male victims of sexual violence were especially silenced, as their vulnerability threatened each side's nationalist narrative of triumphant masculinity. How different from the official version are Cigelj's words: "I heard [about] Serbian women [who] suffered as well. ...

To me, crimes against women are crimes regardless of whether they are committed against a Muslim, Croatian, or Serbian woman."

But despite the private agonies and social fears, and the physical dangers of testifying against powerful warlords, many thousands of survivors came forward to testify. Cigelj explains her reasons:

"If I kept silent, how moral would that be? ... I gave my first testimony in this building... Comprehensive, but still full of holes, because the most horrible things you push into your subconscious. And then, after that first conversation I realized that it's no good to close yourself up and carry the truth inside. You have to help those who stayed behind...

"I felt the need for revenge, and the only way to get revenge was by collecting testimonies. I thought that by making them public I would be able to get revenge...

"In the beginning, the need to tell the truth was strong and I hoped we would speak out. Other women arrived from Omarska. I organized them and told them that we had to tell the truth, no matter how painful it was."

Sivac says, "We were brought out before a firing squad, we thought we were finished. But then we said, 'Maybe one of us will survive and one day tell all this, to the public, to the whole world... Maybe then the world will realize, for once, what's really happening in Bosnia and Herzegovina...

"It's a new shock every time you talk about it, but I feel some kind of obligation... toward all those women, friends of mine who are now gone, who were killed in the camp, toward all those people who were dear to me... and who are now gone... If the story is not told, then no one will know about it, right?"

They speak of life in the camp as a continuum of horror, particular to each and yet shared among all the prisoners. In contrast, they mourn the way their particular torture was exoticized by the thrill-seeking West. Reporters would often introduce themselves by asking, "Which ones are the raped women?" Serifa Halilović, founding member Association of Women of Bosnia and Herzegovina, explains, "A lot of people were interested in rapes and they offered money only to raped women. You can't understand that there are, lets say old women that are here with their daughters and daughters-in-law, and they know that all the men in their family have been killed... And you can imagine how it is for them."

The women understand better than anyone the cold rationale behind the evil inflicted on them, without fantastic theories of sub-human beasts or ancient hatreds. Sivac explains, "I had only one wish, like everyone else, to run away as soon as possible from the city which we loved... [The camps existed,] simply, to destroy their spirit, to make those women realize that they can't live there anymore. It was all planned, none of it was coincidental."

As the documentary concludes, Cigelj does not speak of blaming any ethnicity, nor does her blame end with her former torturers and their bosses. In carefully parsed anger, she accuses, "...a heap of uninterested people, millions of uninterested people. Those who aren't hungry, who aren't getting shots fired on them, who would only wake up if a grenade exploded on top of their heads, or if a knife appeared. For whom it's terrible if their car breaks down. For whom the war is boring because it's someone else's, or interesting only as entertainment with popcorn and peanuts, as a TV program at night after work, who main preoccupation is to accumulate as much money as possible.

"Who, with their actions, finance and encourage the war."

In Sarajevo, I flip through stacks of CDs and DVDs in folded photocopied sleeves piled on a table tucked under a walkway. A man, perhaps with a German accent, asks the patroness of the makeshift shop about the price of his selection—just like all the others, about one dollar. He pauses, confused then distraught, and finally asks, "Wait—these aren't originals?!" She shrugs without looking up, and he briskly walks away.

The patroness looks up at me as he leaves, and says, matter of factly, "The only thing original here is us Bosnians."

I cross the street and walk past the Olympic stadium, Sarajevo's pride during the 1984 games. Across the street, gravestones cluster and stretch long and dense over land never meant for such use—Turkish-style turbaned spheres, crosses both Orthodox and Catholic, an occasional communistic star, giving way with later dates to wooden slats with plastic letters and numbers. The birth dates range over most of the 20th century, but all end in either 1992, 1993, 1994 or 1995. Sarajevo, Yugoslavia in miniature, a living ideal, ravaged by forces wanting to remain part of the country still called "Yugoslavia." Murdered by forces calling themselves Serb, while one of the city's top Generals was himself a Serb, and the "Muslim government" (so-called by western diplomats) as multi-ethnic as Yugoslavia.[82] Staring at the names, my mind stops, I sit on a bench between the rows. How could this city have survived? My mind sits. Stupid, stupid. Is that really the word I want? Survive? Suddenly I start, an elderly woman is staring at me from between the graves.

Pausing a moment, she asks in gentle Bosnian, "What's wrong? Are you alright?"

Embarrassed, I manage to smile and thank her for her concern before shuffling off.

DALIA AND I STARE OVER THE CITY AT SUNSET, FROM THE place on the hill that Marko showed me. This is my favorite moment anywhere. First one speaker from a minaret deep into the city to the right cries distantly, *"Allahu Akbar..."* A minute later, to the left, another muzzein starts his improvisation on a tone acutely dissonant with the first, at a different tempo and with a completely different melodic shape. Another, and another, and their mix shifts with the wind. Suddenly, a speaker only a hundred meters away blasts another intonation of the call, distorted and crackly, drowning out the previous ones. In the long silence between its phrases, dozens of simultaneous calls rebound from the hills encircling the city, each passionately isolated yet all blending like firmament of pulsing stars, or nutrients in a rich bed of soil. This, right now, is my favorite thing. This wasn't like this before the war. Maybe if this really is one thing, maybe it is not my favorite thing, but the thing I hate most. No, these things are one only by polyphony. I won't believe that this dynamic rush of infinite interplay is drowning out into one lone shouting voice.

Land of Opportunity and Success

Had any Serb run off with her...
Howe'er painful 'twere to me
But when I heard she'd gone with the Turks,
No time was there for vain reflection
Full after them in chase we straight did go...
And killed the brothers Alitch on the spot,
But, fell mischance! among the Turks the bride!

—P. P. Njegoš, epic poet of old Montenegro, *The Mountain Bride*[83]

THIS IS WHERE EVERYONE DRINKS A TALL CUP OF TURKISH COFFEE TO GO TO SLEEP. IN THE CENTER OF BELGRADE STANDS A STATUE OF ALFRED JARRY'S UBU ROI, PATRON SAINT, KING OF THE ABSURD, A BIT BURNT, DRAPED IN A CIRCUMSTANTIAL NECKTIE LEFT IN OFFERING. AND THE GRAFFITI—"COLOMBO, FUCK YOU FOR YOUR CURIOSITY." CONDOR TACO, ADVERTISES ONE SNACK STAND. COFFEE IS LABELED "BAMBI SUCCESS," ICE CREAM IS CALLED "TOP GUN—MY REALITY."

An elderly woman walks past with a shirt reading, "This time it's love. Next time you pay." Another T-shirt boasts "Yugoslavia, European Nightmare." Graffiti: "It's Spring, and I live in Serbia." Down the pedestrian mall, the ancient fortress still dominates the city, advertising an epic loser's heroism with a collection of the arms used by assorted enemies to attack the city—fifty-four times since 1 AD. Graffiti: "We Are Not The Champions." Roma musicians tap their tuba bells in front of the train station; a young teenager runs through a Turkish scale on his trumpet and lingers on the third, the tone faltering, pitch dipping, in a studied casual agony, bored.

MY FIRST DAY IN BELGRADE, I VISIT BORBA. HE IS RUNNING around like a very large headless chicken, screaming and laughing constantly, making last minute preparations for the upcoming protest. In this morning's national newspaper, an interview with Borba appeared, in which he spoke against a meeting in Canada of eight of the world's great economic powers, called the G8. Most of the interview consisted of reasoned discussion of the G8's role in developments of the global economy, why people should oppose it, and about anarchism's vision, in which wealth is owned by those who produce it and decisions are made directly by those whose must live out their choice. At the end, though, the reporter couldn't help but ask if the protest would be violent. "We're not planning on burning anything down," smirked Borba. "But there's no guarantee."

Both Borba's phones are ringing off the hook. He spends most of the afternoon yelling into both at once, one per ear, stuffing his face with bagel chips and cookies, sucking down liters of Coca-Cola. He has donned what he calls his "Osama hat," which spookily matches his wispy beard. A kitten lustily sucks on his earlobe.

"Serbia right now is a lot like Spain was before the 1936 anarchist revolution," he explains between calls. "Communalist traditions are being threatened, but many are still intact. Most people have little or no faith in this government, but don't have any warm feelings for foreign domination or the international market either. Titoism gave people ideas of self-management and worker's councils, even if it didn't carry them out. And the current system certainly isn't getting people much."

After another call, he continues. "Nobody pays taxes here, nobody puts their money in the bank. There's even these

commercials—'Trust banks! You can put your money in them!,'"
he howls with laughter.

I ask him about the billboards I've seen around Belgrade,
which answer the question, "Why Privatization?" with answers
like: "To live a normal life"; "To make order"; "To bring new
machines." He brays, "Ah, I love those! People here are still very
suspicious of capitalism. We have been handing out a couple
thousand of our newspapers every month in front of factories,
and most of the workers already agree with what we say. Some
of them told us the last time, 'We read the paper last month,
we agree with everything, but when are you going to give us
the guns?' We told them we don't have guns yet, but we'll see
what we can do.

"Anarchism is becoming a trend in Serbia. The situation is
simple here, the classical model—call me a vulgar modernist,
but it's right out of Marx or something. Everything else is either nationalist or neo-liberalist, sponsored either by Nazis, or
by Non-Governmental Organizations, NGOs, liberal shits who
want to bring the worst kind of neo-liberal capitalism here.
They're always talking about civil society this and that; we are
against civil society. We want a worker's society. We don't want
tolerance, we want everybody to have control over their own
lives."

I ask if he expects the police to try to stop the protest. He
shrugs—he's already been arrested dozens of times and is usually
beaten in jail, and he's not even twenty years old yet. He tells me
that his name—given, and the same as his grandfather's—means
"Struggle." When we later go into the police station to register
me, I meet "Legs," a towering Addams Family reject who usually

volunteers to beat Borba when he's in detention. He smiles widely at us, and we nod back politely.

Before I dismiss Borba's self-confessed dogmatism, I ask him if, when he calls himself a "vulgar modernist," that means he sees class exploitation as the basis of all oppression. He waves the question away. "Of course, you need every kind of liberation. Last year, I almost got killed at the Gay Pride march here. I was waving the red-and-black anarcho-syndicalist flag, so 50 or so fascists surrounded me and kicked me for five or ten minutes. Finally, one of them asked, 'Are you Albanian?' They thought their dream had come true, that they'd found a gay Albanian in downtown Belgrade, since the Albanian flag is also red and black. I told them I wasn't, that it was an anarchist flag. 'Are you a faggot?' another one asked. 'Not exactly,' I told him. So they walked away. I went into the nearest bathroom and smiled at myself in the mirror; so long as I can smile at myself in the mirror, it's OK. But my kidneys still hurt sometimes."

I tell him that at the Gay Pride march in Zagreb, the Nazis were yelling, "*Idite u Srbiju*," Go to Serbia. He laughs hysterically. "The day after Gay Pride here, the newspaper had a survey: 80 percent of people believe that homosexuals should be deported from Serbia. But only 75 percent of people thought it was unnatural. So five percent of people think homosexuality is natural, but that they should still be deported from Serbia!" I pull out my can of Go Gay hairspray that I bought here the other day, and we choke on sobs of laughter. The phone rings again. He wipes his eyes and takes a deep breath before talking to the next reporter.

I STILL CAN'T TELL IF THEY'RE KIDDING ABOUT THE molotovs: a group of 30 or so kids, probably surrounded by police, throwing molotovs in the middle of the day at the Canadian embassy downtown seems a bit, well, precipitous.

"Will the police shoot us or join us?" I ask Miroslav, the surrealist poet with the gigantic handlebar mustache.

"Nothing like this has happened before, we don't know what to expect either," he says nonchalantly.

We leave for the protest without filling any bottles with gasoline; I guess we got up too late for molotovs. Instead, someone leaves a single unlit molotov on the steps of the Canadian embassy, wrapped in a wreath someone stole from a cemetery memorial for the White Russian forces, who fought against the 1917 Russian Revolution. The bottle is wrapped in a cloth that says: "Our sincere regards to the G8, from ASI, Anarcho-Syndicalist Initiative. Next time it'll be lit."

The protest blocks the main street for a few minutes before the police shove the protesters onto the sidewalk. "We don't like capitalism either, just don't block the street," one cop says. We spend most of our time handing out the fliers that Miroslav wrote for the occasion: "Capitalism is like this: When you eat spaghetti, food with a lot of protein, your shit is firm. But when you eat spinach, your shit is soft, without form. Capitalism is like this shit—without form. But when you've found your way out of it, you know you've done it." Everyone either shrugs at the flier or sympathetically shakes our hands; no one seems offended.

In the park afterwards, after the police take Borba away presumably so Legs can beat him as usual, the bored cops ask us casually before leaving, "So which one of you is in charge?"

Miran explains that we don't have leaders: "If you were fighting against authority, why would you want a leader to do it?"

The cop struggles with the thought, then says, "Well, OK, so who is it that gives you orders, tells you what to do?"

After a silence, Miran offers up: "Well, God, I guess." We laugh and the cops leave without another word.

POLICE WALK INTO OUR TRAIN compartment and sit down on either side of me. Emma, Frank, and I raise our eyebrows to each other. "Shut the door so no one can hear," says one cop to the other. They look at me for a minute, and I smile weakly. "So, how do you like Yugoslavia?" one asks. When he learns I am from Sacramento, he gives me a high-five for Vlade Divac, Serbia's greatest star—domestically as well as internationally. The Sacramento Kings basketball player, who left Belgrade 30 years ago, is so popular in Serbia that the pop-punk band Deca Lošíh Muzičara, Bad Musicians' Children, has a top-ten song in his honor. Romani brass bands cover the song, and everyone around gives a thumb up for Divac. The cop tells me how he watches every Kings game on the city square, which is always packed for Divac's games, even the ones that play here at three in the morning. He almost cries when I tell him I've never seen a game in person. Hastily, I repeat everything I've heard people say about the Kings, and he listens with childlike contentment.

He pulls out a little pile of photographs from his bag. "My family is from near Sarajevo," he says in Serbian, "so I also volunteered to fight in Bosnia. But most of these are from Kosovo." In one he is posing in a ditch with a machine gun; in the next he caresses a mortar. "Why does America bomb Muslim terrorists in Afghanistan but help them in Kosovo?" I cautiously tell him that America, like all states, just wants power for itself, and doesn't really care about this or that religion, or if anybody is right or wrong, or anything. He pats my shoulder approvingly and nods. He shows me a picture, smiling in his soldier's tent with a friend. "*Znaš*," he says, "*rat nije strašan. To je normalno.* You know, war isn't terrible. It's normal. Once you get used to it," he continues, "it's just like any other way of life. You just plug your ears and act like a professional. People can get used to anything."

My Serbian sticks in my throat as I try to change the subject. His partner stares at me, bored. "Do you know how to swear in Serbian?" the first one asks. I assure him unenthusiastically that I know the common expressions: Up your mother's cunt, Fuck your life, Fuck your God, Fuck your mouse, I hope your mother gets fucked by a dog. He laughs at my blank delivery, then teaches me how to say a series more. I try to forget them as soon as he tells me. Gun is gun. He whispers when he tells me the different ways to say, "Girlfriend," so as not to offend Emma, though she hasn't understood a word of the conversation. She gets the three of us to pose, and his quiet partner jokingly covers up his badge and says, "Don't take us to The Hague!" They shake our hands warmly and wish us a good stay.

I STRUGGLE TO UNDERSTAND THE DEBATE: ARE THEY STILL arguing about whether or not to join the international anarcho-syndicalist federation, or are they talking again about whether to legalize their union locals with the Serbian authorities? Jovana, the quiet metalhead psychology student, humbly accepts her election as international secretary. I realize that everyone in the room, except for us internationals in the observation rows, has argued at some point. And now, is this possible—consensus? In the Balkans? With a bunch of anarchists?

Thunderous debates are punctuated with showers of laughter. Massive stacks of plastic ballot boxes teeter over our chairs. How in the hell did a bunch of anarchists get a room in City Hall to hold their founding congress in, anyway?

SMOKE, THE FIRST ROMA PUNK I'VE MET, PASSES ME BACK the pack of Smoki flips. The train lurches. He insists I have some of his peanuts. "Belgrade is the worst, the most dangerous city on earth," he says, soft-spoken as always. I realize I haven't been to the neighborhood Smoke grew up in. I want to ask him about when Belgrade residents recently blocked the freeway to protest construction of a Roma housing project, but don't know where to start. "PUNK" is tattooed across his throat. His big eyes race around with edgy compassion, his expression sad and somehow reckless. I ask him about the two Roma children kicked to death recently by skinheads in Belgrade. "Strašno," he says, terrible, in a tone of voice that makes me hesitate to continue. I want to ask him about the protests, where Roma and punks organized together in response to the killings. The protest was a success, bringing much public discussion to the situation of Roma in Serbia. I want to ask about the all-night party that followed the protest, about the punks explaining to Roma grandmothers how skinheads dress differently than punks, and everyone getting drunk together. But Smoke changes the subject: "I can't wait, there hasn't been anything like this festival here for a very long time," he smiles.

The train pulls into Subotica, the northernmost city in Yugoslavia. Gingerbread houses loom alongside the tracks, urban Hungarian fairy-tale architecture. As good a place as any for a punk festival, I guess.

A punk couple from the northern city of Novi Sad shares their food with me on a bench out front of the park, nodding approval as I pull out another bag of Smoki. Her English is excellent, so she translates his quick Serbian for me. He came here from Sarajevo during the war; she is from here, from Vojvodina, and only spoke Hungarian when they met. Neither could speak a word when they went on their first date, but they fell in love anyway. They were relieved to find out they still liked each other when they started to learn one another's languages. I blush as they pause to kiss between every few sentences. "We're an example of Vojvodina's diversity, of Yugoslavia's," she says, unself-consciously. "Though of course, it's less diverse now." He says something emphatically to me, and she translates: "This war was shit." She explains that at least here in Subotica, we don't have to worry about Nazi skins, because the Roma and the punks there got together and drove them out.

I ask them if all the bridges into Novi Sad are still destroyed from the NATO bombing. "People in Novi Sad have a saying," she says. "The Danube is a miraculous river. Most rivers go under bridges, but here, the Danube goes OVER them!" We laugh. She explains that the city now depends on the world's first floating pontoon bridge, which, though interesting for architecture students, prevents any passage of river traffic. "NATO bombed the hell out of Vojvodina, even though most people were in the opposition, the majority here wasn't even Serb," she says. "They bombed everything only because there is military transport through here." I notice a shrapnel pockmark on the sidewalk not far from our bench. "The opposition to Milošević was based here, but after the bombing started, people started to hate NATO even more than Milošević. And now that the Hague took him, they're even marching for his freedom."

"Did you go to the Monte Paradiso festival in Pula?" I ask.

His eyes light up, but he chuckles as he says, "No, Monte Paradiso, no."

"We would have loved to go," she says, "but it is very difficult for any of us to get a visa to Croatia. And he still doesn't have any identification papers, so it would be impossible to leave the country. But we are very excited to be here at this festival in Subotica, we've been looking forward to it for months." We decide it's time to go inside.

The first band, from Banja Luka, Bosnia, plays like recent Pink Floyd, but with soul. I am surprised to notice myself enjoying it. As they finish, punks seep up from every crevice. AK-47, the premiere anarcho-punk band from Croatia, takes the stage. Its members are famous not just for music, but for their involvement in anarcho-syndicalism, anti-fascist struggle, and yoga.

The guitar hits the crowd like a molotov, the bass and drums smash our heads to the floor, and the singer kicks in our ribs with hope, with fury, with love. The crowd explodes.

After the show, we pass the *rakija* bottle and hug each other's bruises. Friends exchange patches and zines, others buy records so the merchants can afford to get back home. Rumor has it that the festival has been canceled already, but everyone is too busy drinking and singing with their old friends who've moved to distant towns to worry about anything. We pass out laughing and singing in the tents.

The next day, we meet one of the organizers on a tram into town. The organizer hasn't slept for three days. She is whispering to Emma, since she's lost her voice. "It's true, there's no more shows. You could have your money back, if we had any. I've been working on this six months, but it'll take years to pay off the debt. Lots of people, even some people I thought were my friends, stole the tickets, sold them for half-price, and pocketed the money. Hardly anybody came anyway, and I understand, since $7 is too much for people here to pay for a three-day festival. But $60,000 is a big debt for us.

"We hired a boxing club to do security, and didn't realize how many of them there are, or how expensive they'd be. Last night, they approached us and said, 'It's fine, you don't have to pay us. We'll just beat the hell out of everyone here.' These guys are big. So we gave them everything we had, everything out of our pockets, and begged them to leave everyone alone. The bands didn't even get money for gas." She points to the kids sitting next to her. "I have to feed these poor souls." She is taking one of the bands to her mom's house. We give them all sympathetic nods. They get off in the rain, smiling weakly back at us.

That night, seventy-five or so punks gather in front of the local grocery store, in what becomes a spontaneous festival. Everyone is arguing, flirting, juggling, spinning fire, singing, sharing food and drink and cigarettes, laughing and yelling and dropping bottles. I spend hours talking with Maja, a young local who pauses long before answering questions, but categorically states her answer once she's decided on it. I scavenge for questions for the pleasure of her answers. One kid tells us he just finished school and received his conscription notice to serve six months in the military. He won't try to get out because of psychological problems, like many people do, or get a civil service position which, he says, still supports the military. He is going to state publicly in a week that he refuses to serve. He expects to get three years in prison. "It has to start somewhere," he shrugs.

Someone walks up and asks me if I dislike Serbs. Drunk again, unable to manage subtlety, I blurt out in Serbian: "Serbs don't exist. And Croats also don't exist. Bosniaks, Albanians, they don't exist either. How would I like or dislike someone that doesn't exist?"

One drunk friend sneers: "Yeah, only Americans."

I look back at him. "Especially, especially Americans don't exist." He stares at me with glazed eyes. Across the lot, our friends are breaking up a fight. We realize we're all getting tired.

On the walk back, Frank remembers that it's been Emma's birthday for several hours. We tear off our clothes and jump into the lake at the park's edge. "You know," says Oliver, "there's a Tomahawk cruise missile on the bottom of this lake that never exploded. Really." We laugh and wonder if Emma will get an extra-special birthday candle.

Back in the tent, kids are passing around a guitar. I end up singing "Mesečina," the popular Serbian folk song, for everyone; somehow they haven't heard it, but they approve. Maja takes the guitar. She gingerly picks and strums for a few minutes, then slips into "The Man Who Sold the World." I didn't think I liked David Bowie, but I shiver at her rendition.

In the morning, running to catch our train, we pass a wall. Red brush-painted letters in dried drip spell out, in English:

> *All I get is red guitar*
> *The rest is up to you.*

"What do you think of Belgrade?"

"I love it, it's crazy. It reminds me of Sarajevo." Her cigarette jerks. I recognize the gesture as my own, from back home, like in America when someone mentions Vietnam or Hiroshima, or the more than two million people in prison—the characteristic gesture of consensual blindness. I change the subject.

Tonight is another perfectly formed gem of madness and passion. The city has erupted in riots of dumb energy after the national basketball team won in overtime against poor Argentina, perhaps the only country in the world to have fallen as far as quickly as Yugoslavia, but we sit in our bar lost in our lives, sneering at the nationalist-three-finger-saluting, flag-waving mob. The brass band plays the Serbian classics "Đurđevdan" and "Mesečina" over and over until even I am tired of them, but Emma, Frank, and I can't help running out and dancing in the streets. Our Serbian hosts are mildly annoyed, as they've long ago tired of this "barroom banalisation" void of any "noble patina of expression." For them, the wild bravado of the mob is anything but interesting.

Ksenia, the linguist, whose deep raspy voice overwhelms the horns in my ears, posits and refutes and taunts and apologizes without calculation, with a direct gaze, until I am beaten with sweetness. *Niko ne zna šta to sija*, no one knows what is shining, moonlight or sunshine, admiration or rejoicing or infatuation or brilliant friendship, or love.

Borba, self-conscious for the first time I've seen, yet still in good form, dismisses the whole world as complete idiots as he drowns in his faith in people. The two of them shake their heads and laugh tragically for Bor, where her cousin lives. The smelting plant burns radioactive waste until green smoke fills the sky, the miners work in the largest open mine in Europe and are paid $35 a month while politicians admit stealing millions without remorse. The only measure of pollution is one man who watches the smokestacks and takes note when a plume looks particularly thick. "Anyway, a machine would break as soon as they turned it on," she says. This week, Borba tells us, 12,000 miners just voted to blockade the highway during their strike. ASI (the anarcho-syndicalist union) forged close relations with the miners when Borba and Miroslav, the surrealist poet, spoke to a packed crowd in the union hall. The miners have even dissolved their traditional union and are forming a more radical organization. Or perhaps they'll join ASI—50 punks this week, 50 punks and 12,000 miners next week, shrugs Borba. ASI's newspaper, with 50 subscribers in Bor, speaks not only of direct action, sabotage, and the general strike, but gay pride, animal liberation, and alchemy.[84] Emma and Frank return to the table after making out in the middle of the brass band, kicked out for speaking English, or maybe for not putting any money into the trumpet bells.

On the way back to Ksenia's place, we pass a shop window broken in the riots. We nurse mineral water at her home well past dawn. She tells me of her recurring dream of finally going back to her childhood vacation home in Zadar, Croatia, and speaking Icelandic so her previous neighbors would not hear her Serbian accent. Her brother has a recurrent dream, identical, except that he pretends to be Greek. She tells me about sneaking out at night, past her parents, during the bombing. I try to imagine the empty apocalyptic streets. Then she tells me of an Italian she met, who opposed the NATO bombing because of his thorough knowledge of Serbian history, "not just because he was some hippie who thought it wasn't fair." When I laugh in disbelief, she says: "No, no, I don't have anything against hippies!"

HERE IS A GRINET CAFE COFFEE CUP, TO GO. I GUESS "Grinet" is supposed to sound like English. Starbucks green on white, fancy scribbled font à la pseudo-Français. Checklist of drinks on cup, hot ones with asterisk—čokolada!*, moka*, cappucino*, filter kava*, caffe latte*, frappe, freezer, ice caffe. Freezer? When I seek out the asterix, it says, "PAZI VRUCE," beware of heat. Can't I be reckless with my cappuccino if I want?

I heard a member of Otpor, or "Resistance" (the student group recognized as largely responsible for organizing the overthrow of Milošević), speak in Philadelphia. After looking around in the US, he was not only astonished at the Third World conditions in North Philadelphia, but also by the matchbooks. "One of them said, 'Don't Eat The Matches.' This is the problem with you Americans, you get so used to being told what to do, you forget to think for yourselves, you forget that you already know not to eat the matches." Ironically, Otpor—like most of the former opposition—advocates policies that look a lot like a political Grinet cafe cup. House Blend: Open markets, privatization, and liquidation of social spending, with a shot of MTV. In one friend's words, "Otpor does not always translate as resistance."

"Caffe" itself is an abomination of the populist phonetic spelling tradition in Serbian, started by Vuk Karadić. Here, James Joyce is spelled Dzejms Dzojs, and Jazz is Dzez. Coffee should be spelled "Kafa." But "Caffe" pronounced in Serbian sounds like "Tsaffuh." No Turkish coffee, no espresso, the two universal drinks here. But this filter coffee is nearly unknown. Borba told me, "It's so funny, there's this new terrible watery coffee, and they call it 'American Coffee' just because it's so weak and bad!" and then I tell him with embarrassment that it's actually what we drink back in the states. When I order a normal espresso, they check off caffe latte, no milk. Like the scene in *Five Easy Pieces*: if you don't have toast, give me a chicken salad sandwich without the salad and toast the bread—that is, if Jack Nicholson were entrepreneurial foreign direct investment capital. Or like in Mississippi diners, where if you don't want sugar you have to order "unsweetened tea," if those diners were global McCoffee shops.

"Don't forget to mark your bonus card," the cup warns. "One free cup with every ten purchases." One cup here costs the same as in America, one dollar. A cup in any of Belgrade's numerous sit-down places, where the waiter cooks the Turkish coffee for you, or an espresso in a sit-down pre-fab kiosk, never cost more than 30 cents. Why not charge an honest price and ditch the coffee card? At least the price is still a round 60 dinars, not 59.95, the "psychological pricing" my friend Maja wondered at when she visited London. But how long until such dishonesties follow? Is it a coincidence that Grinet Cafe opened about the same time as the first appearance of consumer credit lines?

MIROSLAV LOOKS STRIKINGLY LIKE ALFRED JARRY, OF WHOM he is a great admirer. He wants to make a movie revealing that Quetzalcoatl was the last manifestation of the pre-historic being Karl Marx, whose second coming is approaching. Miroslav is the one stoned, not me, but his ideas make me unsure. He tells me that when you land in Belgrade and leave the airport, a giant sign greets you with, "Welcome to Serbia: Land of Opportunity and Success," despite the 30 percent unemployment and dollar-a-day wages.

Miroslav tells me about "Gusla Nights," a festival here that celebrates the one-stringed bowed atonal (and to many ears unlistenable) traditional Gusla of Montenegro, over which Homeric bards sing day-long epics of ancient conquests. The last festival featured some modern compositions in the traditional style, such as, *Oh God, Why Did NATO Bomb Us?* Borba and Miroslav laugh themselves to tears. Another Gusla epic, among the first wave committed to vinyl in the early '60s, is called *Death in Dallas*, detailing in Slavo-Homeric epic verse the entire tragedy of John F. Kennedy's death, from Lee Harvey Oswald's childhood to JFK's child John Jr. saluting the coffin at the funeral.

Borba and Miroslav cut each other off with nostalgic enthusiasm as they tell me about the Yugoslav soap operas of their childhood. For much of the '80s, every time *Better Life* came on television, the streets would be empty. One of the actresses, when asked in an interview what her favorite thing to do was, replied, "Perfumes!" But the other actors had been distinguished theater stars before starring in the soap, and their acting was top quality. The show was an almost real-time reflection of a totally average Yugoslav family. "Why do people want to watch on TV what they can't stand to think about in reality?" wonders Borba. The whole country lamented along with the show's theme song, "I want a better life, a better life, but better lives are for better people." But before long, *Better Life* was canceled and replaced with *Happy People*. The actors of this show were terrible, especially a cloying child actor, and the show often revolved around an Irish Setter named Sima. Soon, families were repeating the one-liners and everyone had an Irish Setter named Sima.

"The new show's popular idiocy was symptomatic of the beginning of Milošević's reign," Miroslav explains grimly.

Borba cuts in: "During the war, you would watch the Croatian channel and it would say, 'Today, Serbian monsters killed these heroic Croatian warriors,' and show a gruesome photo of a bloody head. Then you turn to the Serbian channel, and it would say, 'Today, Croatian fascists slaughtered an entire village of unarmed Serbs, just like in WWII.' The Bosnian channel would have their version. And you look at the heads—it's always the same head!

"Have you heard about the Valium scandal? Just this week, the government declared that they were going to start requiring prescriptions for tranquilizers, which people had been buying over the counter. Maybe there will be riots, ninety percent of the people over forty in this country are addicted to it. Everyone is like: 'How am I supposed to deal with all this shit without drugs? Now I'll have to talk to grandma if she's not wasted on pills all the time.'"

I tell Miroslav of a book, *The Culture of Power in Serbia*,[85] in which the American author spoke to a middle-aged supporter of the regime during Milošević's reign. After a long conversation, the Milošević supporter summed up her differences with the interviewer by saying, "I understand why you think the way you do because you live in America and watch American television. But I live here and I watch Yugoslav television, so I think differently." Miroslav puts his head in his hands and groans.

"Do you know the last thing Milošević did to try and stay in power?" he continues. "On October 3, 2000, the first day of the protests, he decided to play a pirated version of *Titanic* on the state television station, before it was even released in the US. It was a tough decision for people, but somehow two million people gave up DiCaprio long enough to overthrow the government.

"And you must know about Turbo-Folk. Imagine taking four-teenth century songs about protecting your homeland from hoards of invading Turks, then setting them to a techno beat, with synthesizers and electric guitars. My God. Lyrics like: 'We are Serbian supermen, we fight against the world.'"

"It was like, genocide pop?" I ask.

"Of course. I just saw an old music video of two guys with big curly hair slicked down on the sides and, how do you say, mullets in the back, in army uniforms, standing by the museum of WWII artillery in Belgrade's center. 'I'm writing a letter to my Orthodox brother to come fight with us,' one guy rapped. Ceca, the most famous turbo-folk singer, only sang love songs, but her husband was Arkan, the most famous war criminal from the wars in Bosnia and Croatia. He also owned *Crvena Zvezda* [Red Star], one of the big soccer teams here, until rival mafia assassinated him last year."

I muse out loud for a moment. "Hannah Arendt wrote about the banality of evil, how when she went to see Eichmann on trial, he was just a normal, boring guy.[86] But I think these days, it's not just that evil is banal, but that banality is evil." Borba tells me he doesn't need a liberal academic to tell him that, but I remind him that Hannah Arendt was a worker councilist. He's impressed.

Miroslav has been listening to only Black Sabbath for two days. I accuse him of being a real modernist, since he always accuses me of being a post-modernist. "Of course I am a modernist," he says in his accented, careful English. "If I was a post-modernist, I could be a frog, or a grandmother, or Japanese. But I am not a frog or a grandmother or Japanese, I am just a poor boy born in a backwards time in a strange land." I wonder what the miners in Bor made of Miroslav when he delivered his speech to them.

Borba tells me that last night, the Minister of Privatization an-nounced on TV that things are going fine in Serbia, except that groups of subversives, certain anarchist groups, have been handing out anti-privatization propaganda at factories, and foreign investors are starting to pull out. "Our paper only has a circulation in Serbia of 1,500, and that's all we need to scare away investors?" Miroslav interjects with mixed pride and incredulity.

I suggest changing the sign in the airport to: "Welcome to Serbia: Land of Surrealism and Anarchy," which I'm sure all parties involved would find more accurate. As I walk out the door, Miroslav shouts after me, "Welcome to Serbia: The Land Where Things Still Happen."

I LOOK UP *OBRAZ* IN MY DICTIONARY: CHEEK.

"Cheek?" I ask Borba.

"Honor, metaphorically."

"Why is it spray-painted all around town, with the alpha and omega?"

"It's a group. A few years ago, the Serbian Orthodox church realized that they needed more youth participation, so they offered theology scholarships to some youth who were very proud of their heritage: Nazi skinheads." As we walk on, we pass a full-color poster with an Obraz logo in the corner: "All Serbs are Radovan"—the man widely held responsible for the genocide in Bosnia. Further on, another reads, "1942, 1992—Petričevac."

"That's the place the Pope visited on his recent trip, the only place he visited in Bosnia," says Borba. "There's not even any Catholics around there. It's also the place of one of the worst mass killings of Serbs in WWII, in '42. It's like they do these things as favors for Obraz, to help them organize."

One of Borba's friends went to interview Obraz in their office for a research paper. At one point, she giggled because the guy used a word from a fifteenth century dialect to refer to going to the bathroom. "What's so funny?" he growled at her, glowering. She swallowed hard and assured him she'd been thinking of something else.

"Obraz is very active," Borba says. "They were certainly responsible for organizing the attack on the Gay Pride parade, when I got kicked. One American photographer, Ron Haviv, recently toured Serbia with these amazing photographs he took of Serbian paramilitaries during the war. Obraz raided several of his showings: in Novi Sad they beat up the organizers of the showing, in Čačak they beat up the visitors. In Uzice they burned newspapers as 'globalization propaganda' or something. Several galleries canceled showings on the rest of the tour."

Obraz's Alpha and Omega seal, Belgrade, Serbia.

"What about Šešelj?"

"Ah, Šešelj... Milošević created him as the official opposition, so people wouldn't dare vote opposition. He likes pulling guns and rusty knives on people in parliament, they're always having to drag him out by force as he's threatening to kill his fellow parliamentarians. Šešelj's 'Radical Party' still advocates expanding Serbia's borders. He's in The Hague now for war crimes in Croatia, Bosnia, and Kosovo, which is really saving his career."

"What? Why?"

"Šešelj has become a sort of hero, along with Milošević, now that the international courts have 'kidnapped our boys.' You've seen that graffiti, 'They're killing Serbs in The Hague'? The saddest thing is, even many people who were imprisoned, even tortured for protesting Milošević during his reign, now go to protests holding his picture. The same thing is happening in Bosnia and Croatia too, you know—'We're all Radovan' was taken from a similar Croatian poster, 'We're all Mirko.' After the war, the far right lost power. Now The Hague has brought them into power in all three countries after they were on their way out. Everyone remotely sane doesn't bother going to the polls anymore. So it looks like Šešelj's party might actually win the upcoming elections."

"Does Obraz support Šešelj?"

"Šešelj isn't nationalist enough for them. They support some psychotic party or another. Until recently, they supported the Royalist Bloc, led by the King of Serbia. The King was born and raised in London as a financier, just came here for the first time, and doesn't speak a word of Serbian. But hey, he's the King. Anyway, the good King was at a party and someone offered him pig meat and a shot of *rakija*, and when he stood up after dinner, it appeared he'd shit his pants. No Serb wants a King who can't hold his pig meat and *rakija*."

SICH SPEAKS HUNGARIAN BETTER THAN SERBIAN, HE explains, though his Serbian still sounds fluent to my struggling ears. He tells me about the communal farm he lives and works on with his two best friends in Vojvodina near the Hungarian border to the north. Underneath his straggling day-glo braids, Sich beams a benevolence that could turn sand into rich black soil; I envy his vegetables. He explains that after years of such intense life at close quarters, he is ready to spend more time in neighboring Ada, population 12,000.

"Is there much of a scene in Ada these days?" I ask.

"Oh yeah," Sich nods. "We are starting a radical infoshop and library there, and already many local kids are interested. At least twenty kids are involved in DIY projects and politics there, lots of zines and bands. We have already had some effect—our ecological group forced the city to put trash cans around town to cut down on litter. And there exists an underground direct action group as well. There is no McDonald's or anything in Ada, but the food store has a Coca-Cola refrigerator out front, and several times the refrigerator's window has been smashed in the middle of the night. But the police soon figured out who was to blame, and told members of the group that the store's local owner, not Coca-Cola, was the one to pay for the windows, so the actions stopped."

"It sounds like Ada has a more active scene than many big cities in America," I offer. Sich doesn't seem surprised.

Neša tells me about his hometown of Sombor during the NATO bombing. "A man was sitting on the toilet when a bomb fell and blew out his eardrums. He looked up at the ceiling which wasn't there anymore, and saw a pig flying gracefully through the sky. Really. Many people keep farms around their houses there.

"Martial law was in effect the whole time, it was crazy. You got 60 days in jail automatically if anyone told the police they thought you were a spy. Imagine! Dissent against Milošević became so much more difficult. I think if you are trying to encourage people to overthrow their government, bringing about martial law and dropping bombs on them probably isn't so effective."

All of Serbia was bombed for their supposed support of the Milošević regime, demonized for their alleged support of the wars, even after what can be called "...one of the most massive campaigns of draft resistance in modern history."[87] Many young men hid as long as they could from the police who would come to collect them; the police responded with near kidnapping. One friend tells me that while he was trying to hide from them, he returned to his apartment at 3am to find military police waiting inside his apartment, who then escorted him to the conscription center. Military police would routinely search trains for young men trying to get away. Even in such conditions, 200,000 draft resisters left the country. The rough equivalent for the United States would have been if 5 million draftees had fled to Canada to escape fighting in Vietnam, with the borders sealed and police scouring streets, homes, and transport. "According to Center for Peace in Belgrade, 85% to 90% of the young men of Belgrade who were called up to fight refused to serve. In Serbia as a whole, the figure was between 50% and 80%. And even among those who did serve, there were massive desertions from the battlefield."[88]

A whole generation raised on protest and repression. Every time the fighting stopped, Milošević was in danger of being overthrown. Before the war in Croatia even began, a week of huge protests rocked Belgrade, in March 1991, demanding Milošević resign—700,000 workers walked out on strike. "Political commentators in Belgrade were predicting the imminent fall of the regime." Milošević called out that army to put down the demonstrations, but had to result to more insidious means of stopping them.[89] Later, after fighting had nearly stopped in Croatia but was looming in Bosnia and Herzegovina began, all the major cities of Serbia were again turned over by giant protests, which many were sure would drive Milošević out.[90] Exit polls showed the oppositional presidential candidate, Panić, to have had nearly ninety percent support in 1992, but massive election fraud kept Milošević in power. Like Yeltsin, his good friend, Milošević dissolved parliament when his grip was loosened.[91] Protests against the war in Bosnia first were frequent, but became impossible as the war exploded. In 1996, after the end of the Bosnian war, two hundred thousand (again, the proportional equivalent of over five million people for the US!) filled the streets every day for *three months* demanding Milošević's resignation; the government responded with violence against its own population, and disdain for their demands. Then the war in Kosovo intensified, and NATO did its part to keep Milošević in power. Finally, in October 2000, two million people in the streets managed to wrest him from power.

"It's impossible to defeat Milošević in Serbia. All our internal problems have dissolved in the war," said Goran Djindjic in 1991. Perhaps the question of Serbia in the 90's is not about primitive ethnicism or even resurgent nationalism, but the means with which formally democratic systems can fail, and the most impassioned of populations demobilized into ineffectiveness.[92]

THE MAN I AM SITTING NEXT TO ON THE TRAIN STARES at me and asks where I am from, where I am going. He is not impressed that I am taking the train across the border into Croatia. "Were you in Croatia in '91?" he asks flatly. The village woman sitting across from him with a colorful scarf over her head looks out the window and clicks her tongue, *tsk tsk*. If you are a journalist, he continues, tell people that Croatia is... I shake my head, I do not understand, can you write it down? He takes my book and writes "*genocidalan narod,*" a genocidal nation. "I am from Osijek, in Croatia," he explains, "but now I live in a village near Šid, in Serbia." The border crossed him, so he had to cross the border. Perhaps that's why half of his thumb is missing, with a bit of bone sticking out.

"Why are you going to Croatia?" he repeats.

"I have friends there," I answer politely.

"No you don't," he replies. "Croats only live for themselves."

I cautiously reply, "Not all."

"Yes, all," he retorts, "they're all the same. All."

"Some of my friends in Zagreb are Serbs," I tell him.

"No, they're not," he replies. "Not if they live in Zagreb." The woman with the colorful scarf on her head continues looking out the window silently.

After a long silence, I say, "America is a genocidal nation. But there are some good people there."

He looks at me concernedly, shakes his head, and says, "No, I don't think you understand what I said."

I stare back: "Yes I did. America is a genocidal nation. And there are some good people in America, and in Croatia too." I elect to leave Serbia out of the conversation. He looks at me curiously. The three of us stare out the window.

As the train pulls to a stop at the last town in Serbia, the man stands up and grabs my shoulder. "Serbia to Tokyo!" he bellows laughing, slaps me a high-five, and salutes me with the Serbian nationalist three-finger salute. I shake his hand goodbye.

An hour or so later, after crossing into Croatia, I awake confused, everything tumbling. The village woman is digging her fingers into my shoulders, shaking me violently. I stare up at her. Assured I am awake, she grabs my hand, squeezes it as if it were a plow handle, and shakes it with determined force. She nods, smiles, and walks off the train.

BACK IN BELGRADE, ANDREA LIGHTS UP ANOTHER DRINA cigarette. "The problem is that people always tell themselves, 'It could be worse.'" Her boyfriend Neša brings us another round of Turkish coffee and returns to his drawing table. Her energy and focus, the joy she obviously takes in precise articulation, her intense smile, make her words seem incongruous. "We try to help things, you see, we are doing a distribution of political music, we make shirts and patches with our ideas, but in a situation like this it is so difficult you cannot even imagine." She pulls out a pile of silk screened shirts. "Look at these, for example. We paid for high-quality ink, but it all comes off in the washing machine, so it looks gray instead of white. And the silk screens we used were supposed to last for a very long time, but we had to throw them out after we made only these few, because our water pressure up in this high floor apartment is too low to get the ink out."

Ice cream advertisement, Belgrade, Serbia.

I ask Andrea about stories I've heard about opposition groups not being able to afford paper to print their newspapers on during the sanctions. She nods. "The records for our distro—can you imagine? We can only send cash when we order records from other countries for our distro, and only about half of the records ever arrive. The average income here is one-tenth what it was when I was growing up. Our passport used to be one of the best in the world, and now it's even hard to get a visa for Croatia. We are trapped in this country like a prison. It's hell, a real living hell. Can you imagine?" I search for a response, but Andrea is already up for another pack of Drina.

One day during the time of Milošević, Andrea was sitting on a city bus with her friend. "He was going insane from the tension, and really hated middle-aged people, since they are Milošević's main supporters—they think it's still World War II. The bus was completely packed, with arms and legs sticking out of the windows. With the sanctions on gasoline, buses would only come once an hour or less. The bus would stay for five minutes at every stop while people had a fight to get on. At one stop, the doors opened to a man, begging, cajoling, yelling to be let on. 'There's a spot over there, I can see it! Come on, I've been waiting an hour, I need to get home!' People on the bus kept telling him there wasn't any room, but he kept trying. Finally, he gave up and whimpered, 'Why can't I get on the bus?' My friend yelled down at him: 'Because it's all your fault, you voted for Milošević!' The bus totally exploded, the old people yelling, 'What does that have to do with it?' and the young people laughing and yelling, 'Yeah! You tell 'em!' The bus drove off, leaving the man at the bus stop shaking like he was having a nervous breakdown.

"The buses here, you can't imagine. Another time I was on a bus on the main road, and the bus started weaving back and forth, in and out of traffic. Everyone's heads swung left, right, left, right. At first we ignored it, then started looking at each other, until the tires were squealing, and we were afraid it would tip over. One guy yelled: 'What are we, potatoes in a bag?' A young guy jumped up and ran to the front to yell at the driver, I guess to beat him up. When he got to the front, he spun around, pale, and yelled: 'He's asleep!' Everyone panicked, but someone woke him up in time and it turned out OK.

"Everyone here was going crazy from the situation, from all the tension. My mother was riding with one of her friends once on another city bus. Her friend was very frustrated, she worked in a land management office, and everyday saw corruption up close, had to rubber stamp all sorts of schemes just to keep her job. As she was talking, an older woman pushed past and elbowed my mother's friend in the nose. 'Excuse me, you just elbowed me in the nose,' she said. 'So what?' sneered the older woman. My mother's friend screamed, screamed some more, didn't stop screaming until the whole bus was staring at her. She started cursing the older woman, saying, 'It's all your fault, all you people who voted for Milošević, people like you make all our problems.' Things like that always happened, every day.

"Many people had cars in that time, very nice cars, since you could buy a new Mercedes for about $5,000 from the mafia, who got it from Germany or somewhere. But nobody had gas for them. Once I was hitchhiking, and finally I got a ride from a nice guy, who didn't have a gold chain around his neck or anything, kind of a hippie type. He pulled over and bought a coke bottle of gas from a kid at the side of the road—the black market was the only way to get gas at that time. We had just got out of town when the engine started clattering, asphyxiated. We realized the kid on the road had sold us colored water. There was nothing we could do, his car was completely dead. We wished him luck and got out to hitch again.

"In the war, people could do whatever they wanted. If we're just sitting here and I decide to, I can just shoot you, just like that. It happened a lot, everybody just sitting around, they start drinking *rakija*, joking around and then *pow*, I shoot you. A lot of people miss that."

I ask Andrea what people tried to do against the war. How could Milošević wage three wars when half of the population of Serbia, and four out of five people in Belgrade and Vojvodina, refused to obey the draft? "What can you do in such a situation? There were many protests, and we went to all of them. In '96, hundreds of thousands of people marched every day, filling the streets, for more than three months. I joined several peace groups, NGOs. There were so many dirty tricks you'd need ten lives to find them all out. The leaders of every single one were just pocketing the money. I used to hang out at the Women in Black office, but when I would just go for a coffee and to talk to a friend, people would constantly be taking pictures of us. The next time I went, the pictures would be on the wall, or in some pamphlet printed only in English, talking about how the center 'facilitated mediated peace discussions,' until I couldn't take it anymore."

I tell her about Trivo Injić who later became Serbia's ambassador to Spain. He'd been a bookkeeper for Women In Black, until he noticed that the US government was making sizable contributions, and quit in protest. Andrea isn't surprised. "Does it sound like they'd refuse money from anyone?"

I tell Andrea one story I read about the opposition candidate Vuk Drašković. He had been speaking for some hours in a village in rural Serbia about the terrible effects of Milošević's rule. One peasant emphatically agreed. "So I can count on your vote, then?" Drašković asked. "Oh, sorry, no," the villager answered. "But I thought you were agreeing with everything I said?" Drašković asked, bewildered. "I do agree with everything you say. As soon as you are in power, I promise to vote for you," said the villager. Andrea nods gravely.

I ask Andrea if she votes or not. "Here, I don't even have the choice not to vote, like anarchists in other countries," she answers. "If I don't go to the ballot box, then my ballot will magically go for the ruling party, so I have to go to the ballot box and write in, 'None of the above.'"

"We still tried to get together and do things. I was always having friends over, my house was like a youth hostel. My mother didn't mind, but she was embarrassed that she couldn't be a good hostess. Often we didn't have food, or coffee, or cigarettes to give. Milošević funded the war with this incredible inflation. Everyone had to sell whatever they had, family heirlooms, wedding rings, whatever, just to eat. We hardly got any money for such things, the prices were very low—the market was flooded with gold. The soldiers were selling everything they got from robbing people's houses, besides all the gold teeth they brought back.

"These nationalists have no memory. They are in denial of their history, their roots, who they really are. People in Serbia don't look Slavic, like the Russians. Look at my hair! It is dark, and often here our skin is dark. In all these wars for all these years, all the men were always killed... Who made the babies then?" I tell Andrea that I can't tell the difference between Bosnian and Serbian turbo-folk, and she laughs, "Neither can I! The nationalists talk about purity, but the most common Serbian word, 'bre', is from Turkish, the same as the Greek word 're.'

"Of course, it's not just Serbs here. One of my neighbors in this building, an elderly Jewish woman, lived through Auschwitz. She's still afraid to ever leave her apartment. How do you think she felt when Tudjman, the president of Croatia, said that the Holocaust was exaggerated?"

Andrea tells me that during the bombing, Belgrade was the liveliest it had ever been. The streets were full of people every night, everyone was constantly drunk and stoned, movie theaters were full of kids smoking pot. I tell her about Marko's stories from Sarajevo, the basement concerts and car-battery dance parties. "You see, when you finally decide you have nothing left to lose, only then you are free!" she says with elation. "Imagine if you found out you only have a month to live, would you stay at home complaining?"

It is ten in the morning, and none of us has slept. We sit back and sip our coffees. Maja puts on a record of Macedonian folk. Suddenly, we are all dancing, beer replaces coffee, the living room has become a dance party.

I COULD MISTAKE THE WAY THE FRIENDLY MAN SPEAKS for a series of punches in the face. "Where are you from?" he bellows in English. I respond in Serbian, and make the mistake of telling him the truth. "AMERICA! USA! You are Yankee Doodle!" He shouts in absurd English. No one yet has taken it amiss, but I am not sure I want everyone on this silent, packed bus to know that I am from the country that recently bombed them. "I am from Australia! I am Aussie Doodle!" Emma looks over her shoulder, and he violently pats her head. "Don't worry, little one!" Emma stiffens and he forgets about her. I pretend to sleep, but he ignores my feigned escape. He tells me about his wife and two kids in Australia, and I shudder to think of their home life.

"Last night, who was that actor in the carrot movie?"

"Carrothead?" I lazily offer.

"No, no," he yells, karate chopping for clarity.

"Bruce Lee?"

"No, no," he yells, angry at my stupidity.

"Van Damme?"

"No, no," he says, "the actor was the Lonely Ranger, but what is his name? Aren't you from America?" I try to force myself to sleep, to think of anything but his talking. Sleep finally comes as I exhaust myself with the effort. Now, he is shaking me awake. "Here is my family village, now I get off here." I nod my head and smile him farewell. He shakes my hand, then narrows his eyes. "Don't get lost," he says with sagely gravity. "But if you do—remember, you can always ask someone for directions." Gazing at me to make sure I have got his meaning, he disappears out the door.

"BAČKULJA IS A CRAZY GUY," SAYS POP. "DURING THE first night of the bombing, when all the rest of us were in the bomb shelters, he sat on his balcony, a glass of wine in one hand, a bag of glue in the other, Velvet Underground cranked all the way up on the stereo. He said that when they hit the chemical factory, the flames reached the clouds. During the heavy bombing, when shrapnel was flying this way and that, he used to lay on his back in the main square for a good view. On October 5th, when Milošević was being overthrown, the new leaders—Koštunica and Djindjic—were standing on a balcony overlooking a crowd, ready to assume control. Of course, they were surrounded by rows and rows of bodyguards. And between them, who else—Bačkulja! I have no idea how he got there, but there he was, the glorious future of Serbia. Crazy Bačkulja. You know, he owns a factory? He's only twenty-five or something, but he's got six employees. I can't imagine how the factory works, he's always drunk and stoned."

THIS VISIT, I RUSH TO SEE BORBA. A FEW MONTHS AGO, local mafia assassinated Prime Minister Djindjic, an ex-anarchist who translated Kropotkin in his youth and who was a key figure in the opposition to Milošević. Djindjic was also a criminal who used his own mafia connections to benefit from the neo-liberal reforms he implemented; when Germany donated a fleet of buses to Belgrade, Djindjic managed to re-sell the fleet to the city like they were out of his own garage. Borba was arrested because ASI published a communiqué on the Internet that voiced these "public secrets." Borba was released after some days, then re-arrested and interrogated. Just after his release, I called him from Zagreb. "Sorry if I sound tired, I stayed up all last night in the station, partying with the secret police," he quipped.

During his initial arrest on the pretext of being a suspect for the assassination, Borba was housed with hundreds of Belgrade's finest, associates of the "Zemun Gang" who might have information about the assassination. They had names like "Skunk," "Blade," and "Roach." According to Borba, When they learned why he had been arrested, the guys in his cell unanimously agreed that he, as the man who had stood up to the government, was their hero. "You are our intellectual voice," they told him. Borba decided it wasn't the time to discuss his anti-nationalism, or other sticky points. They accorded him the most comfortable bed and took turns surrendering their meals so that he could eat double portions.

I ask Borba about the interrogation. "Ah, this is amazing! First, they had an Obraz poster on the wall of the station where they booked me. In the interrogation room, they had a poster of Al Pacino on the wall, and kept playing some terrible pop love song over and over, like 30 times," he shudders. "They sat me down, tried to scare me, slapped me a few times. And get this—their first question was: 'Who was behind October 5th?!'"

We all laugh in horror. On October 5th, Milošević was overthrown by two million people in the streets, and soon after replaced by the neo-liberal opposition coalition. The question revealed how little the overthrow has affected the internal workings of the state, and how little the neo-liberal reforms have had to do with democracy. The police didn't seem to have noticed that the October 5th overthrow succeeded.

Borba pulls out an issue of *NIN*, Serbia's most widely-read news magazine. He opens to a double-page spread of his photo and an article about his arrest. "They wanted to write about me, the young intellectual arrested for saying what everyone already knows. But I didn't want them to write about me. I told them they had to write about oranges."

One of the men in the cell had approached Borba to tell his story. "This huge, huge guy, with this little itty bitty voice," squeaks Borba in imitation. Z had been a junkie for years, until his parents sent him to a rehab program in Russia. When he returned to Belgrade, he didn't do heroin anymore, but all his friends were still junkies. He decided to be a dealer for them. Since he'd known them for years, he was equitable in his deals, and soon got a reputation as an honorable businessman. One day, a car pulled up to Z's house, where he still lived with his parents. Members of the Zemun Gang told them they'd heard of his good reputation, and would be honored to include him in their business. Z understood what refusal of their offer would mean.

Borba describes how, in the cell, Z's back was so blackened with bruises that he couldn't sleep, how his already huge knees had doubled in size from the police interrogators' baseball bat. Z showed Borba burns from the cattle prod, choke marks on his neck. "He was just a street dealer, why the fuck would he know anything about the assassination?" Borba yells, eyes moist, more upset than I've ever seen him. The police finally told Z that he had two choices. Either he could find himself at the bottom of the river, like some people whose disappearance Z had already heard about, or he could point out Djindjic's assassin in a book of mug shots. Z pointed at three faces at random and signed his testimony.

"He told me in his little teeny voice how if he ever makes it out, he'll do everything his parents tell him to from now on. He said that he doesn't ask much from life. All that he really wants is to smoke pot, and to eat oranges. Oranges are his very

favorite thing in life, he said, he really likes them. And tulips, he wants to make money with a little tulip farm in his parents' backyard, he said he has a talent for growing tulips. I visited him after I was released and brought him a book on how to grow tulips, and he was really happy.

"He didn't even remember what faces he pointed at in that book. He realized that if the police use his testimony and release him, those faces or their friends will be waiting for him when he gets out. He knows, the way he was talking about oranges, what will happen to him. I made some calls to some groups, and the magazine article did talk about him and his oranges... Maybe if news gets out about how he was forced to falsely testify, maybe that can help."

DALIA PICKS AT HER TEETH, SPITTING, AS WE WALK OUT of the pre-fab aluminum-block restaurant. Our stomachs are stuffed with spicy baked beans. "Every toothpick I've used here has broken in my teeth, so I had to pick it out with another toothpick!" Like an IMF loan.

This 500,000,000,000 dinar bill from 1994 might as well have been a napkin. Ksenia told me how during the worst of the inflation of the Yugoslav dinar—32 million percent in August 1993,[93] the highest inflationary rate in world history—you would go to a restaurant and order a few beers with some friends. The waiter would bring the beers and the check, which might be worth ten dollars in dinars when he brought it. You would then tell the waiter, "Stick it on my tab," sit around talking with your friends for a few hours, maybe order another round. By the time you paid the tab—now for two rounds—the total might come to fifty cents worth of dinars, due to the inflation during those two or three hours. Those who still had credit cards were especially happy—whatever you could put on your credit card this month would be nearly free a few months later when you paid it off. Many people in the cities purchased apartments in dinars and paid them off after a few months, often for around ten dollars.

When Tito died in 1980, Yugoslavia had the highest per-capita income of any socialist country, and was generally lauded as an economic miracle. The public did not know about the twenty billion dollars Tito had borrowed from the IMF. Two years later, the IMF gave another loan to Yugoslavia, on the condition that it institute "an anti-inflationary macro-economic stabilization policy of radical austerity, trade, and price liberalization, and institutional reforms to impose on firms and governments monetary discipline and real price incentives."[94] Twenty years later, Argentina, the most prosperous country in Latin America and another "economic miracle," would be given the same advice, with very similar results. At least in that case prescribed systematic idiocy, and not conspiracy, was enough to destroy the country.

Scheduled blackouts, gas shortages, and food rationing began the same year. By 1985, the value of the currency had fallen by ninety percent of its 1979 value. Imports flooded the market as trade was deregulated, destroying demand for locally produced goods, and half of the state banks closed due to imposed reforms, choking off investment for local industry. The reforms facilitated buyouts and liquidation of struggling businesses. Nearly two thirds of industrial workers were classified as "redundant," and, as the austerity measures required firms to fire such workers, unemployment skyrocketed—especially in Serbia, Bosnia, Kosov@, and Macedonia. Then, in 1989 with the fall of the Berlin Wall, Yugoslavia lost its privileged position as a buffer-zone between the sides of the Cold War, for which it had previously been so readily rewarded. The IMF, instead of granting more loans, recommended more severe austerity measures.[95]

A year later, during a match between the main soccer teams of Zagreb and Belgrade, fans poured down from the stands and tore each other to pieces. The entire country stared at the TV, all at once.

KSENIA AND I ARE GETTING DRUNK IN THE CAVE, A GIANT pothole of a club filled with techno-heads under strobe light. We compare bad consciences—I know that back home I was protesting as the bombs fell here, but that doesn't quite make me feel comfortable enough. She becomes upset with generosity, promises me that no one here would hold me responsible for what my government did, but I assure her it's not others' opinions I'm thinking of. She tells me that she recently watched a documentary on Srebrenica, a town in Bosnia where Bosnian Serb forces killed thousands of men during one weekend. I tell her she can't hold herself responsible, that she was protesting whenever she could and speaking out, that no one could have thought she was supporting the war, but she shrugs.

Ksenia is cautiously, critically proud of the aspects of Serbia, and especially of Belgrade, that contradict the nationalist reductionism of Serbian politicians. She tells me that it's politically correct now to hate everything here, to reverse the denial of the nationalists by claiming that people here are all monsters wholly responsible for everything that happened in the war. She tells me with quiet pride how when the head Imam, or Islamic religious leader, of the Balkans was recently searching for a location for a new Madrasa, an Islamic theology school, he decided on Belgrade. There's already an Islamic university paid for by an international Islamic organization to the south in Novi Pazar, in the majority Muslim area of Sendjak. Ksenia tells me some of her friends are a bit threatened by it, but she assures them that the school probably has more interesting things to teach than how to cut off Serbs' heads.

Ksenia's mother grew up a Croat in the town of Knin, the capital of the Serbian majority area of Krajina within Croatia, itself a minority Republic within Yugoslavia, the only Non-Alliance Pact country in Europe. A minority within a minority with a minority within a minority. She moved to Belgrade with her husband a couple of decades ago and says that she has never experienced discrimination here for her Croatian accent. I am impressed that, while so many people in this area have drawn their mental map in such a way as to view themselves as the aggrieved minority—Serbs in Croatia or Kosov@, Albanians or Croatians within the federation of Yugoslavia—Ksenia's mother seems to pass up the category of victim-minority. Or is it that I'm impressed with the di-

ABOVE: Pancevo train station, Vojvodina, Serbia.

BELOW: Romani woman and man, Zeleni Venac market, Belgrade, Serbia.

versity of Belgrade, or Serbia? Can I assume her experience is typical?

Every time I go to Ksenia's house, her mother buries me in homemade pleasures: walnut *rakija*, Turkish delight, Turkish coffee, sausage, cheese, sweet jams, until I lose my will to ever stop eating. Ksenia, like most of her friends, still lives at home. The doubling of the city's population with refugees and the economic collapse have made housing hard to afford for most people in their thirties. "Do you think we're spoiled here? I mean, just living off our parents for so long? In America, don't you have to move out when you're eighteen?" I assure Ksenia that the idea hadn't occurred to me. "People here still work to live," Ksenia observes, "not like in Western countries where people live to work.

"Do you think people here are more sexist than in America?" she asks me. Again, I don't know what to say.

"Women here seem more assertive and confident in general than what I'm used to. But they're also suspiciously skinny. I see more spousal abuse than I'm used to, but maybe it's just more out in the open. Men here know that they have history at their backs. Maja tells me 'tradition is patriarchy' here, and the word somehow means even more than when people say it back home. I mean, the Orthodox Church is led by 'Patriarchs'." Ksenia tells me how in the villages, at least until recently, people still lived in *Zadrugas*, clan-households of around 50 people, led by a single patriarch with final say.

The radio plays a cover of "California Dreaming" with lyrics in Bosnian, as Ksenia and I sip our beer together in an outdoor cafe. She tells me about a friend's brother, who ran away to Israel after a year in the Yugoslav army in Croatia, and who then had to serve in the Israeli army for three years. In high school, during the war, two of her friends got in a fight, and one of them got mad and yelled: "You're such a fucking Croat!" to the other. Then the other said, "But you're a Croat too!" and the first paused, thought, then said, "Well, I'm not the kind of Croat you are!" Another of her friends is trying to move to London, where he thinks he'll be happy because he'll finally have enough money. "Look, I've worked five years without a vacation, and I'm 27," he complained to her. "I spent ten years that should have been the best years of my life in protests... I don't want to hear anything more about politics, I don't want to do anything for anybody else anymore."

"Many people my age are tired of spending so much of their lives struggling," explains Ksenia. "Even if they are critical of NGOs and the IMF, most people still hope that capitalistic changes might make their lives better. But then again, I was speaking with a taxi driver the other day in Novi Sad about the October 5th revolution that got Milošević out, and the current situation, and he said, 'You know, we should have an October 5th every year!'"

Ksenia tells me about the time she forgot the name of Tito's dog in elementary school. Her teacher refused to let the matter drop. "Don't you know that little Rex saved Tito's life?" The teacher screamed, *"Where would we be without Rex?"* If little kids were screamed at for forgetting the name of Tito's dog, I am suddenly not surprised that adults sometimes might be sent to labor camps, such as the infamous Goli Otok, on similar grounds.

Bilja, our waitress, joins us for a drink. She emanates self-possession, yet lectures Ksenia that her shoes aren't feminine enough. Bilja looks ten years younger than her age, and tells us her secret to a long youth: "I have done a lot of things in life, but I've never bent my back for anyone." When I tell Bilja that I am writing a book about the Balkans, she locks my eyes and says, "No sane person can understand what happened here."

When Ksenia visited London, some people recoiled when she told them where she was from, demanding: "Why do you hate Muslims?" She and her brother walked into a bar on the same trip. At one table sat a man with Drina cigarettes, a type made only in Sarajevo. Ksenia impulsively grabbed them, overjoyed to see them for the first time in years, but the man grabbed her hand without looking at her. "I'm sorry, I was just excited to see them again," she apologized. "Spare me," answered the man. She left the bar. "I mean, he was right, I totally understand," she says.

She hands me another cigarette, and we smoke together in silence for some minutes. She finally shakes her head and mourns, "You know, 'we' hate 'them' because 'they' hate 'us.' But meanwhile, another country is taking over the world!"

Another night of stumbling through the early morning streets with Ksenia; I cannot pass a window display of all the new refrigerators, the gas/electric stoves, the new models of wash-

Bunny dealer in underground passage, Belgrade, Serbia.

ing machines, and the recent wave of dishwashers, without falling to my knees in admiration. "Appliances! Appliances!" I cry, and search in vain for an exact definition of the word for Ksenia. That night, I dream that I am at a party. Turbo-folk is blasting, we are all dancing in the smoky apartment. I appear with a gigantic gold washing machine around my neck, on a

Kids' tricycles, Belgrade, Serbia.

thick gold chain. "Hey," I slur coolly to a woman dancing next to me, "check out my appliances." Ksenia can't stop laughing when I tell her my dream.

ON THE MAIN PEDESTRIAN STRIP IN BELGRADE, A MAN sells nationalistic buttons and postcards. "We are very strong," in Serbian, with the logo of the football team. "Fuck the USA," and then a picture of NATO's stealth bomber shot down by Yugoslav forces, with the words: "Sorry, we didn't know it was invisible." A series of postcard photographs from the bombing, burning skyscrapers, the shell of the massive Chinese embassy. I notice an "Obraz" button to the side.

"*Odakle ste?*" he asks me. Where are you from?

"*Iz Amerike.*" I answer.

He beams, "*Ova zemlja, čudesna je, bre?*" This country is *čudesna*, miraculous, isn't it? In the literal sense. Back home, I'd get accused of exoticizing, but he was the one who asked. I nod back—*da, da, čudesna je.*

On the train seat across from me sits a giant of solidity. The lines across his hands and face suggest decades of factory work. A large airborne seed, as if from a huge dandelion, floats in through the open window. We both eye it as it lazily swirls across the compartment, dropping and lifting, drifting away and returning. The man blows at the puffball; it circles and floats over in front of my face. I puff at it, and it returns to his sphere. Without expression, the man blows it back to me. I blow underneath it; it floats up to the ceiling and slowly drops over his head. He blows it back at me, but it is suddenly sucked back out the window. We both peer out the window at the passing countryside.

Munching cookies on Borba's bed, I flip through two volumes of police documentation of civilian deaths from the NATO bombing that Borba somehow obtained. Hellishly placid corpses leisurely loiter any old place, a relaxed foot without its leg, a distracted head with no body, a gesturing arm that forgot its shoulder. Most of the photos strike me as more absurd than horrific—a thing that used to be a person is the essence of horror, but a single tennis shoe standing defiantly among mute concrete rubble, this is hardly even a whole thing. Tragedy made for consumption is extra-real, but somehow, this seems insufficient. I tell Borba what Tvrtko had told me in Zagreb, that although one might expect the government to exaggerate the casualties, he believed that the official figures for the war in Croatia were very low. People might not be so proud of their national victory if they realized how much of their nation had died for it, not thousands but some tens of thousands. Borba told me he was sure the same happened here, since Milošević somehow claimed proudly that they'd won the NATO bombing, with only 3,000 civilian casualties. "Who knows how many civilians were killed in three months; who knows how many more in the army." He takes the books away. "Why are you looking at that, anyway?"

Borba tells me how the Yugoslav police magazine *Bezbednost* (Security), wrote that PUNK stands for "*Pomozite Ustanak Naroda Kosova*" (Help the Kosovo People's Uprising), and that the circle-A symbol stands for greater Albania. The conspiracy must have seemed very wide-reaching, since both were painted all over the city.

Borba isn't mystified at all by the cause of the wars here. "The old communist politicians were losing their jobs, since the Cold War had ended. They had to make a new constituency, so they became nationalists and made war." He can't understand why radicals other places sided with this national cause or that one. "Why would I pick a favorite bourgeoisie? It's just like any nationalism anywhere, the local bourgeoisie trying to become the biggest fish, and convince the workers that it has something to do with their liberation to kill each other."

"What about the genocide in Bosnia?"

"Sick, tragic, terrible, but how does NATO taking a side help? Even the humanitarian aid convoys that activist groups from the West sent made things worse—they only sent aid to the Muslim population, reinforcing ethnic divisions. Many Serbs in Bosnia were starving, too, since all the money Serbia was secretly funneling in was going for guns. The Serbs were more convinced than ever that the world was out to get them, that there was no way out except to win, without negotiation."

Pop and I disagree with Borba, uneasily. Imperialism is terrible, but maybe genocide is worse. Insofar as the NATO bombing in Bosnia ended the slaughter of civilians, it served a good end, however accidentally. Any use of the bombing for legitimation of future imperialist conquests is terrible, but sometimes the wrong people do the right thing for the wrong reasons. Borba laughs at us. "Listen to you! Now that Bosnia is a neo-liberalist protectorate, far more people are going to die of capitalism than if the war had been played out, maybe not in Bosnia, but in the whole world... They're going to invoke Bosnia again and again to do whatever they want."

Borba visited the US a couple of years ago, just after the NATO bombing. It seems everyone here dreams of going to the US, but Borba and Jovana were the only people I encountered who'd made it. Jovana told me that people in Vallejo, California, were just like in Serbia, that she made good friends and enjoyed herself. I was surprised, until she mentioned that she didn't meet many white people.

The guy sitting next to Borba on the flight spilled red wine on Borba's white shirt, so he was rendered "a suspect from a terrorist country with a bloodstained shirt," in Borba's chuckled words, and searched by the airport authorities. He was supposed to stay two months, but went home after one. "I was bored and miserable. The people I met didn't know anything about the rest of the world, they couldn't hold a conversation. Everyone was completely narcissistic, I couldn't stand it."

BACK IN THE US, I OPEN UP THE SEPTEMBER 4, 2003, *New York Times*. A headline catches my eye:

> Rights Group Urges Inquiry on Torture in Serbia
> BELGRADE, Serbia, Sept. 3 (AP)—Amnesty International is demanding an investigation of allegations that security forces tortured suspects arrested in connection with the assassination of Serbia's prime minister in March...
> "We believe that the use of torture and ill treatment during Operation Saber was widespread, particularly against those perceived as low-level criminals, out of the public eye and unlikely to have their allegations widely publicized," Amnesty International said. "Allegations of torture by security forces of detainees include asphyxiation by taping bags over the head, beatings, electric shocks to the head and body, and mock executions," the report said. "These are extremely serious allegations," the report continued. "And we are asking the Serbian authorities to allow us and other human rights groups unfettered access to interview any of the detainees privately, so that we may ascertain the true scale of the problem."
> There was no immediate response to the report by the Serbian authorities, who have denied such allegations from other human rights organizations.

ONCE AGAIN, I FIND MYSELF WITH A GROUP OF SLOVENES trying to be Serbs, but this time in a way I love.

Sitting in the train out of Belgrade, with the next two compartments full of Slovene youth drinking and laughing and screaming and sitting in the overhead luggage racks, I can fully imagine my Slovene friend's adventure in France a few years ago, where a nice little school skiing trip ended in riots that tore up the whole resort. Maybe I'm a bit of a Slovene myself—nice, calm and friendly most of the time, but I just don't feel myself without an occasional blowout.

Heartbreak is so much easier to deal with singing along with partisan songs, passing the frothy plastic bottle, and yelling at the guy who keeps farting, while two of the Slovenes protect my luggage in the next compartment by rolling around beneath it. At least if I'm not doing it with the one I love, they are—with the one they love, not with the one I love.

Skopje, Macedonia.

SHARE THAT TASTE

THE OLD LADY WITH A GOLD TOOTH, ACROSS FROM ME, REMOVES HER SHOES FOR A NAP BETWEEN BORDERS. AN OFFICIAL OUTSIDE THE TRAIN WINDOW PICKS UP SOME LEAVES AND LAYS THEM ON A LOG BEFORE SITTING DOWN FOR A BREAK. ON THE BORDER, THE GUARD ASKS ME: "TRANSIT GREECE?" "TOURIST," I ANSWER. HE ASKS, "OHRID?" AND I NOD TO THE TOWN I AM GOING TO, AND JUST AS I THINK I'M GOING TO HAVE TO BUY A VISA, HE ADDRESSES ME AS "AMERICA!" IN THE VOCATIVE ("HEY YOU") NOUN FORM, LIKE, "HEY YOU, AMERICA!" HE STAMPS MY PASSPORT AND HANDS IT BACK. A MINUTE LATER, ANOTHER GUARD WALKS BY, LOOKS IN, AND SAYS, "AH, AMERICA..." IN A EXHAUSTED TONE, AS IF HE IS SAYING, "AH, LIFE IS TOO LONG."

"Please be quiet" post office, Skopje, Macedonia.

First sight of Macedonia: relaxed soldiers with Kalashnikov AK-47s walk through sunflowers. Overturned cars lie everywhere, not from war but from laziness, or possibly aesthetic sense: I see a neat little circle of them on their sides in a grove of trees beneath me. A giant, shining, hammered-copper mosque roof stands across from a Macedonian Orthodox church. People fish in the river, water up to their knees. An old man in a wide field plays with two tiny kids. At the station, toothless old men laugh and listen to frenetic Balkan folk-pop, not checking my ticket as I walk past. Feral cats and dogs share their cafe with me, minding their feral business. The language is just different enough from Serbian to keep me attentively confused. Everything so far is sketchy but manageable—the instant I look lost in both train and bus stations, anxious looking young men approach me with mysterious suggestions, but leave without fuss when I wave them off. Sarah in Zagreb told me not to speak Serbian, just in case I ask a KLA veteran for directions, and meet the same fate as the Bulgarian tourist last year who asked the wrong person for the time: He got his head cut off. So everyone gets a chance to pleasantly mock my English. At the train station, a woman who doesn't even work there ran around translating and negotiating as I tried to refund a ticket. Then she wished me a good trip so warmly I wanted to buy her a drink. The shameful intrigue of war is at a comfortable distance, unless the bus breaks down near Tetovo. Everyone in line stands charmingly close, even when counting money, when they stand in line at all. Every face is harshly unique; genetic diversity mixed in every combination, the accumulated stretches of expressive faces through extreme times.

RISTE IS MY FIRST FRIEND IN OHRID. I ASK HIM THE TIME as I get off the bus, and he ends up spending two hours helping me find the beach that Sarah from Zagreb told me to sleep on, and showing me Ohrid's sights. He reassures me that the scorpion we saw at the beach isn't common, the first he's ever seen. We stare down into the Roman coliseum, watching ghost gladiators show each other who's boss, watching ghosts of lions eat their fill of ghost Christians. Then I leave Riste to find his friends, and don't see him again. Soon I am summoned to a table by a "Hey!" from a woman in a tank top with "Miss America" written over a US flag. By the time I summon the nerve to sit with her, she's been joined by an overbearing man.

"In America, they think we are banana people," he tells me. Every sentence is punctuated with a jab of his finger into my nearest available body part. Though he resides now in Sweden, he hasn't forgotten his Macedonian roots. "America is waging a war to destroy the Serbs, Orthodox Christianity, and everyone who doesn't think like it does." When he finds out I'm from California, he says, "Ah, there are a lot of fags in San Francisco." I don't mention the Zagreb march to him, responding with a silent poker face. He finally leaves, Miss America on his arm.

The next morning, I awake to the sounds of water splashing just by my head, and chickens running to their feed. Lizards everywhere run up to the water. I try to remember what country I am in. The old lady feeding her chickens doesn't shout at me for sleeping on her beach, but instead invites me to have breakfast at the cafe a few meters away. I realize the mountains across the lake are my first view of Albania, shrouded in mist, as expected. I'm glad I decided not to sleep in the enclosure that was, as I feared, the old lady's garden. A sixteenth century Macedonian Orthodox church looks straight down on us from its rocky perch.

In the cafe, as I play with twin black kittens, a series of family translators files out to make sense of me. A kid no older than seven is playing in a rowboat in the water, maybe unmooring it. No one seems worried. My fourteen-year-old waitress chases the cats away, but they return with a full list of demands once my omelette arrives. Last night I had almost decided this place was malevolent, between the scorpion and the Swedish Bananaman. But now I'm not so sure, as a man dives from this cafe straight into the lake, as I eat this perfectly seasoned omelette that wouldn't need pepper even if they brought it, and as the young waitress tells me I'm sitting directly beneath the apartment of Sarah's late grandmother, who was the first translator of Henry Miller into Serbo-Croatian.

In the town center, the Muzzein call blasts across the street. This could be Saudi Arabia. The restaurant is playing sentimental pop love songs that could easily be Peter Cetera singing in Macedonian. Total discordance, yet somehow uniting in an ecstatic higher harmony. Reciprocally, they reinforce each other's passing perfection. This moment is seemingly impossible yet immediately realized. The Clash of Civilizations Theory is disproven by this moment. The modernity of the amplified Muzzein call and love pop, of tractors, of hospitals, of the ubiquitous and homogeneous punk movement that has my friends wearing the same clothes and listening to the same music in every country I can find them, is an opportunity for reconciliation. The mistake of thinking one has broken with history results in the fact of historical synthesis. Failed attempts at homogenization result in a diverse common ground of attempt. The menu lists "Sexy Salad." Dare I order it?

As impossible as Хот Дог = Hot Dog, Помфрит = Pommes Frites, Хамбургер = Hamburger, yet there they are, sold in the stands. Like ordering an exotic-sounding local dish, "Momsko," which turns out to be two large naked hamburger patties, fries, onions, and navy beans. Or the clothing store here named "ASSPORT." My cap with crosshairs, that reads, "Uncle Sam Streetstyle." Everyone here wears counterfeit FUBU—For Us, By Us. Fubu Roi. As the Americans sitting behind me at a folk festival said, "There is logic to it, but still!" A bit later, they gasped with an articulate choke, "This is *very!*"

At a parade in Ohrid the musicians and dancers are from everywhere, but this quartet has no dancers, just pounding meter-wide drums and meter-long double-reed zurlas, shrill in their cutting frenzy: Albanian. The police trail them, a kid in front holding a sign naming their village, and below that "MACEDONIA" in huge letters, an elegant refutation against possible suspicions of Albanian separatism. They came late, seeming almost to invade the parade. None of the Macedonian folk dancers can keep step, but a big group dances the Slavic circle dance *kolo* around the Moroccan trance music anyway, and everyone seems content with the inconsistency. Are the police there to protect or contain the band? Maybe it is just the police, or is there something tentative and tense in the air around them? One guy eyes me and aims his super-zurla at my head, the sound so focused that the melody is closer to me than my own body. Drums thump and chatter aggressively. The beat pounds in Turkic time signatures I can't pretend to count out. Their sensible, calm smiles, as their instruments let out such a perfectly ordered madness, win my confidence instantly. This is why Maja's Macedonian family, from a village near Tetovo, invited an Albanian group to play at their wedding. This is why Albanian families there still invite Macedonians to their weddings.

IN THE ANCIENT NARROW STREETS OF OHRID, BLOWN CLEAN with breezes from the oceanic lake, a kid cries, "Hey punk!" as we pass. He wears a T-shirt of the Minneapolis punk band "Destroy." His patched and spiky garb fits the universal punk standard: BEWARE! The Nature of your Oppression is the Aesthetic of our Anger! I return a solid nod. He asks in English where we are from—Branka's waist-length dreadlocks and my green afro have perhaps made us stand out. "Do we drink?" he wants to know. "We don't do much else," Aaron replies. He invites us to a place he calls "The Underground."

The Underground is a stretch along the lake's edge, something like an urban alley, but otherwise too amenable a spot to deserve such promising infamy. Rowboats substitute for the docks. A dozen of the town's youth sit scattered across the lot, hugging their knees and passing a wine bottle. Stepan, our seventeen-year-old host, introduces himself, then shows us off to all his friends. We meet the town's two other punks, and I compliment their fashion—where do they find accessories in Ohrid? Sometimes they go up to Skopje, the capitol, but most of it they make themselves. Stepan shows me the "No Gods, No Masters" patch he painted by hand, from the punk bank Amebix, identical to the silkscreened one that I recognize from punks in California, France, Mexico....

"You are from Sacramento?" asks one punker excitedly. "Do you know the Deftones? I would like one day to go to America, only to see the Deftones."

"Is it true that in America," another friend asks, "you get arrested if you wear a Che Guevara T-shirt?"

"You know, we are a very ancient country," Stepan tells me after a few beers. "Have you heard of Alexander the Great? He was a great man, for he brought many people together in his multicultural empire. He did not seek to control, only to give different people a chance to live together in peace." I'd never realized Alexander was so punk. Stepan's voice cracks with indignation as he tells me how some people even try to claim that Alexander spoke Greek, not Macedonian. I tell Stepan that I speak some Serbian, a Slavic language which arrived in this area nine centuries after Alexander's Hellenic empire; is Macedonian similar? "Yes, very similar, the Serbs are good people, warm and open," Stepan tells me as he holds his hand to his chest.

"We have many problems here with the Albanians," he continues grimly. "You know they are Muslims, and Islam is a religion of genocide. We have often had problems since they arrived." I start to object, but several kids explain with polite reserve that I cannot understand since I am not from here. After an awkward pause, the Deftones fan says quietly, "Things are hard for Albanians. But things are changing, I think for the better."

The last wine bottle is emptied. Branka and Aaron return to their hostel, but Stepan refuses to let me sleep on my beach; I must stay with him at his sister's. I'm sad to leave my idyllic beach on the lake, all but its smell. "Is that from pollution?" I ask as we climb down for my bags hidden in a cave. Stepan's friend assures me: "Only from flora and fauna." We pass an ancient church, one of little Ohrid's 365 Orthodox churches. Stepan crosses himself, washes himself carefully at the fountain, and crosses again as he leaves, Amebix patch notwithstanding. For the price of a cup of coffee in a local cafe, a taxi takes us across town to his sister's. She lives on Ulica Pariska Komuna—Paris Commune Street. Stepan jokes, "I live here because I'm an anarchist."

Ivana and her friend are shouting at each other over the TV as we walk in. "*Slušaj me!*" Listen to me! Ivana pounds the table. She graciously offers me a seat and continues yelling as she disappears into the kitchen, returning with an unsolicited platter. "Do you like pancakes?" she asks as an introduction. "Tomorrow I will make you pancakes, with maple syrup." Then she reverts to berating her friend in Macedonian. The friend responds stoically, and I realize they're not fighting after all.

Ivana grabs my journal as I take notes, and starts reading it before I can stop her. To my horror, she opens directly to a page on which I've written about my fear that I'll fall in love with someone while traveling and end up married. Her eyebrows rise, and she nods wisely: "Aha! I see." I grab it back and beg her to change the subject, but she relishes several minutes of my discomfort first.

On Ivana's bookshelf, underneath a series of Buddhist meditation paintings, I am surprised to find a large selection of English language books about Islam, printed in Saudi Arabia. "My boyfriend is Muslim, he is from Turkey but lives on Staten Island. He sends me those books, I love how they are written. Have you been to Staten Island?" I tell her that I've been to Turkey, but only driven across Staten Island. "I love Turkey, it is a real place, civilized. They know how to live." We compare recollections of tea gardens, hookahs, spicy lentil soups, giant mosques and ancient ruins. She jumps up as I ask about the several books on Malcolm X. "You know of El-Hajj El-Malik El-Shabazz? He is like a hero for me!" She ruffles through her desk, and pulls out an essay written for her English class.

It began with a quote from its subject: "History is a people's memory and without a memory man is demoted to the level of the lower animals." The essay summarized his life and thought, including his transition from Nation of Islam sectarianism to the widely-embracing anti-imperialist struggle of his last years. "He was willing," I read, "to go through anything to gain the rights of Blacks; humans." Ivana tells me that the paper was given a B, because the teacher believed Malcolm X to be a "terrorist."

Wasn't Malcolm X translated into Serbo-Croatian in Yugoslavia? I would expect Tito to have been friends with him, as an important non-aligned revolutionary leader. Ivana laughs. "Are you crazy? He was a Muslim nationalist. They would never have translated him. Besides, I can't read that language."

"Isn't the Serbian alphabet the same as Macedonian?" I ask her. "Aren't the languages similar?"

"Serbian hasn't been spoken much here since Macedonia broke away from Yugoslavia. And anyway, it's an ugly language," she retorts flatly.

Stepan appears in a long Sex Pistols T-shirt and pajama pants. "Sex Pistols are for sleeping," he says. Ivana teases his hair, he swats her hand away. They kiss each others' cheeks goodnight, and he disappears. Ivana opens another beer for me before I can object. She calls a friend at 3 a.m. to bring her cigarettes, but he has just crashed his car and is depressed. He is trying to go to sleep while doing a lot of cocaine. She calls up a taxi to go buy her cigarettes. "It's a normal thing to do here," she explains.

After we have been talking about Dostoyevsky, Ivana asks me if I have ever heard of a very good but perhaps obscure author from America; he writes much about the situation of African-American people in the US. "Give me a try," I urge.

"Do you know of a book called, er, something ending in 'Bones'?" I'm uncertain, so she continues. "The author, his name is Stephen King, have you maybe ever heard of his work?" I have, I assure her, but I was unaware of this particular work, and indeed such a focus of his writing. She is surprised to learn that he has written books on other subjects, as well.

The sun rises as we finish off the pack brought by the taxi. Ivana readies her bed. As I stand up to sleep in Stepan's room, she proffers a tired conclusion to our conversation: "You'll hear a lot of stupid things, don't be surprised. Many people don't like each other here these days. It wasn't like this two years ago, even in 2000."

After my afternoon pancakes with maple syrup, Stepan takes me into town. We walk out the door into a turmoil of joy; the Roma neighbors are filling the street with music and dancing. "This was a wedding, but they are always doing this, finding some reason to party," Stepan nods approvingly. We take the long route, as Stepan wants to show me the Turkish neighborhood. One mosque dates back 400 years, but the houses and block apartments are modern. He translates a bit of overheard Turkish. In the center of town, I promise to meet him at the Underground, bottle in hand.

Every night for the rest of our stay, when I get back to Ivana's, she teases, "So, did you marry anybody today?"

ONE NIGHT, SEEKING PROTECTION UNDER A TARP FROM the sudden rain that interrupts the folk concert, I meet Joe, a European Union employee who works around Tetovo, the center of the current conflict in Macedonia. His position is the "reconciliation of the Macedonian and Albanian communities." He puts multi-ethnic soccer teams together, though almost all of the interested youth are Albanian. Recently, he tells me, he was in a village in northern Macedonia, near Kosov@. He talked to one man there, who explained that Albanians have only been in the Balkans since the 1920s, not since pre-history as is usually thought. "You see," the man explained, "when Mussolini invaded Ethiopia, the Italians needed people to row them back to Italy. As the Italians are not accustomed to rowing their own boats, they recruited a large number of Ethiopians to do it for them. When they returned to Italy, they did not want to keep them there, so they put them all across the Adriatic, in the land that is now called Albania. So you see," he explained, "the Albanians are actually Ethiopians."

"Have you ever seen an Ethiopian, even in a picture?" asked Joe.

"Of course," answered the man. "I see them every day. They call themselves Albanians."

When Joe asked the man where he learned this, he whispered: "From shepherd of our village. He lives up on that hill. He is the wisest man I have ever known."

IVANA WORKS FULL TIME, 5PM TO 10PM DAILY, AT HER MOTHER'S clothing store for children. Like most businesses along the main street, it has a short table surrounded by chairs out front: a precaution against the temptation to waste working hours working. Today five friends are already sitting out front when I come to visit Ivana. We stare at each other until I manage "Ciao," then they realize I am the American. Immediately one tall, clean-cut hyperactive woman asks me what in the hell I'm doing here, I try to explain in mixed English and Serbian, she says, "You come to see how we live? Fuck off!" with a laugh and a big smile and I laugh back, then she yells "lazes," you're lying, she keeps going and I don't understand, her brother who does a lot of coke asks me something I don't understand, she again asks me what the fuck I'm doing here, what do I do? I try to say I'm trying to write a book, she doesn't understand, says "lazes!" with a smile and asks me how old I am. I say 29, she says, "Lazes! Starac magarac!" I think she's asking if I speak Hungarian ("madjarski") and I emphatically answer no, then they are confused, then me too, until I ask Ivana who seems uncomfortable what magarac means, she says "donkey," and I laugh and say several times, "Ja sam starac magarac!" I am an old donkey, and we all laugh and I keep laughing and she asks me what's funny, and I say, "Absurd situation," which she doesn't understand, so I say, "because I'm an old man donkey," and she says, "This is not funny, it is sad you're an old man donkey," then her brother asks me if I like her, she girlfriend? And everyone looks at me so I shrug but look at the ground, she says, "Do you have a girlfriend?" and I emphatically, fearfully say yes, yes, she is beautiful, I am very happy with her, and they ask how long will I stay in Ohrid, where do I go next, and I say Albania, and she says, "There's nothing to see in Albania," and I say, "But it is a very unique country," which she agrees to. So I try to explain again about the book, but she again says "lazes" before I can explain anything. She leaves, and returns with a chocolate bar called "Kandi" she bought for me. I say "thank you," she says, "You Are Welcome," importantly, and then they all leave.

Ivana later told me how Tanja, who told me "Lazes," is studying sports therapy in Beograd. Ivana tells me that when she introduced her boyfriend to Tanja, Tanja's first words were, "I'm going to tie you to a chair and rape you and no one will hear you scream." He wasn't sure how to respond to her either.

I CAN'T THINK OF ANYTHING TO SAY AS WE STARE AT THE smashed, burnt-down mosque in Prilep. Momir tells us the story. In 2001, a convoy of ten Macedonian soldiers was ambushed and killed by KLA guerrillas. His cousin was one of the casualties. They had been ordered, against all regulations, to sit on a pile of explosives in the back of a truck, which blew up when the ethnic Albanian guerrillas attacked. A small group of locals attacked the mosque that night in revenge, then moved down the street to burn down an Albanian-owned pastry shop. We walk up to the still-closed, burnt-out shop. The police showed up before the mob to the pastry shop. One of Momir's friends had been present, and heard a cop tell one of the vandals, "Don't do that again—in front of me." The newspapers reported the next day that police valiantly attempted to defend the Albanian businesses, but a massive mob had overpowered them.

We stop in a shop to buy white wine and soda. I pick up and stare at a chocolate bar named "Greedy." We head back to the park to join our other friends.

Over our Prilep spritzers in the park, Momir continues the lesson. The concert inside can't be as interesting as wine with Momir. If anyone is someday going to write a Howard Zinn-ian "People's History of the Balkans," Momir is the one. "Anarchism has a long history here," he says. "In 1903, anarchists were essential in the establishment of the Krushevo Republic, in what is now Macedonia. The Republic lasted only 13 days, but is remembered daily in Macedonia and across the Balkans. In it, all ethnicities were declared equal, farmland became common property, and bread was free for all."

Momir hands me an article from his backpack, entitled "Down with the Sultan, Long Live the Balkan Federation!" by Bulgarian historian and anarchist Georgi Khadzhiev:[96]

> During the Transfiguration uprising the question of state power was never raised, and no decrees were issued. The population of the liberated villages nominated and elected

not mayors and presidents, but commissioners from among their own number. The commissions were to administer, not to rule. Never was there any talk of establishing any authorities, albeit new ones... This was quite natural and also a matter of necessity, because decisive power was now in the hands of the people in arms, and its fate was in its own hands...

[Like the Makhno movement in the Ukraine, 1917–1921, the militia leaders] left the issue of the social system to the councils which were chosen by the local population. One of the Makhnovists' appeals to the population reads, "The revolutionary insurrectionary army sets itself the goal of helping the villagers and workers... and does not interfere with civil life... It urges the working population of the town and surroundings to immediately begin independent organizational work..."

[Krushevo Militia leader] Gerdzhikov writes: "We somehow began setting up our own institutions... The population was rejoicing, in the villages people danced and held feasts. There was no more 'This is mine and that is yours'—in the hills and forests before and after the congress we had set up storehouses: the whole harvest was deposited there as flour and grain in common stores. The livestock also became common property... We issued an appeal to the ethnic Greek population in Greek explaining that in taking over territory we weren't fighting for the re-establishment of a Bulgarian empire, but only for human rights; we explained to them that as Greeks they too would benefit from this and it would be good if they would support us morally and materially..."

Khadzhiev goes on to write:

[T]he fate of the formerly Ottoman lands and their population was determined above all by the states striving for power. This will to power is a distinguishing mark of every state, be it feudal, monarchist or republican, be it capitalist or socialist: it is a motor force behind the very existence of the state as such. The same striving for power also dictates the behavior of the small states in the Balkans... Even today the political problem of the Macedonian and Thracian population still needs to be resolved, and the social aspect of this problem is even more serious.

In all of the Balkan states nationalist poison has constantly been injected into public discourse and artificially maintained in an appropriate dosage in the consciousness of citizens over generations. Nationalism is a well-tried instrument, as too is religion, for maintaining each state's striving for power.

A political solution to the significant problem of Macedonia and Thrace—these two geographical regions with their exceedingly mixed population—is only possible through a federation

of the Balkan peoples, which they would participate in as autonomous territorial units.

I hand the article back to Momir. "You know, Basil Davidson,
the most famous English-language scholar of African history,
made the same argument about Africa in *Black Man's Burden:
The Curse of the Nation-State in Africa*.[97] Areas with such mixed
populations can only exist peacefully as federations of regional
autonomous communities, never as nation-states. He uses the
Balkans as an example for Africans, and he wrote it in the 1980s.
What finally happened to the Krushevo Republic?"

Momir sips his spritzer. "After three weeks, Ottoman authorities
sent 40,000 troops, who burned 200 villages, raped more than
3,000 women, and killed nearly 5,000 people. The Republic's
leaders shot themselves under the proclamation, 'Better death
than slavery.' The Ottoman general was so impressed with the
leaders' heroism that he gave them burials with full honors."

Anarchists in Macedonia continued to struggle against the
Sultan's rule, while displaying prophetic awareness of the danger
of western capital. "Most of them didn't make it to their mid-
twenties," says Momir. Several made unsuccessful attempts on
the Sultan's life. A series of bombings succeeded in taking out
an Ottoman bank and a European bank, and sinking a French
trade ship, as well as eliminating the idealistic perpetrators.
At first, anarchists and nationalists found common cause in
fighting the Sultan. Soon, though, they realized how opposed
their ends were, and relations soured. One time, a national liberationist from Solon, now Thessaloniki, was sent to assassinate
an anarchist in Prilep. When he arrived in town, he searched
out a local contact whose address had been given to him in
Solon. His local contact laughed when the would-be assassin
told him of his mission. "I myself am this anarchist. Go back
to Solon."

We get up to go into the concert. FPO, Forever Positively Obsessed,
gets on stage. Vasko, our host from Skopje, grabs the microphone.
Vasko howls, curls up, and springs into the crowd. Elbows slam
into my chest like a mother's embrace. Marko, a twelve-year-old
member of the Peace Office anti-militarist group in Skopje, springs
past. I struggle to keep up with the clean-living youth, who put
me to shame with their overdriven spirit of fun.

Marko hops over to me during the set of the next band, Brain

Ghetto. He grabs my ear and yells over the music, "This song is called, 'Just Another Civil War for Them.'" I thank him for the translation, and he throws me to the ground.

As we file out of the show, the crowd from Skopje return to the park and begin unrolling their sleeping bags. Momir and I pour another round of spritzer. A little drunk, I ask him what he thinks is most responsible for the wars here. "Wars? It's all been one war. In Macedonia, NATO openly transferred KLA troops out of the village of Arachino when they were surrounded, and threatened to bomb the Macedonian troops if they interfered. Two KLA troops were recently captured, and the KLA took one hundred hostages for their release. CNN and BBC reported, 'One hundred Albanians taken hostage.' And have you ever heard of MPRI—Military Personnel Resources Incorporated? They are a group of retired American military personnel, supposedly private military advisers. They've been advising the Macedonian army since '95, and now, it doesn't even have snipers. MPRI also advises the ethnic Albanian forces. Have you ever heard of both sides having the same generals before?"

Momir refuses the offer of a sleeping bag, and stretches out contentedly on the grass. What does he think the motives are? "The Trepcha mining complex in Kosovo is one of the most important in Europe, and you probably know about the proposed Balkan oil pipeline from the Caspian Sea. Also, the US and EU now have permanent bases all over the Balkans, in an area where they never had excuses for bases before. They pressure the Macedonian government to let them stay for a year, and the Macedonian government asks them to leave after three months. They compromise on a six-month stay. Then the international forces announce, 'At the request of the Macedonian government, we have agreed to keep peacekeeping forces stationed another six months.' Besides that, the bombing gave NATO something to do when there was a lot of talk about disbanding it. Also, Yugoslavia was large and independent; divide-and-conquer is the first rule of Empire. They have a lot of reasons."

My drunken head sloshes with Momir's words, and then with the words of Tvrtko in Zagreb: "The international forces didn't do much to help, but I think in the end it was local causes." Besides both being well-read, well-traveled, and deep, fair thinkers, Tvrtko and Momir are kindred spirits. Twisty melodies from an all-night wedding drift into my sleeping bag as I fumble with my knotted thoughts. Vasko and his straight-edge entourage still joke cheerily, and I try not to resent their energetic sobriety. Dreams of airlifts and napalm spill through my mind.

In the morning, the straight-edgers shout us into consciousness like revolutionary cheerleaders. The blurry world comes into focus through my hangover. Vasko's cheer proves contagious enough to make me laugh, and finally I claw my way into wakefulness just in time to catch the train.

IN SKOPJE, EVERY HOME IS ROASTING PEPPERS. THE AUGUST earth is baking, and its vapors drift up from the many cracks in the sidewalk. A bus passes with the words "SHARE THAT TASTE" pasted across the side, in English, advertising nothing. A Macrobiotic fast-food stand boasts Walnut Salami. Horses graze the traffic meridians. Police pass by wearing silk-screened "POLICIA" T-shirts without badges. Do freelance cops ever make their own uniforms? I stop at a little metal box on the street to take it all in. Without the bother of electricity or seats, the proprietor spins the metal Italian soda holder—lemon, orange, mandarin, raspberry—and mixes me up a glass for the equivalent of 15 cents. This is definitely the most noble business on earth, I reflect, licking the raspberry syrup from my lips.

In 1963, a massive earthquake leveled Macedonia, then still a republic within Yugoslavia. Yugoslavia was given assistance by the rest of the world. Every country contributed its national version of '60s experimental architecture, all in matching concrete. Consequently, Skopje looks like "finals day" in a high-school architecture class for giant mud monsters: massive pagodas beside five-story ski-slope roofs, tumbling postmodern glass plates stretching over the roads, pre-fab building blocks thrown atop each other, all enclosing an ancient castle surrounded by Socialist Realism sculptures.

On the edge of town, a gargantuan Christmas-light cross glowers down from a hill. After a recent ruling against having an official state religion, the state apologized to the Macedonian Orthodox church by giving them around two million dollars for the cross, complete with its own elevator. In Belgrade, Maja told me she figured it was there to keep the Albanians in their place.

A few days ago in Tetovo, a car proceeded when police motioned for it to stop. The police opened fire; the people in the vehicle fired back. Two people in the car were killed. A few

days later, also in Tetovo, some Macedonian kids who'd just graduated high school were playing basketball. A car drove past and sprayed them with a Kalashnikov, killing one and seriously injuring two or three others. In protest, high school students around the country staged a walk-out. Most of the kids marched against ethnic violence, but some groups walked around afterwards beating up anyone who they thought looked Albanian, especially anyone wearing Muslim skullcaps. For a few days, groups of around 40 kids walked around attacking people. Macedonian kids beat up suspected ethnic Albanians, and Albanian kids beat up suspected Macedonians. One group of ethnic Albanians boarded a bus, asked to see everyone's ID cards, and beat up those with Slavic last names. The beatings stopped only two days before our arrival.

Francisco and I cross the bridge to the Albanian section to

Skopje, Macedonia.

check out a towering mosque that looks like a brick smoke-stack from a Dickens novel. One friend told us that he hadn't taken a bus across the bridge for years, after being harassed during his last attempt for being Macedonian. We stop in the old Turkish bazaar for lunch. We fill the only table in a small shop for hours, slurping our bowls of soup, as the proprietor chats with us warmly, curious about the US. We cross back over the bridge, to the ethnic Macedonian side, in the sleepy mid-western afternoon. Five horses drink from the concrete and brick river, next to a couple of fishers standing with their pants hiked up.

FRANCISCO IS STARTING TO GET EXASPERATED WITH MY promises. Skopje seemed a lot friendlier when we thought we had a place to sleep. He stares at the river and clicks his walkman back on when I return to tell him the youth hostel is closed. I go back into the Post Office and call my friend's mother again, underneath a sign that chides: "PLEASE BE QUIET." Again, she fervently explains to me just what I need to know, in Macedonian, and again I tell her I don't understand, in Serbian. After several minutes of taxing her graciousness with my despair, I thank her and hang up. Hours later, on the last credits of my third phone card, a friend in Zagreb gives us a number for a friend here, whom we reach at 10 p.m. He gives us the address of the new Peace Office.

We just have time to drop our bags and make introductions before we're back on the street. Our hosts take us to Mickey's, a rough-and-tumble B.Y.O.B. ping-pong and pool hall that doesn't seem to accept money for anything. As we wait our turn for the cue stick, our friends tell us about their office space. Their group's main focus is to introduce provisions for Conscientious Objector status in Macedonia, and to provide a forum against militarism in general.

Damyan tells me that when the KLA came to Arachino, not far from here, many locals went on picnics to watch the fighting. He tells me that his school was near the US embassy, and that sometimes American guards would train their sights on him for fun when he walked past. This is why, he says, at many protests here people smash the windows of cars parked outside the embassy, and break the windows of the Embassy itself when they can get away with it. He brags about the diversity of the neighborhood, bordering on the largest Roma community in the world, and that his neighbors are Sudanese. "I love this," Damyan says. "I can't understand these people who talk about purity. Color of skin is like color of eyes." We share a painful silence. After he bounces a corner shot, he puts down the cue stick. "You see, this country is an aquarium."

GEORGI'S SQUARE JAW AND GOOFY SMILE MISLEAD me: back in the US, this boy would be varsity material. After a few days, his persistent overtures of friendship in choppy English start to win me over. I figure anyone sleeping on the floor of a Peace Office can't be all bad. Soon he embarrasses me for my previous prejudices.

One day, Georgi sits me down. "Macedonia, as a state, got just what it deserved from the Albanians. What can it expect from such long neglect of their rights?" he demands. "Now, 'when trees become green,' like we say here, many Albanian kids, especially the less educated, fourteen or fifteen years old, join the KLA and run to the front. My friend, who fought in Tetovo, said most of the KLA 'soldiers' were just kids with Kalashnikovs, obviously without fighting skills. He said many, many more KLA soldiers died than anyone admits: Macedonia doesn't want the bad reputation, and the KLA wants to seem stronger than it is." Georgi looks at the floor. "I don't know who is right. Everyone is wrong here. But maybe now that the KLA have representatives in the parliament and the Macedonian nationalists have lost the majority, the fighting will stop.

"Do you know about the privatization here?" he prods. "At first they came in promising to reform 'weak' industry, to buy those industries already failing and bring them to work better. They promised that profitable, successful industries would still be owned by the public. But once people trusted them, the reverse took place: successful industries were sold off and the public was left with only the failing old monsters. In Prilep, where I come from, a 'first class' marble mine was sold to a Greek interest. The workers were paid an average of $17,500 for their shares: a lot of money here in Macedonia, but still so much less than the shares' real value. The rest of the company was thrown in dirt cheap in the deal, but of course including a big 'provision' for the government officials who arranged the sale."

"Even worse, Deutsch Telecom, through Hungarian Telecom, just bought the Macedonian telephone company. The Macedonian phone company had been a 'golden chicken,' sure to lay golden egg after golden egg. The former Prime Minister, Ljupcho Georgievski, admits that the sale was a great mistake. His provisions from such sales, however, have helped him rise from humble beginnings to become the richest man in Macedonia."

Besides privatization as a condition for loans, Georgi says that the IMF also demands total transparency of the entire economy. "That's colonization, when somebody knows everything about your resources. The IMF are telling speculators which factories will work and which won't.... Imagine what a stock market is like, if you know everything your competition is going to do."

An older punk friend had described the differences over time to Georgi in this way: Even when Macedonia was the poorest republic of Yugoslavia, the punker could always afford to split a bottle of cognac with a couple friends, some sandwiches, cigarettes for all, and still have some spending money left. Now, in post-communist FYROM (Former Yugoslav Republic of Macedonia), most kids often don't have enough money for a single beer.

"A few weeks ago," Georgi begins, "I was on an elevator and this old lady got in. As soon as the doors closed, she turned to me and said, 'What's wrong with you young people today? Why are you so quiet?' I didn't know what to say. 'In my day,' she went on, 'people would take to the streets if we didn't get paid, we protested at everything. We made some real noise. I can't understand how young people just sit at home when they have nothing to eat. You sit still with your PlayStations, so obedient. You deserve all you get if that's how you're going to act.' Then she just walked off the elevator, before I could get a single word out of my mouth."

STAYING WITH THE COUSINS OF MY KOSOVO ROMA FRIENDS, the father tells me about his job as the former head of electrical engineering of Obilić, the largest power plant in Kosovo. Now, he is nearly penniless as he receives no pension—he fled Kosovo as a refugee, so Serbia will not pay him his pension, and his application for asylum has just been rejected by the Macedonian government. His two sons work as physical laborers, earning $10 a day each for 12 hour shifts. Their application for asylum here has also been rejected, and the Macedonian government has told them to go back to their town in Kosovo—go back and live with neighbors who have explicitly told them they'd be killed if they return. The United Nations High Commission for Refugees, in a rare act of sensibility, intervened and forbid Macedonia from sending them back to certain danger. But the family's status remains up in the air, and they fear it could change any day.

In other countries in Eastern Europe, Roma had been forcibly assimilated into the industrial economies by being put into recently created, "economically artificial" jobs. When the old system fell, these jobs were the first to be made redundant.[98] Here, or in neighboring Kosovo, where Roma were relatively integrated, even head engineers of the largest industries in the country have ended up destitute, if they're the wrong ethnicity.

Djafer tells me of the family's journey here, during the war.

Roma were caught between armed Serbs shooting at anything that moved, on their ground, and a triumphant KLA (Kosova Liberation Army) rushing to cleanse and claim as much territory as they could, on theirs. Terrified and surrounded, some five hundred Roma left together, in a giant column, and walked toward Macedonia. Kosovo was happy to let them out, but the Macedonian border refused to admit them. There, between the Kosovo and Macedonian borders, 500 people sat freezing and waiting for eight long, cold days for an answer. The international forces, busy with their military humanitarianism, did nothing to help. After eight long, cold, terrible days sleeping on the frozen ground, Macedonia allowed them to enter, and put them in a refugee camp in the middle of the countryside, then, after a year, in a camp adjoining Sutka, the largest Romani settlement in the world. After several more years, the Sutka camp was closed and most Roma have found housing within thriving Sutka itself. But, if even this once well-to-do family is looking at repatriation to a country waiting to kill them, what will happen to these tens of thousands?

TODAY IN SKOPJE, AS I TRY TO GET ACROSS THE RIVER TO find times for buses, police approach me, suspicious of my wandering. Italian president Silvio Berlusconi is in town for an Eastern European/Italian business conference, so the streets are swarming with police. I cheerfully explain to them that I'm trying to find the bus station, but they are unimpressed, particularly when I reveal that I don't have my passport or any picture ID on me. Nor am I staying in a hotel they can call, nor do I have phone number or exact address of "my friend's house," which is actually an NGO office, where I'm staying. "You see," I explain in gestures of forced cheer, "I went to a concert last night and didn't want my passport to fall out while I was dancing—you know, dancing?" I demonstrate dancing. More police gather. Each scowl seems more severe than the last. I state my case over and over, increasingly slipping into Serbian, which makes them more suspicious. They begin to toss the word "špion," spy, around with frequency. Searching my bag, they find: CDs that they are suspicious to learn I just bought; a camera that confirms their suspicion; a book on Kosov@ by an Albanian author they, to my immense relief, do not appear to recognize as Albanian; a copy of *The Economist* which they flip through with great care; and a bag of peanuts which arouses a strong but ambiguous reaction. Finally, one explains something to me: I believe he is offering to have an officer drive me to my friend's house, on Partisanska Street, where I can produce my passport, to which I agree with great relief. A *carabinieri*-style military jeep pulls up, full of eager-looking rookies, ПОЛИЦИЈА (*POLITSIYA*) stenciled on the side. I began to climb into the front, but with a chuckle they pull me out and show me an entirely steel-encased cell in the back, with no windows, and handcuffs welded to the floor. "Get in," the officer instructs in fine English.

I am amazed by how cold steel can get on a winter day, and what aggressive drivers Macedonian police can be. When the door finally opens to light, I climb out and try to orient myself.

"*Partisanska?*" I ask. I am met with curious stares. We are still far from Partisanska—but I see a gray building guarded by a Kalashnikov-wielding young fellow.

"*Ah, ne Partisanska! Politsiya!*" They all laugh heartily at my bewilderment and lead me past the Kalashnikov into the lobby, where they search my bag a few more times. I am very glad I left my souvenir Albanian-flag cigarette lighter at home that morning. "*Albanski? Romani? Bulgarski?*" one cheerful fellow asks me, and I cheerfully shake my head "no" to each, not sure if he was asking about languages I spoke, or my real nationality. "*Ne, ne, Amerikanski! Turist!*" They switch shifts as they get impatient with my responses. I realize they are serious when they don't offer me any of the coffee they are drinking—practically torture by the standards of Macedonian hospitality. They leave, and I sit alone, smoking the last of my "Filter 57" cigarettes. I hear my name repeated over the phone to various listeners, none of whom seem to recognize me, even when reminded of the "*špion*" possibility. No one can decide what to do with me.

After they exhaust all other options, and I still haven't broken under the no-coffee treatment, they give me an ultimatum. "You go in taxi, you get passport, then you come here. Bag, keep here." I am insulted that they estimate me of being such a cheap spy that I couldn't even afford to replace the camera, CDs, and peanuts they keep as collateral.

When I return with my passport, after amusing my friends and checking to make sure no one had any marijuana lying around, the cops have thought of a few more questions. I have won enough trust by returning that they don't take me to the basement, which my friends have just told me has been, in times past at least, the favorite spot in Skopje for intensive interrogation. They again call their various listeners, now that they can figure out how to spell my name, but still I don't ring any bells. Forms are completed. Sternly, the elder in the station calls me in and points at my bag. "Take." It doesn't seem any lighter, or heavier, than when I left it. "*Zdravo*," I say, the old communist salute, and am greeted in turn.

As I walk out through the lobby, one of the coffee-drinkers asks in Serbian, "What are you doing here?"

"Tourist," I say with firm conviction.

He pauses. Then he holds my eyes with his. "Bush. Iraq. BOOM BOOM," referring to the ongoing bombing, and prophetically to the future war. I nod gravely. With gravity and honest despair he asks, "*Zašto?*" Why?

I'm shaken. "You know Bush lost elections?" He nods hesitantly. "This is also how he makes bombing," I tell him. He thinks for a moment, then nods with firm approval. His friend then shouts, "Bin Laden!" I answer with a shrug. Again, he shouts some Macedonian, then, "Bin Laden!" I gravely shake my head and shrug again, then suddenly he puts me in a headlock and gives me a nookie to his own gut-wrenching laugh. With a pat on my back, I am free to go.

"*Zdravo*," I say.

"*Zdravo*," they salute back.

A LETTER, IN ENGLISH, PRINTED ON THE FRONT OF EACH of a pile of T-shirts I see in the Skopje market:

Dear Mary, I hope you understand after all the time we've spent together, I think you are very special. You are the most special person in my life, and I really mean it. We've had conversations about a lot of things, and I know I've told you that I care about you a lot, and you told me the same thing. But there's something I never told you before, something about how very much I really care about you. You might be surprised. The time has come for a special question. I can't wait any longer to ask you, it's driving me so crazy to just be like we are and not more. Mary, will you be with me forever? I hope you won't say no. Love, John.

Central Mosque, Prizren.

Eating Your Family

"Sifting through the names in the Decani charters, he found many cases where the father had an Albanian name, and the son a Serbian one; or vise-versa; or stranger combinations involving three generations. Thus we have a father named Tanush (Alb) whose son is called Bojko (Srb); a father called Bogdan (Srb) , with a son called Progon (Alb); and several pairs of brothers such as Gon (Alb) and Drajko (Srb). Stanojevic's explanation is twofold: intermarriage, and sheer fashion."[99] —Noel Malcolm

Francisco and I are pulled off the bus. The Kosov@ UNMIK (United Nations Mission in Kosovo) border guard from Bangladesh needs us to identify our bags. I stare at an army tank, surrounded by sandbags, across the road. As he's opening the trunk, a tall, domineering man walks up like the protagonist in his own action movie. He asks the border guard urgently, in English, with a strong Scandinavian accent, for some phone number. He barks angry orders into his cell phone in Albanian and hangs up without saying goodbye, wincing like a practiced cynic.

"Is this what we heard on the news?" the Bangladeshi border guard asks.

"No. That's nothing," says the Scandinavian.

"Are we going to stop the truck?" asks the border guard.

The Scandinavian dismisses his question with a wave and walks off. "These are your bags? OK, you can get back on the bus," the border guard tells us.

TEARS OF GRATITUDE WELL IN MY EYES WHEN AGIM PICKS up the phone. We hadn't been looking forward to sleeping outside here. "Hello? We are friends of Ardian in Tirana, we would love to meet you." Agim suavely tells us he'd love to meet us, to wait for him in a nearby cafe. His English is strained, but I don't address him in the Serbo-Croatian he has grown up with here. I thank him in a hysteria of gratitude and race off to tell Branka and Aaron the good news.

Agim and his friend Bashqim greet us with firm handshakes and deep smiles. They lead us to their favorite bar, sitting at the foot of a massive ancient mosque. We stare happily at each other for some moments. Bashqim works with Americans in his job as a police forensics investigator, so his English is good. "Before the war I was an elementary school teacher," he smiles. Agim is a law student. I ask him if it is difficult to study law here, while it is still being written. "I have to know three legal systems: Yugoslavian law, Kosova law, and International law." He shrugs humbly at our astonishment. "It's not so difficult as he says," teases Bashqim, "he's just doing divorce law. He wants to meet divorcées." We laugh as Agim denies the charge.

Agim starts up his cell phone in the pause. He leans over and translates the start-up screen for us: "Enver Hoxha is my idol." The plastic phone cover is decorated with a wafting American flag. I stare in wonder. Enver Hoxha made himself unpopular in Albania by maintaining rule for forty years through absolute isolation, suffocating repression, and continual bloody purges. In Albania these days, few young people idolize Enver Hoxha. To his credit, he also distanced Albania from each side of the Cold War, and he might have felt uncomfortable sandwiched with an American flag in a cell phone cover. "I never thought of that, it is kind of a contradiction!" Agim laughs. Branka and I exchange looks of amazed relief to finally be safe after our morning in Albania. After an exchange in Albanian, Bashqim asks, "Do you think Agim looks Japanese? Everyone here calls him the Japanese Guy." We admit the resemblance. Agim shrugs and smiles handsomely. Agim may be the most immediately likeable person I've ever met; spontaneous, effortlessly charming, viscerally honest, clownish. He insists on paying the tab, and leads us to his house.

Aaron nods out the back window as we drop our packs on Agim's floor. Behind Agim's apartment sits a collapsed and burnt-out house. Agim shows us his bedroom, neatly decorated in lush colored fabrics, then the small but inviting kitchen. He points towards a framed photo hanging on the living room wall. "This is my father, he died from the Serb police, and also my brother, this one here." He points to another. "That is my other brother with his three children. Now the children live with their mother and grandmother in the village. Just a moment." He walks across the room and pulls some papers from a dresser. "This is his university degree, he was a graduate student in agricultural engineering. Should we go?"

Agim and Bashqim joke in Albanian in the front seat. Bashqim tries to translate for us but gives up, laughing too much. Bashqim slips the car confidently around the mountainous curves, twisting over snaking rivers. "We grew up Muslim, but we have no problem with anyone for religion. No problem any religion—no god, same god." Bashqim points out the window. A mountain goat stares down at us from a massive granite cliff. He parks the car on the shoulder, and we get out.

Agim stops us again and runs ahead. With a sheer drop to the clear, churning river on one side, and zipping cars brushing our sleeves on the other, we kneel together as he takes another picture. He must be using up an entire new roll here, just on us. "Very beautiful, yes? Beautiful rock cliffs?" he asks us. We nod enthusiastically. "Beautiful stream? The sound also of the stream is beautiful, yes?" Agim checks with us to make sure we are still in the same world, and we agree again and again, hypnotized by his questioning, the roaring river, and the dusk that steals the cliffs into its darkness. "The mountain goat we saw, see, very beautiful?" Yes, very beautiful, and we are all simply and completely happy together.

Back in town, they bring us to another outdoor bar, along the main promenade. Young people stroll along the river, flirting and teasing. I don't think I've ever heard so much laughter, such immediate cheer, so much fun in the air. This is not what I expected. Proud of each other's presence, we sit for a long time sipping our beers. Agim insists we smoke his cigarettes.

"Most of these buildings seem OK. Did the war destroy much of Prizren?" I ask.

"No, not so much in the city," Agim says. "Many villages. My home village, how do you say?" Agim takes out his lighter and flicks it. "Burned? Burned. Also that suburb over there, and some apartments." He offers us another cigarette.

Agim's cell phone rings. He covers his conversation with his hand and speaks softly.

"Agim has many women," says Bashqim. "But this is his girl-friend." Agim is clearly laying on the consolation. Bashqim laughs. "She knows, she is not really angry. He tastes, but he does not eat."

When he gets off the phone, Branka asks: "Which girlfriend was that?" Agim feigns embarrassment. "So, our Albanian Casanova!" He pretends to wave her away, but is obviously eating it up.

"Kosonova!" I yell. Agim loves it. We order another round.

Agim asks, "Do you want to learn how to say, 'I love you?'" We nod. "Të dua."

I pipe in, "In French, je t'aime. Te amo in Spanish."

Agim adds, "Like Italian!"

Aaron says, "Volim te," the Serbo-Croatian phrase. Bashqim starts chewing on his straw.

"Aha!" shouts Agim, who points at Bashqim. "Nationalist! Nationalist! You're a nationalist!"

Bashqim looks over, hurt. "No! I am NOT a nationalist."

Agim apologizes to his friend and laughs, "OK, OK, I know you're not a nationalist."

On the way back to Agim's house, we stop for fries. Agim leaves us to talk to three younger women. At first, they eye him with disdain and suspicion, but soon they're laughing at his clownery. They're obviously impressed with him. So are we. Bashqim asks one for her phone number, and she laughs him off. I smile blankly, and one of them sneers at me disgusted before looking away. Agim kisses them each goodbye.

At his house after we'd drunk our fill, Agim asks if we'd like to see more photos. "This is when I was joining the UCK, or how do you say, the KLA?" This photo shows him with a Kalashnikov, this one with two handguns, this one with a handgun in one hand

and a Kalashnikov in the other. "Here is my father meeting with Enver Hoxha's wife. And this is one of the first meetings of the KLA." The photo shows a huge number of men sitting on chairs in a field. "Here I am in the war," smiling at the camera, prone, alongside a large machine gun on a tripod. Then a photo of him in his living room, with his guns. "I was in Germany when the war started. I didn't want to be here, but when my father and brothers died I had to come back."

"Can we see your Kalashnikov?" asked Branka.

Agim looks hard at her, his cheer for the first time strained. "No, you don't understand. No, no, no more Kalashnikov. Guns are bad. Better no guns. When the international forces came, everyone gave up their guns. I was happy to have no more gun. You understand, no gun?"

Aaron mentions a video he has from Albania on Enver Hoxha's life. Agim begs to see it. We settle on the floor around his TV. The video, told in absolute monotone, with crackling muffled recordings of communist orchestras playing anthems in the background, shows a young Hoxha at school, studying hard. Soon, he has become one of the country's leading intellectuals, but one who knows the meaning of hard work. Now, scratchy photographs show him leading his unit of partisans in the mountains, heroically beating back the fascists, despite the enemy's vast advantage in numbers and arms. Finally, he signs the victory accord, putting an end at once to both the curse of fascism, and Albanian King Zog's exploitative, merciless rule. The communist period seems to consist of a series of important meetings with world leaders, establishing for the first time Albania's dignity as an independent nation. The video extols Hoxha's unequaled compassion for his people, as time and again he walks in their streets, giving ear to their needs. Agim watches with absolute attention.

"Would you like to see my gun?" offers Bashqim. He checks the chamber of his new Glock, standard now for Kosovar police, and hands it to Branka. Aaron and I beg to see it next. I ask if I can dry-fire it; Bashqim shrugs. On the TV, Hoxha kisses another baby.

SITTING ON THE BUS, I HAVE TO RESIST THE URGE TO take a photo of the American military base outside Prizren. Instead, I flip through the pages of Sebastian Junger's *Fire*.[100] In a quotation on Cyprus by American journalist Scott Anderson for *Harper's*, published one month before NATO peppered this area outside the bus window with depleted uranium ammunition and cluster bombs, Anderson wrote:

> To a degree I've not encountered in any other ethnic conflict zone in the world—not in Bosnia or Sri Lanka, certainly not in Israel—the Turkish Cypriots appear to speak as one, and they have chosen [President] Rauf Denktash to do the talking. ... Rauf Denktash is obdurate and unyielding and steeped in history because so are his people.
>
> ...If the history of Cyprus—indeed, the history of most of the world—reveals anything, it is that there is no such thing as justice: You live in your house until the day someone comes along and throws you out, and then he lives there until someone else comes along to throw him out. Just where do you pinpoint the moment in this island's history and say, "Here, we will right this wrong," and let all the previous ones go by the wayside? Obviously, you cannot afford to go very far back, because in Cyprus, as everywhere else, there is always a prior victim.
>
> So perhaps what has passed as "The Cyprus Problem" all these years has actually been "The Cyprus Solution," and perhaps the diplomats who periodically wring their hands over the ongoing stalemate on this island should actually be taking notes and trying to export it elsewhere. This would require new thinking among the power brokers of the West, and perhaps especially among those in Washington, embroiled in the latest crises in the Balkans. Maybe what most needs to end is all the chatter about exit strategies. Those in power must recognize that there is no exit from bad history and that at certain times and in certain places the best that can be done is to simply stand between the fighters indefinitely and hope that someday they'll get over it and move on—not in a year, not in ten years, but maybe eventually. Until then the least costly solution, in terms of both blood and money, is to give the Bosnians and Serbs and Kosovars of the planet what the Cypriots already have, a "dead zone" across which they can hurl accusations and threats in safety. At least it will give them something to talk about, and all that the rest of the world will have to suffer is the hearing of it.[101]

I pull out the article that I'm using as a bookmark to re-read it, seven months after NATO troops occupied Kosov@:

> VITINA, Yugoslavia (Jan. 16)—An American soldier serving with the international peacekeeping force in Kosovo was charged Sunday with sexually assaulting and killing an 11-year-old ethnic Albanian girl, the US military announced.[102]

Behind it is stapled an article on the trial by investigative reporter Joe Vialls:

One such case is that of Staff Sergeant Frank Ronghi, who on 24 August 2000 pleaded guilty to sodomizing and killing an 11-year-old Kosovar girl in January the same year. A member of his platoon testified that Staff Sergeant Ronghi disdainfully claimed, "It's easy to get away with this shit in a third-world country."

The "shit" Ronghi referred to is described here by the US Army Pathologist for Europe. "Her right jaw was fractured, practically bisected," said Lieutenant Colonel Kathleen Ingwersen. "We found evidence of sperm and semen in her vagina, mouth and rectum," she testified to a hushed hearing. "There was trauma to the neck muscles, the trachea and the carotid artery," Colonel Ingwersen said, adding she had found evidence of "blunt trauma" as the child was apparently beaten, choked and forced to kneel, face to the ground, as she was sodomized.[103]

Back home in the states, I clip out an article on Cyprus, from the May 17, 2003, edition of *The Economist*, written four years after Anderson's[104]:

By May 15th, as many as 250,000 Greek-Cypriots and 70,000 Turkish-Cypriots—about 40 percent of the island's combined population—had visited what each community calls "the other side." The enthusiasm of both sorts of Cypriot for getting reacquainted after 29 years of official hostility has shocked the politicians and offered a new glimmer of hope.... Tearful reunions of elderly neighbors from villages where Greek and Turkish populations once lived together are being shown on television on both sides of the island, with grandchildren fraternizing cheerfully in English.

A growing number of Turkish-Cypriots are starting loudly to question the need for some 30,000 Turkish troops on the island. Many accuse their government of corruption. In February a huge demonstration—at one guess, 70,000 people, a third of the Turkish-Cypriot population, including prominent businessmen and trade-unionists—marched through northern Nicosia shouting slogans against Mr. Denktash, with placards that read, "Yes to peace, Yes to the EU...."

Back at the Nicosia checkpoint, Mr. Advinli, the car mechanic, confidently declares that in the end "people power" will prevail. "Turkey, Denktash, the UN: we won't listen to them anymore," he says. "We shall reunite our island ourselves."

ILIR HAS BROUGHT FRANCISCO AND ME TO HIS COLLEGE.
Francisco tries to convince me that we owe it to our host to speak
to his class. But how will I tell them where I've been for the last
four months? What am I supposed to say I'm doing here?

The English professor walks up the stairs, talking to an admin-
istrator. His class was supposed to start half an hour ago. Ilir slyly
throws his cigarette behind him; Francisco tells me he remembers
the gesture from the days of school under the Shah. Before Ilir can
ask if we can talk to the class, the professor is lecturing us extensively
on the tragic underfunding of the school. "The students, without the
proper material resources, have no possibilities of success. Have
you seen the pitiful condition of the rooms? Even Priština has better
resources! But you must visit the library before you leave; it is the
school's pride." Students keep sticking their heads out of the room,
retreating inside when they see the Professor.

"I am so sorry, but we must catch our bus!" I shrug, feigning
grief to the Professor. "We had time before, but now it is getting
so late." Ilir looks at us, disappointed. The Professor excuses
Ilir from class to show us the library. The shelves are filled
with Serbo-Croatian books, a few Albanian titles, and a series
of Reader's Digest Condensed Books jealously guarded behind
glass. The books cannot be removed from this room; no one is
sitting at the long clean reading tables.

On our way to the bus, Ilir points out a little wooden house
along the road. "That is a Serb's house, you know?" Francisco
and I look at the house, indistinguishable from those next to
it, aside from the layers of razor wire in which it is wrapped.
"Yes," I say, "Agim told me about it. They have left and do this
so no one will break into their house?"

"No, no, you don't understand. They have not left. They are still
living there." I ask him again to make sure I have understood, and
he nods vigorously. I wonder what it's like to be inside. How long
until the cause of Albanian national liberation grabs a crowbar?

On our way to the bus, Ilir tells us of his work. "When I can
find work, it pays almost nothing. I do not even make enough
to eat my family."

Francisco corrects gently, "You want to feed your family, not
eat them."

When Ilir understands Francisco's words, he stops walking
and starts to laugh. Francisco and I stop. The three of us stand
on the sidewalk, laughing.

BEHIND THE ENDLESS STRETCHES OF RAZOR WIRE, A PATCH of grape vines still grows in a small farm plot, in diffident mockery.

A YOUNG WOMAN SITTING ACROSS THE AISLE FROM ME ON the bus asks me where I'm from. "Military?" she asks. I tell her I am a tourist. "You mean, business?" I assure her I am only here to visit friends. "American friends?" No, Albanian friends, Kosovars. She eyes me curiously, then shrugs.

"Where did you learn English?" I inquire, since she speaks nearly without an accent.

"It's my job, I'm a translator here for the American soldiers."

"What're the worst questions Americans have asked you?"

"One of them asked me: 'Do you know what school is?' I speak five languages fluently, I'm a professional translator. Another time, one asked, 'Do you have cancer here?'" She looks at me until I laugh in astonishment.

I catch my breath. "People in America think that people in the Balkans are primitive, stuck in history. I guess that's why I want to write about here, to change that idea."

"We *are* stuck in history," she says. "I mean, did you notice what happened here?"

"But what about that other history, the history of multi-ethnic anti-imperialism, the very reason Yugoslavia was founded, at least in 1945? Wasn't that true too? Or the multi-ethnic miners strikes in the 80's against austerity plans? I mean, this 'ancient history' everyone talks, is it really the only history? I tell her about living in Zagreb and in Belgrade, about how many people I have met who refuse to think in terms dictated by that kind of history. "I mean, OK. My friend Neša in Belgrade once told me he thought that even the old textbooks during the Tito era had problems. The Turks were always portrayed as evil imperialists, which perhaps made scapegoating Muslims easier in the 1980s and '90s. But that was a misreading."

After a pause, she asks, "How is life in Belgrade now?"

"People are poor, frustrated, they have one tenth of the money they had a few years ago, they can't travel like they used to. It's hard. I don't understand how people get by."

"Good. Good for them." Her look is calm. My throat dries up a little. "Are you surprised I say that?" she asks.

"I don't know if I'm surprised," I say. "Give me a minute."

"Look. Serbs are animals. I didn't use to think so, it was fine in Macedonia, but since I've been working in Kosova, I see things differently."

Through my dry throat, I ask slowly, "Neša in Serbia, who told me about the textbooks, is he an animal?"

She looks away, impatient. "Of course not. My roommate is Serbian. I tease her: 'No, you can't have a cigarette, you damn Serb!' But I'm kidding, we're good friends, we share a room. But the Serbs who were in Kosova..."

I look down, not sure what to say. Her polite voice lapses into a sudden scream: "WHY CAN'T YOU UNDERSTAND ME?"

I stare in horror, but already she has composed herself. "You should get a job as a translator," she says, and awaits my response.

After a breath, I manage: "I'd like to learn Albanian, but I don't know any yet."

"It doesn't matter. I am from Macedonia, so I only make $1,000 a month, translating for American soldiers, even though Albanian is my first language. That's good money for here, but the American translators make five times as much, even though they can hardly order a sandwich. I guess they don't trust us with their secrets."

We exchange a polite farewell when she gets off at the next stop.

IF I WERE A REAL JOURNALIST, I WOULD TAKE OUT MY CAMERA right now. "Excuse me, can I take a picture of your daughter?" Across from me in the train seats, a Roma mother and her two daughters patiently sit out the train's bumps. The mother chats intermittently in friendly tones with a middle-aged man to my left in Serbian. One daughter gets up every few minutes to stand at the window. The other, around six, sits quietly with an expression somewhere between a pout, helplessness, and fear. Over her right eye, she has a growth the size and shape of a fleshy carrot. This, where they have boarded the train, is the area most saturated seven years ago with depleted uranium shells. A United Nations study conducted after the bombing, the only source quoted by Tim Judah in his popular book *Kosovo: War and Revenge*, found "no indications of contamination" from the use of depleted uranium shells. NATO even refused to confirm whether DU was used at all, and "if it was, where and how much, [thus] it was impossible to come to any conclusions." I can't help but wonder if the flesh carrot protruding from the sad Roma girl's face isn't such a "conclusion." Should I take a picture and bring it to the UN, show it to my friends back home? The mother might well be glad for the chance to share her troubles. The little girl looks up at me, distant, pouty. I smile weakly and she looks away.

ON THE TRAIN THROUGH SOUTH SERBIA, THE STRETCH WHEN I usually feign sleep to avoid conversation, the man sitting across from me offers me a cigarette. He must have noticed me staring at his tattoo—a large peace sign in bold, home-tattoo lines. And, higher on the same arm, another tattoo—the Serbian nationalist symbol, within the handle of a dagger. This time, as I am here to write about neighboring Kosovo, I take a breath and accept his cigarette. His wife maintains her distant gaze through the window as we step into the hallway.

"*Znaš, Srbi su pacifisti.* You know, Serbs are pacifists," he begins. I have never before heard this claim for a people who have a tradition of throwing a three-day party when one of their sons joins the army. Only marriage and death are feted to the same extent. "Croats are fascists," he continues, perhaps noticing from the tag on my bag that I boarded the train in Zagreb. This is the conversation I had hoped to sleep through, particularly as I keep dropping Croatian words throughout my Serbian.

"The state was," I agree, "but many Croats also fought with the Partisans."

"No, they were all Ustaše."

"But Tito himself was half Croat!"

He pauses. "Tito was good. Peace, prosperity, brotherhood and unity..." I decide not to press him further to acknowledge Tito's heritage, and move on. At the moment, I am here to find out about a subject close to the hearts of Serb nationalists, and tell him I am heading to Kosovo, to write on the situation for minorities.

"You are a writer. Will you write about this conversation?" I tell him I don't know yet. "I was in Kosovo." He points to his shoulder tattoo. "You don't want to go there, too many Albanians now. Albanians are bad—they rape women, kill children. You know, they are Muslims?" I nod sternly. "Well, Muslims are terrorists."

"Not all!" He asks for an example, but I hesitate to say Bosnia, the first example in my mind. I fear my very limitied Serbian is not up to the task of defending the one and a half billion people of the Umma in one swoop, but I see no way out. *"Teroristi su samo u posebnim situacijima."* They're only terrorists on special occasions.

In the next train car, someone's radio blasts one of these strange American-sounding pop songs such that I have never heard outside the Balkans. "Everybody has cheated everybody, in the 21st century. Time to make sure, you don't lose..." I begin to doubt my own sanity. Am I projecting my paranoia in radio waves?

The train enters Niš. He points out the Mahala, the Romani neighborhood, which seems to be going about its business as we pass it. We exchange waves with some kids. I tell him I've been studying Romani in America. He tells me he speaks Romani, as well as Russian and, of course, Serbian.

I tell the pacifist how I am worried what will happen to the Roma if Kosovo becomes independent from Serbia. "Kosovo will never become independent," he states with complete resolve. "It's the sacred ground of Serbia, as Jerusalem is for Israel." I follow the simile through in my thoughts, but decide to keep it to myself. "Like, the heart?" I offer. "Yes, the heart of Serbia."

He offers me another cigarette, but I apologetically explain that I am exhausted from my voyage. Attempting to recline sandwiched between passengers on each side, I squeeze my eyes shut and focus my very awake attention on appearing to nap deeply. After twenty minutes, he shakes my shoulder, not convinced. *"Amerikanac!"* Realizing I have little choice, I accept a cigarette.

"Ja, Srbin." I, Serb. I had guessed as much, but respond with a manly nod. *"Žene, Albanka."* My wife, Albanian. This I had not expected. I cannot hold back my astounded smile. His face still serious, he shrugs, *"Ljubav."* Love. Apologetic, almost embarrassed. "You see, I am not a nationalist, I am a pacifist."

Yes, I tell him, I think I am going to write about this conversation.

AND HERE IS THE TEXT THAT LED TO THE MOST INTENSIVE intervention ever[105]:

> NATO personnel shall enjoy, together with their vehicles, vessels, aircraft, and equipment, free and unrestricted passage and unimpeded access throughout the FRY including associated airspace and territorial waters. This shall include, but not be limited to, the right of bivouac, maneuver, billet, and utilization of any areas or facilities as required for support, training, and operations.—Appendix B, Rambouillet Agreement[106]

Tim Judah, again the most widely read English-language author on Kosovo, claims that this Appendix B, the basis of Milošević's rejection of the Rambouillet agreement which then precipitated the NATO bombing, was accidentally included when the treaty was copied from standard UN peacekeeping drafts.[107] As part of the treaty, it was not up for discussion, as the internationals were tired of Milošević's manipulation of the negotiation process. I happen on a more credible explanation by a character not exactly known as an antiestablishment thinker, Henry Kissinger:

> The Rambouillet text, which called on Serbia to admit NATO troops throughout Yugoslavia, was a provocation, an excuse to start bombing. Rambouillet is not a document that an angelic Serb could have accepted. It was a terrible diplomatic document that should never have been presented in that form.[108]

A FEW MINUTES PASS AFTER THE PACIFIST AND HIS WIFE DESCEND from the train until another, older man offers me a cigarette. We smoke in silence for some time, blowing our smoke out the window as lush fields of Southern Serbia race by. "*Amerikanac?*" he finally asks. I smile.

"Every bridge on the Morava river, bombed. Every electrical system, bombed. Water systems. We are not a rich country but we cannot live like *this*." I nod, staring in his eyes, unsure where to start. "That's *my* infrastructure." He is not even pretending to smile at me.

After a long silence, he sweeps his hand across the scenery. "Look how peaceful these mountains are. The Vranska Bora. This is what America bombed."

He pauses to keep from losing his voice. "I used to eat everything, I loved food, like I loved women. And now, they had to take it all out." He lifts his shirt to reveal a long scar. "Carcinoma."

"My sister died of it. I probably will too. Sixty percent of children in this area are born with carcinoma or leukemia.

It's going to be eighty years until this land is livable. I mean, I have to live here, all my life."

"I could throw you out the window right now, like the Americans tried to throw me. But I won't, because I am hospitable and civilized." He is staring at me, shaking.

I start in, "I am worried about people feeling like that in Mitrovica, but I figure that people want..."

"Communication. They do. My father died fighting the Nazis, and three of my uncles. When the Americans attacked us, you know our army was three percent the size of theirs? They dropped more munitions on us than both sides dropped in all of World War II, on this small country. But we still managed to get to them, a couple times... You know, we knew before the bombing that they were using heat-seeking guidance systems. One day, we heard they were coming to bomb one of our airports. We rolled out sheets and sheets of aluminum foil, right next to the real runway, and weighed it down with tires. The Americans came by and couldn't believe how good their reconnaissance systems were! They rained bombs down, over and over, until the foil was shredded. The real runways were fine. I'm sure they were high-fiving each other up there in their precision bombers, and couldn't believe how hot the bombs made our runways burn—which were of course just the tires. Once everything had cooled off, we'd run out and roll out another bunch of foil, just like that. They'd fly over one last time, expecting to survey they success—and the "runways" would show up like nothing had ever happened. Maybe they thought Serbia has some kind of supernatural runways. And you heard about all our cardboard decoys?" He burst out laughing. "Took them a while to understand how we could have so many tanks. Must have cost a lot of American taxes for all those missiles."

"The Americans were so mad about the decoys that they intensified the bombing—and managed to bomb an old folk's home in Vranje, where I live."

I pause for a moment. "I have a big question, about the Roma... The Albanian forces drove out 100,000 Roma claiming they collaborated with Serb forces, but the Roma I know claimed that they were just trying to stay out of the way. Did the Yugoslav army give the Roma guns?"

He laughs, condescending. "Why would we ever give them guns? What nation would they be defending? They had no more reason to be with us than against us, we knew if we gave them guns they might be using them against us a day later. We'd have to be crazy. Of course, both sides used *cigane* (gypsies)— if someone puts a gun to your head, or your child's head, and tells you to do something, you'll do it. But they never took up guns for either side. Why would they?"

I excuse myself and sit alone in the next compartment. Staring out the window, I try to change the subject of my thoughts, but cannot. I think of friends who'd been driven from their homes, of the civilians killed, of the massacre in Račak... Though by any account, the atrocities were an order of magnitude fewer than in, say, Bosnia, they certainly exceeded anything that could be called counter-insurgency, even a messy one. I walk back into his compartment.

"One more question. I understand completely your position, that you needed to guard your country against 'terrorists,' against ... What happened after the war showed that you were right to fear that." He nodded. "But, since this is probably the only chance I'll have to ask a JNA officer, at what point did the fighting move from a counter-insurgency, from actions from defensive policing, to, how do I say, to *total* war? When did civilians become valid targets?"

I had broken his trust. His look of confidence changes to betrayal and anger. "I killed no one! We were fighting terrorists! We were fighting to protect our country! Who wouldn't do the same? Who wouldn't fight to protect their country?!" His answer communicates more that he was hurt by my question, than any acknowledgment, or refusal, of the distinction I suggest. His answer functions as an end to communication, as the same answer does anywhere. I apologize for disturbing him and leave his compartment.

I DIDN'T EXPECT AN OLYMPIC-SIZED SWIMMING POOL TO BE MY first stop with the Kosovo Roma. It's already too late today to get to any of the refugee camps, explains Adrijan, my host; and besides, don't I want to get out of the heat? I can't argue.

The kids throw themselves on me, all at once, over and over, screaming and laughing as I do my best to hurl them across the pool. Beach pop blares over the speakers. The Serbs, I reflect, are the ones over there with the beach balls; us Roma have to do with laps and splash fights. I have only just met Adrijan's family, and I can't keep the cousins apart from other kids from the village who happen to be there, but it doesn't seem to matter as far as splash fight alliances go.

This pool was built by the international aid workers, pretty much for themselves, explains Adrijan, but mostly they don't come until night. Up over there, all that concrete is going to be a restaurant, says Adrijan, pointing. If they have time to finish it, I don't say, and look around remembering, incongruously, that everybody in the pool could be refugees within a few months. This enclave, and the refugees in the camps I'm here to visit, were created by Clinton's "humanitarian intervention" on the supposed behalf of the Albanians in the first place, but at least they've made a nice swimming pool for the refugees to swim in, when the internationals themselves aren't using it. On the drive back to Adrijan's village in another part of the Serbian enclave, the kids in the back seat burst into a harmonious cacophony of beatboxing and improvised singing. Tapping my head, I realize that some clichés are true.

Back at the house, as Basmah, Adrijan's wife, brings Turkish coffee, Adrijan clarifies the situation. "Without politics, Kosovo would be the best place in the world." I tell him about the Roma girl with the carrot-sized tumor on her eye that I saw on the train, and ask if people seem to be having health problems from depleted uranium. "Not that I've heard of, but it's strange, the weather has changed, and the earth... The fruit has all been small, bad quality, it dries fast. The trees themselves seem to be dying. Perhaps it is this."

Before the war, there were 10,000 Roma in Pristina, another 10,000 in Mitrovica, a pre-war total of around 150,000 in all of Kosovo. According to a year-long, village-by-village study by the independent NGO Voice of Roma, 88,000 Roma fled Kosovo immediately after the war—more than half of the refugees always described as "Serbs fleeing revenge actions by Albanians."[109] The remaining few are mostly inside refugee camps. Adrijan's village has been one of the few lucky ones to end up inside a Serbian enclave, and thus safe, if trapped, in their homes for nine years and counting.

Poverty, however, is still a great problem, since those few jobs within the Serb enclaves are certainly not available to Roma, and the Roma, unlike the Serbs, are not receiving payments from the Serbian government. Adrijan receives some work as a translator for internationals, but even for him it is difficult to support his family. "I can't eat this table, I can't eat my door," he shrugs.

ADRIJAN EXPLAINS TO ME AS WE PULL INTO THE LEPOSAVIĆ camp, "They don't like internationals here. I can understand. Internationals were coming here for years, and taking notes for their reports, and what did they do for these people? Nothing. And it's not like these people don't know that the internationals are getting paid to write about them." As we drive into the entrance to the camp, everybody looks up, and curious kids walk up to the car. Somebody runs off to tell of our arrival. Soon, a man approaches us wagging his finger. "No internationals," and shoos us away. Adrijan explains to him, in Romani, that we are not with the UN, government agencies, or NGOs, but friends of Voice of Roma, a small NGO run by a Rom from Kosovo who now lives in America. The man remembers Voice of Roma, who recently delivered aid money to the camp, and welcomes us, though still it is evident he is suspicious of me. "What questions do you have for him?" Adrijan asks me.

I force myself not to leave. How am I any different? Maybe I'm worse—I don't even have an agency behind me that could help. I fiddle with my notebook. Adrijan knows I am not getting paid to write, but as his nephew said last night in the village, "You are not getting paid to write this? Oh, I see—you are writing to be popular!" I cannot ask him, I cannot ask anyone the one question I want to know from everyone—How do you survive? The man from the camp stares at me expectantly. By default, I ask him the same question I'm sure every international before me has asked, and he gives the same answers.

"Thirty-five families of 235 people live in the camp, which used to be a military parking garage. Many people are going hungry. We do have clean water. Some of the other Roma camps receive aid from UNMIK, Norwegian Church Aid or some Danish NGO, but this camp receives nothing. They visited a few times, took notes, but never brought any help. No, wait—one year, for the Islamic holiday of Bajram, Norwegian Church Aid did bring some food, for that one day. Red Cross isn't interested. For seven years, we have been here, and been visited by many organizations, even by Soren Jessen-Peterson himself, head of UNMIK, but we have got no help from anybody." Despair surfaces through his boredom as he speaks, despite what must be a routine recitation for him. "Some people manage to find work for 5 of 10 euros a day, but only perhaps 3 days in a month. But this is very insecure, few can find even this.

I ask him what would be the best for Roma here. "We have plenty of problems, but we don't want our kids to have the same thing. The internationals tell us, 'No problem, just go back home to Mitrovica, the war is over.' We would love to go back to Mitrovica, but we would be killed. Some have tried, and they were—even Ashkalije (Albanian-speaking people of the same descent as Roma, who are supposedly integrated into Kosovar Albanian society.) We did go back to visit our destroyed houses once, and the Albanians organized to meet us, throwing rocks and shouting, 'What are you looking for? This is not your place!' UNMIK has started building us housing, for 'social families'— before, we had our family homes—but even this is useless if we cannot live in them. The Albanians will take them.

"The best would be to go to a third country, but no one will accept us—we are not refugees, they say, because the war has been over for seven years. Next to this, it would be best of some organization would build us houses, but not where there are Albanians. I don't want my children to be killed. We are not people who want too much, just a normal life, a home, bread, and a job of course. Would you like to walk around the camp?"

The residents have partitioned the former military parking garage with cardboard walls that do not quite reach the ceilings. Blankets act as doorways. I pay a brief visit to my friend's Aunt, who lives alone in a small room. I tell her I am a friend of her nephew, but she doesn't smile, even for the picture I take of her to show him. She has lost her mind, explains my guide, but her neighbors are helping to feed her when they can.

Our guide tells us that typically, around eleven people live in each room. In the entire camp, there are two toilets for men, and two toilets for women—for thirty-five families. Of these, seven of the families are Serb refugees. They receive three meals a day from the Leposavić government, and also aid from UNMIK and Red Cross. "We sent representatives to the local government, they talked, but did nothing. Isn't this discrimination?

"Last time Red Cross visited us was two years ago. They brought us flour, but it was so old it was full of worms, and we couldn't eat it. We are getting no help. Our children will die from the dirt, the hunger, everything. Some children have nothing to eat all day. I myself have small children, and when I have money, I have to go buy milk in Mitrovica, sometimes even from other refugees—they receive enough so they have a little extra to sell. Anything else you would like to see?"

Stepping out of the dark building, I know I have to take photos, but it is the last thing I want to ask. I force myself to ask permission, and by this time our guide's suspicion has relaxed, and he nods, of course. Suddenly, kids run up excited from all directions, competing to pose for the next shot. Each kid strikes their own sophisticated pose for the camera, then runs up after the click to look at the LCD screen on the back of my digital camera. They hold me hostage, and won't let me leave until I have digitally immortalized each of their egos several times over. Finally, we exchange handshakes and waves with everyone like sudden old friends, and drive off.

ON OUR NEXT DAY VISITING THE CAMPS, WE STOP OFF IN MITROVICA to buy an internet card. Just before entering the Serbian area, Adrijan stops the car to take off his Kosovo license plate— obligatory in the rest of the country, but dangerous to have on your car in Serbian Mitrovica. As he stops a construction truck to borrow a wrench, I smile and nod, avoiding conversation. The Serbs have been re-arming and forming militias within the past few weeks, and another opportunity for independence draws near—and the potential for another wave of ethnic cleansing. Then again, within the last month, two British tourists were machine-gunned near here for driving a Serbian rental car through Albanian areas. A couple months ago, a friend of a friend from Zagreb was stabbed in the neck four times in an Albanian town near here for playing Bulgarian music at a "Peace Train" dance party—too close to Serbian for the local Albanians. Our license plate safely in the glove compartment, we drive into town.

I grab my camera to snap a photo of a boy hanging out of a dumpster in front of a UN armored troop carrier, but Adrijan shouts at me to keep it down. At one point, we drive into a road blocked by a Serbian funeral procession. I reach over to turn off the radio, instead accidentally bumping it to screaming top volume, a few seconds of blasting very un-Serbian music before he, in a fluster, switches it off. No one takes notice. I again can't manage to look at this place like a normal city. It is the first time I have been in a city before war has concluded, and in the possible event of independence for Kosovo in a few months, all of these residents could well be refugees. We stop for a plate of *čevapčiči*, in a stand just underneath a billboard proclaiming Seselj a *Srpski Junak*, a Serbian hero, and head off to the camp.

The massive Trepča mining complex alongside Mitrovica is by far Kosovo's greatest economic asset. Or was. With the north half in the bounds of the Serbian part of the city, and the south half in the Albanian side, it has been rusting since the war. I snap a photo of its collapsing buildings behind "USAID" signs until we flee an angry man from the guard's booth. Here it is again—the new paradigm of aid, predated in Bosnia, perfected in Iraq, imported for home consumption in New Orleans. Billions of dollars in funding, nothing, but nothing, on the ground. Bosnia, eleven years after Dayton, still has fifty percent unemployment. Kosovo, particularly in areas like Adrijan's village with no refugee remuneration coming in, still have nearly one hundred percent unemployment, and no water or electricity for most of the day. Back in 1999, would the Kosovars have returned with such vengeance had they not frozen to death for lack of blankets in their months of exile?

Of course, more than money would be required for Trepča to run again, with the north half in Serbian Mitrovica and the south in the Albanian sector. But with such unemployment figures, wouldn't large-scale employment for all ethnic groups, on condition of co-ownership, be a tempting start to co-operation? Would people be able to afford their hatred at the cost of lives like the present, if they had alternatives which involved co-existence? If the stories of ancient ethnic tensions are anywhere true, it is in Kosovo, but even here, ethnic traditionalism was submerged by modernist promises of prosperity throughout the Tito years. The NATO bombing cost the same as *seventy-five* years of Kosovo's GDP.[110] What people *don't* ultimately resort to violence over scarce resources under extreme poverty? Within the poorest ten countries, we find Somalia, Congo, East Timor, and Afghanistan, with Rwanda, Sudan, Liberia, Sierra Leone, Eritrea, Ethiopea, Angola, Mozambique, Chad, Uganda, Cambodia, and Haiti not far up the list. At $400 GDP per capita before the war, the Yugoslav province of Kosovo wasn't far off either.[111]

IN 2002, THE INTERNATIONAL COMMUNITY CAME UP WITH eight "Standards" which were to be its own goals in Kosovo, as well as the preconditions which the Kosovar authorities would have to meet before Kosovo would be considered for independence. However, after the riots of March 2004, UNMIK revised its stance on the Standards, turning them into simple recommendations, that would not likely be followed until after independence was granted. To date, seven of the eight standards are still far from satisfied: Functioning Democratic Institutions, Rule of Law, Freedom of Movement (for all communities), Returns and Reintegration (of all refugees), Property Rights, Dialogue with Belgrade, and an integrated Kosovo Protection Corps.

Only one of the Standards seems to have been taken seriously by any of the parties:

> Standard 5. The Economy: There should be a sound institutional and legal basis for a market economy, a balanced budget, and socially owned assets should be privatised.

On second glance, it may seem strange to make privatization of socially-owned assets of equal importance as Rule of Law or Refugee Return. But it was with privatization that UNMIK wasted no time. I read on the CIA Factbook page on Kosovo, "In order to help integrate Kosovo into regional economic structures, UNMIK signed (on behalf of Kosovo) its accession to the Central Europe Free Trade Area (CEFTA) in 2006."[112] Can they do that?

King and Mason, two former high-ranking UNMIK analysts whose book, Peace at Any Price, documents the failures of post-war Kosovo, suggest several ways the economy could have been developed in a manner to accomplish the other Standards:

> Employment schemes that encouraged young people to work in different parts of Kosovo, for example, might have inculcated a sense of broader civic identity by giving people a chance to develop relationships beyond their local areas. Boarding schools, a multiethnic national service programme and investment co-operatives for young people could have diluted the influence of KLA veterans while building a sense of community that extended beyond an individual's village, region, or extended family. They might even have fostered relationships between people from different ethnic communities."[113]

Such schemes were not considered because these goals were clearly never a real priority. Instead, by Spring 2006, ninety percent of Kosovo's Socially Owned Enterprises were sold off—one wonders how, since many were still legally owned by the Serbian state. Nikolaus Lambsdorff, head of the EU's Economic bureau, or "Pillar," invoked the American legal idea of "eminent domain," "according to which the Kosovo Trust Agency, the privatization agency working under the aegis of the EU Pillar, would have the right to appropriate property and only later pay cash compensation to anyone who could establish title to the seized asset."[114]

The KLA had their own interpretation of "a legal basis for a market economy." Investors received threats for bidding against them. One "entrepreneur, Bekim Kuqi, owned a large department store in Ferizaj/Uroševac. When he showed interest in bidding in a privatisation in November 2004, a car bomb crashed into his store and destroyed it. Kuqi lost $5 million."[115] "Many of the SOEs foundered and were stripped of their assets... The KLA appropriated most of them and, not wanting to rock the boat, KFOR and the police never kicked them out."[116]

Instead of scoffing at and looting the socially owned enterprises, Kosovo's new managers might have done well to read an article entitled "Under Workers' Control" in the November 9, 2002 issue of *The Economist*, contemporary to the writing of the Standards. The article praises a recent wave of worker takeovers of failed factories in Argentina, after their economic collapse in 2002:

> Ghelco is just one of 130 Argentine companies that over the past four years have risen from the ashes of bankruptcy under employee management. Together they provide around 10,000 jobs—not to be sniffed at in a country where one in five is unemployed. They are a small part of the explanation for the surprising resilience of Argentina's economy and social fabric, after its December devaluation and debt default. "IMPA, a manufacturer of aluminium containers, has retained 147 staff ... 'We have shared out what we don't have in solidarity,' [the production manager] says. The workers have responded with improved productivity and innovations such as switching to scrap as a raw metal... Everyone receives the same amount, including the new managers..."[117]

The article ends on a reassuring note for *The Economist* readership: "If all this smacks of past revolutions, from Bolshevik Petrograd in 1917 to 'Red Clydeside' in Britain in the 1970s, that might be misleading. 'This movement doesn't threaten capitalist companies,' says Mr Murrua. 'We are simply taking over companies that don't work.'"

Workers in Zrenjanin, Serbia and Zagreb, Croatia both later followed the Argentine example to retain control of factories that the State was trying to sell off.[118] Frustrated with the legal limbo of privatizing companies they didn't own, even UNMIK finally resorted to collectivism, although King and Mason give us no idea of the success of their experiment:

"One particularly inventive attempt relied on a re-interpretation of hardline communist [sic] commercial laws ... firms were privatised out of their legal limbo by giving power to revamped workers' councils."[119]

I FAIL TO COME UP WITH AN EXCUSE TO MAKE ADRIJAN TURN the car around before we enter the Česmin Luk camp. I try to remind myself, this camp is the reason I've returned to the Balkans this time. I cannot write about the Balkans without mentioning this camp of a few hundred people, this camp and the two adjoining camps called Kablare and Zitkovac. The three camps were built by UNHCR, the UN agency for refugees, adjoining the Trepca mining complex—in particular, near the massive lead slag dumps from the mine. The agency reassured the refugees that the high lead levels in the area would not be a concern for the two or three weeks until they were moved to a better situation. Despite protests of catastrophic health effects from the residents, despite reports and admonitions from the World Health Organization and numerous other human rights organizations, the residents of the camps have not been allowed to leave their toxic homes, a decade (and counting) after UNHCR's promises. Dr. Klaus-Dietrich Runow, on a fact-finding mission launched by the Society for Threatened Peoples, said that residents of the camp measured with "the highest levels of lead ever found in samples of human hair." Local residents speak of greyish lines running through children's teeth, of the glazed look in the eyes of residents after enough time, and of every birth in the camps either possessing massive birth defects, or stillborn.

I ask Adrijan about the razor wire along the fence of the camp as we approach it, and his answer surprises me. It was not put up by the town to keep the refugees inside, but by those inside the camp to keep out fellow refugees who were envious of their shelter in the barracks. The fighting of envy for the unenviable had concluded years ago.

Adrijan goes on to explain as we drive into the camp that I might not want to mention the main question I had for coming on this entire trip. Much of what has been written about lead poisoning in the three camps near Trepca has been written by Paul Polansky, a "poet" from Iowa City who claims to have been sent as a "spy for the CIA" to prove that Roma were collaborating with Serbs in the war. When he found no evidence of Roma collaboration, he "went native," and wrote a series of books in bad verse about the plight of the "Gypsies." As the sole voice for Kosovo Roma in the West, crowds would once greet his arrivals with cheers. For various reasons, his name has since fallen into some disrepute in the camps; now the residents are hesitant not only to discuss Polansky, but also the lead poisoning that he publicized as well. In addition, Adrijan explains, the local Serbs were starting to avoid the Roma as if they had some terrible disease, as the story of lead-poisoning became known. So the Roma were not currently interested in talking about the cause, or one of the worst of many causes, of their present suffering.

We walk into what could be a small schoolroom with a representative of the camp. After introductions and handshakes, Adrijan asks me what I would like to ask the woman about. My mind freezes. I have come all the way here to ask one question, and now I can't ask it, but can't think of what else to ask. So I ask it anyway. "Can you please tell me about lead poisoning here?"

She almost shakes as she begins, "Look, from 1999 until now, lots of people are dying, but maybe it's for other reasons, you can't say it's just because of the lead. And it's not just Roma who have it, especially when the factory works and pollutes the air in all of Mitrovica." Adrijan was right, she is defensive about the idiotic suspicions of contagiousness. She doesn't want to talk about it. Adrijan shoots me a mild I-told-you-so look, his frustration softened with long experience working with internationals. Accepting that I now knew less about this camp than when I was reading reports about it in San Francisco, I let her change the subject.

She relaxes as we moved onto speaking of less contested horrors. For whatever cause, many of the children are very sick, from cold or flu. After even worse initial conditions, the camp finally received aid with some of the hygenic conditions of the camp, and the situation had improved, but still to nothing like decency. "Even we Roma have some culture." The internationals built a terrible little kitchen inside their bathroom, which was also their only water supply. I didn't understand—you mean the only faucets for drinking water are in the bathroom? "No, no," she clarified. "Not faucets. The toilets. The same eight toilets shared by all the families, that's the only place we can get water. This too is poisoning, another reason so many people are sick. Not even animals drink from toilets like we have to."

"We do receive some food aid from Norwegian Church Aid. But much of it is very bad. Sometimes good food, sometimes bad food. A few days ago, they brought us bananas, but we gave them back. One banana was like one liter rakija." I ask Adrijan to translate again, and he explains, "You know, they were brown and so fermented that you would get very drunk from just one banana." I write it down without letting myself envision it. "Catastrofa," she says, without translation. "In the camp is always problems, never without, always new problems."

Adrijan stops translating as she started talking about her own troubles, living in one room with two of her brothers, one's wife, and their child, and explaining that she is soon moving to France and wouldn't come back—how she will get to France, she doesn't bother telling us. She talks about her own relationship problems for twenty minutes more, longer than she had spent talking about the camp, until Adrijan cuts her short and we bid a polite farewell. "There's always people like that, who just want to tell you about their personal problems," he said in the car.

On the way back, we pass another destroyed Romani Mahala, called Fabricka, where no wall was intact. Adrijan tells me this once housed tens of thousands of people. One partial wall, stands, still painted with the word "Majupi"—the Albanian derogative term for Roma.

As we drove along paved roads in surprisingly good condition on the way back to the village, Adrijan explains as an aside, "This road used to be dirt, but the Albanians put mines under it and two people died, so the internationals paved it." I am glad when we arrive at Adrijan's house.

I ALWAYS THOUGHT BEFORE NOW THAT ROOSTERS ONLY CROW AT dawn, when in fact they crow all through the night. Especially when one is lying insomniac with thoughts of the days.

When I have glimpses into the life-smashing weight of actually living here, caught in a moment here and there in a face or gesture, for years, for decades, my mind refuses, shuts down, as it does before images of war, death, and misery. Flipping sleepless through the 2002 photo book called *Memory and Identity* by Laura Trallori, from my friend's shelf, looking at pictures of those who are sleeping downstairs, I have to remind myself to breathe, not because my friends and their families in the pictures aren't managing, aren't proud, aren't happy, but because the pictures open up the long spaces between picture and picture.

I find myself thinking about some families here like, "They're doing all right, they have a stove."

Hen crossing the doorstep with her teenage chicks. Farm cat strolling through coop, leaving the hen a wide berth.

A whole townlet on house arrest, with an indefinite sentence, feared to end in a worse "punishment," for the crime of an assumed but false association. Or, like most sentences, for the crime of historical weakness. Lives destroyed by humanitarian action, imprisoned by another's liberation.

Defiant vivacity.

Parenting by constant attention that allows the kids to fall on their face when they trip. Living rooms of slaving women, too busy, too tired, but with endless time for trading wisdom and secrets. And the men in constant rehearsal and performance of the family's social self, boisterous, generous, considerate, and bold. And the music, the music some magical fetish for so many far away, here not some amulet but only a background, and when occasionally everyone jumps to their feet singing and dancing in the living room, it's they who carry life, not some gem of culture or tradition that carries them.

Roosters and cats checking each other out, chicks weaving through the flowers, sheep wandering from their pen, curious, oblivious that they have two days left of life, pigs shuffling in the Serb neighbors' yard. Kids on swings, making creepily perfect reproductions of the cat-sex howls heard all last night. And a saxophone testing the melody of "Dzelem Dzelem," wrong, and wrong again, then improvised snippets in time to the neighbor-cousin teen's tabouka drum—the sax arrived only two days ago with the visiting family back for the first time since the bombing with German apples and wafer snacks and ostentatious wedding videos … The sadness and frustration, sexual and existential, and despair always reappear but are never final before this Nietzschean force of life, the will to power of the chicken and of the seed and of the fucking around. This despair absolute, then moderated by the crazy cousins and irritating neighbors and Yahoo Messenger call to cousins refuged in Germany—Sartre wasn't thinking of here when he said, "Hell is other people." Maybe sometimes it's true, but this morning, this has to be the opposite.

WHEN WE ARE ALMOST BACK TO THE GRAČANICA ENCLAVE WHERE Adrijan's village lies, he sweeps his hand across the windshield, across a wide stretch of decently-sized foothills to the south of Pristina. "On March 17, 2004, those hills were completely covered by KLA forces. It was worse than in 1999, we had a bigger fear than we had after the bombing."[120]

I again am surprised to find myself feeling naive. "I didn't realize anything happened here, near Pristina! All the news I got in the US, from the alternative as well as mainstream press, just talked about riots within Mitrovica, supposedly spontaneous ones in response to two Albanian kids drowning after being chased into the river by dogs owned by Serbs."

"That was the story, but it's never been proven. But within two hours, all of Kosovo was on its feet, it was very well organized, so I doubt it was so spontaneous. The Albanian forces made a ring around the Serbian enclave where we live—starting here, in these hills—and broke right through the Swedish KFOR lines, who didn't have enough soldiers. Within 15 minutes, they'd burned down 15 houses. After everything settled down, they were able to buy all the land in this village—Čaglavica—for very, very cheap, as you can imagine. Now it looks like Beverly Hills. I think Kosovo has more construction happening than Dubai."

I see Adrijan's point. Outside the window, where two years before had stood a Serbian village, now looked like a downscale Dubai—one giant mall complex after another, with monstrous shining hotels, car dealerships, gas stations, and office buildings towering over the road. In front of one gargantuan concave building, NATO and US flags flew cheerily alongside an Albanian one. I tell Adrijan about a story one of my friends wrote from her trip to Guatemala, when she asked her taxi driver what had stood in the area they were driving through, before its obviously recent development. She knew it had been a Mayan village, leveled by the government in that country's own brutal civil war. The driver cheerily informed her that nothing had *ever* been there before.

Adrijan went on. "If the US Marines hadn't shown up within two hours, they would have kept going. They would have got to our village." Adrijan pauses, the first time I've seen him upset. "My oldest son came to me and said, 'Dad, I'm going into the kitchen now and I'm going to get a knife to cut my throat so I don't have to watch what they're going to do to you.' Can you imagine that train of thinking in an 11-year-old boy?!"

We both remain silent for the rest of the drive.

WALKING THROUGH PRISTINA, SINA COMMENTS, "RAMUSH Haradinaj must be pretty popular!" On both sides of the street, the former ground commander for the KLA's blocky head glares down from posters, captioned with the words, "Welcome Home!" Haradinaj, under strong pressure from Western diplomats, was just released from the Hague. He was acquitted of several war crimes charges, despite the strong objections of Hague prosecutors that they had incontrovertible evidence of his guilt. Sina pauses. "But I guess if he really was popular, they wouldn't need to put up those posters."

How popular, really, was this "Liberation Army?" Despite Mao Tse-Tung's famous adage that the revolutionary is the fish in the sea of the people, a bunch of guns in the hands of a few unpopular thugs can be surprisingly effective. "...[T]he number of armed militants was initially tiny, and they enjoyed no mass support inside Kosovo. Only occasionally did they kill Serbian police officers and Albanians they believed to be traitors."[121] In 1997, neighboring Albania experienced complete economic collapse and consequent uprising, in which the old stores of government weapons were liberated by the population. Kalashnikovs sold for $5 apiece. Analysts doubt that without the bargain of nearly free weapons, the KLA could never have got off the ground.[122]

According to King and Mason, the KLA's first public action

was to threaten to execute anyone who advocated autonomy within Serbia, rather than independence.[123] Assumably, if their goals had been shared by the whole population, they would not have had to enforce them with death threats. Several witnesses were dissuaded from testifying against the KLA in the Hague after being "targeted by extremist groups",[124] and at least one, Ilir Selimaj, was killed before he could testify.[125] Likewise, political rivals were targeted: "Several prominent members of Ibrahim Rugova's LDK, the KLA's only serious political rival, were abducted and killed."[126]

In a strange attempt at bringing order to Kosovo, UNMIK created a 5,000-person "civil emergency force" for the KLA elite, called the Kosovo Protection Corps (KPC). "KLA members were soon to make up the majority of the Kosovo Protection Corps. Many also engaged in various forms of crime. Though agreements with KFOR and UNMIK had already abolished all branches of the KLA several times, in March 2000 the KLA military police, the black-shirted PU (Policia Ushtarake), continued to operate. Among the activities they allegedly engaged in were the coercive extraction of 'contributions' from businesses and individuals, the burning of minority houses, and the expropriation of flats and businesses... During much of the emergency period, such crimes were committed with virtual impunity. Three hundred Serb houses were burned in Prizren; only two suspects were arrested."[127] In the words of General Fabio Mini, commander of KFOR forces, "All members of the KPC were criminals."[128]

The leaders of the KLA—and the new Kosovo government— were often at the forefront of the worst abuses. In one story told by a Washington DC newspaper:

> According to the German Bundesnachrichtendienst (Federal Intelligence Service), Mr. Thaci is one of three KLA kingpins who run the Albanian Mafia rackets in Kosovo. Mr. Thaci is also known for eliminating anyone who crosses his ambitions. During a trip to Kosovo, former Secretary of State Madeleine K. Albright gave Mr. Thaci a kiss on the cheek right after he had just executed six of his top officers. Let's call a spade a spade. Mr. Thaci—nicknamed "the Snake" by his admiring comrades when he was the commander of the KLA, once listed as a terrorist organization by the State Department—should be called what he really is, a terrorist who has taken over the baton as prime minister from another terrorist, the KLA leader Agim Ceku, who, according to *Jane's Defence Weekly*, was linked to two of the grisliest epi-

sodes of brutality against Serbian civilians in the Yugoslav war.

In her book *The Hunt: Me and War Criminals*, Carla Del Ponte, former chief prosecutor at The Hague, reveals the gruesome details of the hundreds of Serb prisoners whose bodies were stripped of their organs during the Kosovo war. According to her sources, senior figures in the KLA were aware of the scheme, in which hundreds of young Serbs were reportedly taken by truck from Kosovo to northern Albania, where their organs were removed.

Miss Del Ponte provides grim details of the reported organ harvesting and of how some prisoners were sewn up after having kidneys removed. Miss Del Ponte also wrote that the claims were made by several sources, one of whom "personally made an organ delivery" to an Albanian airport for transport abroad, and "confirmed information directly gathered by the tribunal." Miss del Ponte further writes, "The victims, deprived of a kidney, were then locked up again, inside the barracks, until the moment they were killed for other vital organs. In this way, the other prisoners were aware of the fate that awaited them, and according to the source, pleaded, terrified, to be killed immediately." Mr. Thaci is accused of benefiting from the trade when he was Kosovo's prime minister.[129]

In 2000, the first elections after the war, the public voted strongly in opposition to the KLA, in favor of Ibrahim Rugova's LDK, which had led the 10-year-long non-violent resistance preceding the Kosovo war. The internationals again and again excuse their complicity in KLA crimes by citing fears of alienating the public; apparently, they could have saved themselves the effort, since the public still preferred their pre-war leaders. But liberal humanitarian intervention brought the KLA into power, and can't exactly go about disowning its newfound friends.

In one illuminating documentary entitled *The Brooklyn Connection: How To Build a Guerrilla Army*, a Dutch filmmaker follows forty-year-old Kosovar Florin Krasniqi around, chronicling his life as a minor construction tycoon in Brooklyn.[130] He also may have armed the KLA nearly single-handedly from his business, beyond the $5 Kalashnikovs. In one scene, he buys a massive caliber gun from a shop in rural Pennsylvania, explaining that it is for his "Albanian Elephant-Hunter's Club." In another, he brags about having smuggled several tons of arms into Kosovo, filling the entire cargo hold of a jumbo jet, hidden under packages of humanitarian aid. The arms he buys in the movie are clearly in preparation for March 2004, and are to be used against UNMIK and Serb and Roma civilians, since, at the time of filming, the Serbian forces have long since left Kosovo. Richard Holbrook, the head US diplomat for the Balkans, and General Westley Clark, head of the NATO action against Serbia and Kosovo, both make surprise cameos as obsequious entertainers of New York's Kosovar lobby.

According to King and Mason, "UNMIK and KFOR ... let down the great majority of people in all communities who want to live in a peaceful and prospering society. International pusillanimity did not honour local mores—it benefited a small minority of self-styled militants and outright criminals who live by extortion."[131] "[T]he international community was bowing to bullies, reinforcing the Balkan [sic] view that violence works."[132]

Kukumi, the first film made in post-war Kosovo, attempts to expose the post-war situation in a rare act of courageous critique, portraying Kosovo as a society ruled through heartless cruelty and force.[133] Love serves only as an invitation for horrible tragedy. One reviewer writes, "The casual brutality that emerged in post-war Kosovo stemmed from an older set of patriarchal laws which were used as an excuse to rob property from the weak and deny care to the vulnerable."

The film's opening night ended with its metaphor invading the literal. According to the same reviewer, "Twenty minutes before the film's end, a bomb threat required the cinema to be evacuated."[134]

TWO MONTHS OF DAILY ENGLISH CLASSES IN THE VILLAGE, EVERY day its pataphysics. Teaching a reading lesson about Amelia Earhart, I struggle to explain the word "disappeared."

"If I take this bottle, first you see it, then you don't see it. It disappeared."

"You hide it."

"Yes, but you don't know."

"Yes, I know, you hid it."

"Er... If I am here, then not here but you don't know why, maybe very fast, not here next hour, even next day, next year..."

"You are lost."

"But you don't know. It's a mystery."

"AHA! Like vampire!"

"EXACTLY! You see me here, but if I am a vampire, and you take a picture of me, maybe to send on Messenger, after you take the picture of me, you look, and I..."

"Disappear!"

"YES!"

So I teach the lesson, about how Amelia was the first woman to fly across the Atlantic, then the first person alone across the Pacific, and almost the first around the world, until her plane...

"Disappeared!"

"PERFECT! Yes. Understand?"

"Yes, understand. Amelia Earhart is vampire!"

AFTER TWO DAYS WITHOUT WATER, WALKING TO THE NEAREST town miles away to fill a few bottles for drinking, Adrijan finally gets fed up and drives to the water utilities office in Gračanica. The office is empty. Neighbors explain that the staff is away on another project. Then Adrijan finds another man, who tells Adrijan that it's his *slava* (religious day of feasting) so he can't do work. Adrijan goes again into the police station (where the Albanian policeman threatens to arrest his son for not being in school, until his son explained where he went, which has had another bomb threat called in today, the third since I've been here, one of which was traced to a Pristina phone—and the cop let him off.) The police give Adrijan a phone number for the water department in Pristina. When he calls and asks them when the water will be on again, they said, "Again? You mean it's off?" They hadn't heard anything. Seven hundred people in the village, no water for three days, and nobody had noticed.

VALON HANDS ME THE WINE BOTTLE AS WE DANGLE OUR FEET over Prizren's majestic river. The Ottoman stone river banks seem untouched since being built centuries before. "Here, we don't have the option of nostalgia, since things haven't changed from thirty years ago, from a hundred or two hundred years ago. So what would we be nostalgic for?"

Prizren's winding stone riverfront road is so congested with sociability that his words seem even more literally true than he may have meant them—not a car is in sight in the center of town, only cafes and promenading locals. "So instead, we become nostalgic for progress, for promises of freedom and prosperity, for new magical technologies. The present is so concretely hopeless that we put all our hopes on abstracts. That's why all Kosovan art is abstract art! We're all future-nostalgics!"

Drita pulls the bottle from my hand, with a crazed smile

under her conflagration of hair. "See that?!" pointing to a trash heap collected on the river bank. "*That* is abstract art."

Valon tells me about his vacation last summer in Sutomore, Montenegro. He met some Kosovo Serbs and joined them on the beach. When they asked him what he was doing, he told them, "I'm trying to be your friend. How are we going to live together in the same country if we can't be friends?"

One sun-bather turned to him and said, "First, we cut your throat. Then, we can be friends."

I tell him about one Serb friend, Ivan, who lives in North Mitrovica. Ivan says he doesn't care about independence either way, as long as minorities are protected, and they can live a normal life. And in the Serb area of the village where I'm staying, how I drank rakija with the metalhead neighbors who told me miss their Albanian friends and just want things to go back to normal.

"Of course, we lived together for centuries, why would it be a problem now? But some of these people committed war crimes, how do you think people feel about them coming back?"

"You know, Prizren is the only city in Kosovo where Albanians never drove out the Roma or the Serbs. We're not so caught up in these new politics, we still think of ourselves in some kind of Ottoman way. And 30% of the population here is Turks, so it's a different dynamic."

My mind jumps. "This hertitage from the Ottomans is great, but also you have this problem of political passivity, like in all of the Balkans. If you have any sense in you, you don't fuck with politics, so the only people who get into politics are all mafia psychopaths. Like Haradinaj."

A few weeks previously, the Hague had acquitted Ramush Haradinaj of multiple charges of war crimes and crimes against humanity. One Roma friend told me many people whispered that Haradinaj had killed more Albanian civilians during the war than the Serbs had, in an effort to trigger Western intervention. Even if he had not literally ordered their killing, the KLA was open in pursuing escalatory politicies that they knew would result in primarily civilian casualties; Haradinaj was an on-the-ground commander of such actions. The Hague acquitted him of war crimes near his home village on Albanian as well as Serb civilians; Carla Del Ponte, head prosecutor for the Hague for ex-Yugoslav war crimes, was furious at his release for what she viewed as reasons of political convenience, and appreciated that Serbs would take this as further evidence that they would never be acknowledged as victims of war crimes, only perpetrators.

"You know Haradinaj still runs the majority of protection rackets in Kosovo? And if you notice all those gas stations and private universities, you know, one every kilometer down the freeway, they're all money laundering schemes that he's got a hand in."

I ask Valon how the universities are here. "They're OK, but you usually can't get higher degrees. I got accepted to study in England, but I was a half-point too low on the English exam." Valon's English seems better than mine, but then, who knows if I could pass the test either. "At the moment, I'm in a Masters program for Philosophy in Bulgaria, at the University of Sofia. The problem is, now that Bulgaria is in the European Union, it's really hard for us, from the other countries, to get a visa. I was supposed to start classes two months ago, but here I am. Imagine, two months waiting to go somewhere that is closer than Belgrade, but that now is 'in' Europe. Fuck Fuck Fuck."

Valon changes the subject and asks about my book. Excited to hear that I am interested in the history of anarchism in the Balkans, Valon pulls out his notebook and shows me parts of an article he recently translated from a zine called *Avanti*, on the history of anarchism in ex-Yugoslavia, stretching back to the 19th century:

> The famous Serbian socialist Svetozar Markovic attested an influence by Bakunin's ideas in the late 19th century, during his time in Zurich. Particularly influential for Markovic was anarchism's focus on Federalism, which he felt would be key for any future form of Balkan socialism. After his departure, Bakuninist anarchism came to predominate in expatriate Serbian student circles. On the terrain of former Yugoslavia, anarchist ideas were often brought back by visiting workers, often including smuggled copies of Johann Most's newspapers *Die Freiheit* and *Der Rebell*. In 1871, Most himself visited Ljubljana, but he quickly had to escape from the police, to Trieste. Miloš Krpan, a teacher in Croatia at the turn of the century, had connections with many anarchist centers across Europe, and tried to bring anarchism into practical expression in Croatia. Despite Austro-Hungarian repression of anarchist ideas, Bosnia and Herzegovina soon became familiar with anarchist thought, with Sarajevo as its cen-

ter. Joseph Voloner and Johan Hable were arrested separately in Sarajevo for distributing Most's *Der Freiheit* among artisans and other workers.

As the night goes on and rakija replaces wine, Drita shouts, "Fuck, why are we talking in this imperialist English language? Pričamo na srpskom! Let's speak Serbian!" On the center steps in town, our conversation, shouted, slides over into Serbian, my Albanian and Turkish friends swearing like their old neighbors.

WHEN ADRIJAN TRIES TO GIVE HIS WIFE BASMAH A CLOTH TO pick up the giant pan, hot from the oven, she waves him off and yells in Romani, *"Mange nasi tato!"* It's not hot for me! She picks up the roasting pan, smoking from the outdoor oven with a whole lamb inside, and lifts it into the oven again with her naked hands. I tell her I will always remember her saying *"Mange nasi tato"* and she laughs hard, and says it to me again in a few minutes, laughing. *"Mange nasi tato!"* Later, Adrijan tells me that there is a saying here, a woman who doesn't fear heat also isn't afraid of her husband. "It's true!" says Adrijan. "I am the one afraid of her!" he says with a big smile.

ALL AROUND ME IN THE SERBIAN ENCLAVE, NEW POSTERS HAVE gone up daily for Nikolić, the candidate for the hard-nationalist Serbian Radical Party, often also featuring the gleaming face of Vojislav Seselj, who now sits in the Hague indicted for war crimes as a paramilitary leader in Croatia, Bosnia, and here. On his campaign recently, Nikolić said, "We are ready to defend Serbia's pride." Were he to win, Kosovo would very likely return to war. The Serbs are hoping to partition northern Kosovo— which borders green-line Serbia like the Serb Republic within Bosnia, and the area could erupt any day. The Serbian Radicals are throwing their lot in with Russia, which may well be eager to assert itself on the world stage by backing regional allies. Such a conflict would not only endanger the various residents of Kosovo. "Of course I want Tadic [the pro-European, less-nationalist candidate] to win," my friend here told me tonight. "If Nikolić wins, he'll cause the Third World War." I'm not sure he was exaggerating.

I turn on the Serbian news tonight to see if the results had come in. Tadić is giving a speech, and his seriousness makes me think he had lost. I was especially confused why he kept seeming to say that it was important for Serbia to follow the "Arabski put," the Arab path, and strengthen its ties with Arab countries, until I realized that the "Eu" dipthong of "Europski" (European) sounds more like the American English /ae/ of Arab, while the A of "Arabski" is pronounced /ah/... Damn the Great English Vowel Shift of the 13th–17th centuries.

I google the election and let out a little cheer that Tadić had won. The teenage son of the family I'm staying with asks me why I was happy. I tell him that the candidate that wants war has lost, and the other one is winning. He beams and gives me a big hug.

Over his shoulder, his mother looks at me sternly. We speak all the time, but I had never heard her discuss anything like elections. Usually, she is too tired from laboring to maintain her large household, besides her day job. "Why are you happy? Nikolic should win," she says.

"But Nikolić is asking for war!" I said.

"Let him. Let there be war. Let the Albanians and the Serbs hate the Roma, let the Albanians and Serbs fight. Let there be war. Either peace, or war. This is not life. I can't live like this anymore. No freedom of movement, no work, no hope for my children's future, no standard of living. You know what happened to me the other day?"

Two days ago, she tried to visit her family, now refugees in Macedonia. At the border, she was turned away because her niece was with her, with a different last name. The Kosovo/Macedonia border is a key point in regional human trafficking, so adults cannot (officially) cross the border with someone else's children. Stranded on the border unexpectedly, she caught a ride with an unofficial Albanian taxi van. He insisted on taking a route around the Kosovo border, though she protested, since as a resident she would have no trouble at the border. He also insisted on a 50 euro ($80) fee for what is usually a 10 euro ($16) ride, which she couldn't pay. The six-year-old niece, who has a remarkable intuition, began crying. After making them walk through wilderness around the border, he picked them up again, now with a number of Albanian passengers in the van. For the entire ride back, the passengers asked her threatening questions, whether her whole family had fought with the KLA during the war, where exactly she lived, and so on. Though also a fluent speaker of Albanian (having grown up in an Albanian village among Albanian friends before the war), she kept silent, shaking with fear for the entire long ride, as the niece continued crying. Finally, they dropped them off at the border of their Romani neighborhood inside the Serbian enclave.

I told her I knew about her ride. She looked firmly into my eyes. "I can't live like this anymore. Let them make war."

Hours later, the first half of the results indicated that Tadić really had won.

"Tadić won," she told me. "No good."

SITTING BESIDE EACH OTHER ON HIS IMMACULATE CARPET, ADRIJAN tells me, "I remember growing up, this road leading to the village would be covered with tents in the summer, foreigners from wherever would be sleeping there without worry, bicycles laying unlocked outside their tents. Now," as he lights yet another cigarette, "people are scared to sleep in their own houses."

ON OUR NEXT DAY OF BUSINESS, ADRIJAN PULLS OFF A SIDE road and drives through the town of Crvena Vodica, near Obilić. As we near the camp, vast stretches of rabble line the road on both sides, which Adrijan explains used to be a thriving Mahala, with 847 residents in 114 houses, to be exact. Now, most of the houses are short piles of concrete. I step out to take a photo, but pretend to be peeing in the grass until a car passes. In the background stands the newly renovated Adem Jashari stadium, named after the Kosovar guerrilla leader who was killed in the beginning of the escalation that led to the war. A few houses have been rebuilt and fly Albanian flags—the inhabitants are not the original ones, explains Adrijan. One old man and a younger boy are picking away at the remnants of a wall, with a wheelbarrow full of square bricks behind them. Suddenly, for the first time I understand why so many Balkan ruins have such clean beams, why they resemble, in more ways than one, a corpse picked clean to the bones. When Bakunin said, "The passion for destruction is a creative passion," I doubt he imagined such a liberation of building materials.

We pull into the Plametina refugee camp, nestled just under the Tower-of-Babel-tall smokestack of the Obilic "Kosovo B" coal power plant, so near that we drive through the mist of the cooling tower. Some youth are doing some construction of their own by the entrance to the camp, weighing down the corrugated tin roof of a shack with some trash. Adrijan explains that the buildings that refugees live in—416 of them, from all over Kosovo—were built as housing for the workers at the plant. Temporary shelter for the construction workers as they built the plant over fifty years ago, clarifies Adrijan, not the ones who worked in the plant after it was built. It looks to me like a crumbling industrial site that I can imagine squatting in for a few rough days while waiting to hop a freight train on some punk-rock adventure. But hundreds of people living here, for seven years and counting, with their whole families, weddings and births and deaths... I mumble *"svaki imaju svoje svaki dan"* to myself—"everyone has their own everyday" but I can't imagine how this everyday can possibly keep going on.

After Adrijan explains to a weary but welcoming camp representative who we are, the camp representative explains that each family receives around $70/month in aid—not much for a large family when food and most other items are more expensive than in the US. I grimly reflect to myself that they are lucky compared to the residents of Leposavić, but choose not to tell the man my thoughts. Again, I cannot fathom how they are not starving after seven years of such conditions, and ask the man if perhaps people have found some space to grow food? "Look up. If we are storing wood for fires on the balconies, do you think we have space to grow food?" They do receive some assistance every other week: potatoes, milk, sugar, flour, oil, and wood. There are a couple faucets in one building that have to provide for every resident in the complex—everyone has to fill bottles for everything there. Sick people are able to go to the doctor in the neighboring Serbian area, but most people don't have any identification papers, and the doctors refuse to help them without official papers. And even if the doctors see them, they don't receive enough assistance to pay for the medicines prescribed. This is a big problem, emphasizes the man. "Many sick people. We have lots of sick old people."

What kind of help do they need most? I ask, not knowing what else to ask, as if I was someone who could file a report that could help them get it. "Food, or more clean water to drink. We don't want to be parasites, I just want a job so I can feed my family with my own salary." I suppose their history has shown them there's nobody else they can rely on. "If a father goes into the village," he clarifies, "his kids will ask him for candy when he comes back. Any father would bring candy, but he has to say, 'I'm sorry, I don't have anything.'"

I ask the representative if he is worried about Kosovo becoming independent. He looks at me for a minute before he tells Adrijan, "It's better not to say anything." Adrijan explains that he wants to but can't. I wonder if someone he knew made the mistake of telling an international bureaucrat something that they then passed on to someone who didn't like what they heard. "Anyway," the man offers, "Kostunica says they won't get it." Adrijan laughs the name of the Serbian President under his breath, "Kostunica!" When I ask if there are any UN checkpoints to protect them, the representative says that there aren't, but that they haven't received any threats since moving to the camps. Perhaps, I reflect, their neighbors are not worried that life in the camps is such that the Roma will want to stay in Kosovo, and thus do not object to their presence.

As we thank the man for his help, he offers us two RC colas in the obligatory gesture of Balkan hospitality. Adrijan vehemently objects, so I follow his lead. The man insists. We object. But the man will not allow us to leave the camp without taking his two cold RC colas. We drive off guiltily sipping from the cans. Adrijan is angry. "I hate that. I really do. You know what those colas cost him." I try to distract myself with the thought that perhaps RC Cola might sponsor the refugees of Plametina as their official cola.

Later, I learn that Kostunica had just paid a visit to Kosovo Polje to commemorate Vidov Dan, the day when Serbs—so the story goes—were defeated in 1389 near Kosovo Polje by the invading Turks. On the same day I visited the Plametina camp, only about 5 miles away, the local Albanian forces bombed the (Albanian) police station for having the affrontery to allow their (technically) own president to visit the site. Hours after my visit, the Roma residents of Plametina camp issued statements that they felt under serious threat and would like to be given shelter elsewhere, as soon as possible. Consistently with the concern shown them by UNMIK since the war, their fears were ignored.

On the drive home, Adrijan turns up the radio. Passing an elderly Albanian man biking the other direction on the freeway,

Leposavić Roma refugee camp in Kosovo, in 2006.

Adrijan honks his horn and waves a big, friendly smile. The man, a bit mystified, waves back with a smile, his bike wobbling a bit as he squints to recognize Adrijan through the windshield. A minute further, Adrijan honks again at a man working his field by the side of the road, and the man returns the greeting, again a little mystified. Adrijan's eyes glow as a he shoots me a giddy look before honking and waving at everybody else we pass on the way home.

STARING INTO THE SUN

NERVES STILL SHOT FROM MY TIME IN KOSOVA, I STUMBLE OFF MY BUS INTO CETINJE AS THE SUN JUST BEGINS TO POKE OVER THE MOUNTAINS. AARON AND BRANKA TOLD ME HOW EVEN, WITHIN CRAZY MONTENEGRO, CETINJE HAS A REPUTATION. THE CENTRAL FOUNTAIN SCULPTURE OF THE TOWN, AT LEAST DURING THEIR VISIT, HAD BEEN TWO GIANT BULLS IN GLASS, ONE MOUNTING THE OTHER, WITH A WATERFALL OF VESICULAR FLUID PUMPING THROUGH ITS TRANSLUCENT PATH THE ROUTE OF THE FOUNTAIN. ALL OF MONTENEGRO'S GREATEST ARTISTS AND INTELLECTUALS HAD ALL LIVED IN LITTLE CETINJE AS WELL, INCLUDING THE GREAT POET NJEGOŠ, WHO HAD SPENT MUCH OF HIS LIFE MINISTERING IN A LITTLE CHAPEL IN THE CENTER OF TOWN.

AFTER EXCHANGING GLANCES WITH SCULPTURES PEEKING OUT
from several corners, I set my pack down in a cafe in the center
of town, and wait for it to open. I decide, sipping my espresso,
that I could use a few days in the company of sculptures and
schizophrenics after a week visiting the refugee camps in Kosovo.
I ask the patron of the cafe, then everyone I find awake on the
street, if they know of any rooms to let for three or four days.
Finally, in the local office of the airline, the young woman
working behind the counter tells me they have several clients
with rooms to rent, and her boss comes in to make the call. The
boss tells the young woman that my host is on her way. The
young woman adds, "That should be five Euro." Her boss spins
around and yells at her for several minutes about down-bidding
one of their clients for a stranger, and the young woman looks
at the floor guiltily. As her angry boss stomps away, she looks
up and shoots me a conspiratorial smile.

It is hardly nine in the morning, but the whole family has
awoken to greet me. Despite my repeated refusals, I am sat
down before a large breakfast, with repeated servings of Turkish
coffee. Father, son, and two daughters eye me curiously, but
the mother directs the series of questions. What is it like in
America? They seem particularly interested in befriending me
to the younger of their two daughters, until I make clear, repeatedly, that I have a girlfriend in Zagreb. The older daughter,
my same age, seems to be reserved to help around the house,
and has a sad, resigned air about her. I attempt to ask them
questions about their lives in between my answers, but their
curiosity leaves little room. I am proud of my Serbian—in general
subjects like this, I am finally able to hold a full conversation.
They are clearly impressed as well, and ask me, flatteringly,
how I came to learn so much of their language.

An hour into the conversation, the father approaches me and
pours a shot of rakija for each of us. I attempt to ask him about
football, which someone in the family is interested in, judging
by their decorations. He points to his son with a smile and pours
me another shot. The mother proudly interjects that their son is
a football player for the local team, to which the son responds
with a straightforward smile, and answers my questions about
his team with a pride free of arrogance. Even if I have begun
my questions out of politeness and a desperate lack for obvious common subjects, the son has already interested me in

his team's struggles. I reflect that in America, I might not feel so comfortable discussing football at ten in the morning with a family of strangers, even with the aid of whiskey. But their openness has won me over.

"*Poznaš-li Arkana?*" asks the mother. Do you know Arkan? I laugh awkwardly, sure I have misheard. "Arkan! Arkan!" Do you know who he is? I figure this is some Montenegrin humor, teasing the American tourist by mentioning the most awkward subject between us. Yes, I have certainly heard of Arkan. Do people in America know Arkan? Of course. Arkan is a very famous man. No one has burst out laughing yet.

"*Mi smo svoja porodica!*" We are his family! They are looking at me with smiles and expectations. "Oh!" I manage. There is an awkward silence. Even fulfilling my role as a good guest, I cannot bring myself to laud the greatest paramilitary leader of the Yugoslav wars. I still wonder if they are joking, until the mother points at a portrait on the wall. Arkan, before he was assassinated by fellow mafiosi, stands proud surrounded by my present company. In his arms, the football player son, at the time just a baby. They keep looking over at me. My lack of reaction sits awkwardly.

"*Čekaj! Čekaj!*" Wait! The son runs out of the room. A minute later, he returns with a DVD in his hand. We pull up our chairs around the TV. A Serbian flag flies across the screen, behind faces of a succession of Serbian kings, as historic Serbian anthems play. Soon, Arkan appears in fatigues, bullhorn in hand, directing his *Tigrovi* paramilitary troops with an inspirational message. Soon, they are at work defending the nation, with mortars and bazookas. The camera turns away from the heroes for a moment to show a house, its stones puffing out with smoke each time a morter shell enters, then beginning to bleed flames. The house looks familiar; I have been to this area of Croatia, I have friends from there, refugees. The family all watch the video with rapt attention, like it was the seasonal play-offs.

Homemade movies from the war have recently been used as central evidence in the war trials in the international court of the Hague. Many were passed around for years, often to show at parties, before copies made it into the hands of the court. The direct footage of massacres and often explicit scenes of rape and torture served as the most damning evidence available, of the very people who had been keeping the videos for nostalgia.

Arkan's *Tigrovi* were known as the worst for such crimes. On the screen, a sniper takes aim with his high-powered rifle.

"*Znaš*," I begin in careful Serbian, "*najgore stvar u ovima ratovima je da umrle toliko civili.*" You know, the worst thing in these wars is that so many civilians die. No one looks from the screen, though I know they heard me. Nervous after a very long pause, I add, "*Znaš, na primjer, u Iraqu.*" You know, I went on, like in Iraq. Still no response. Then, the older daughter says slowly, "*A to je dešava i tu, tako isto.*" It happened here, too. "*Znaš*," I know. The son reaches over and ejects the movie. He then puts a Steven Seagal movie in, which I watch with him as the others get up. This video also has lots of grenades and guns, but at least it's fiction.

THE SON BRINGS ME TO THE OLD CENTRAL MONASTERY, accompanied only by a friend in dark shades he calls "Mafioso." "It is a joke," he clarifies. Mafioso isn't convinced I can speak Serbian, so he asks the football player son all about me. "What religion is he?" asks Mafioso. "Catholic," the son answers immediately. Not particularly wishing to be construed as a Catholic while I sleep in Arkan's family's house, perhaps because I said that I had a girlfriend in Zagreb, I quickly correct him and say I'm not Catholic, that I'm not really any religion. Perhaps Catholic would have been better after all, but my guides just seem amused.

Inside the monastery's museum, an archeology student shows us around the antiquities. Here, the right hand of John the Baptist. There, perhaps the first illuminated Bible to be written in Cyrillic. Bejewelled robes of kings and dented suits of armor cross their arms down at us who still breathe. I stare through the scratchy glass, chiding my limited command of Montenegrin as I try to guess the stories the archeologist delivers with a distant gaze.

On our way out of the door, a spritely older fellow walks out of a door to the side. My host grabs my arm, and pulls me over to the man. My host kisses the hand of the man, and I follow in turn, thinking only of guest protocol. My host introduces me to Metropolitan Mihailo, the Archbishop of Cetinje and Montenegro. The church, which refuses to count itself part of the Serbian Orthodox hierarchy, is still apostate within the larger Orthodox church, and functions awkwardly alongside the Serbian church in Montenegro. The Cetinje monastery certainly seems the Archbishop's turf today, though, whatever the official scandals. He cheerily says, "Hello! Good day!" in clear English, which I return.

I leave early the next morning, two days earlier than my original plan.

IN THE OLD TOWN OF BAR, I HAVE FOUND THE PUNKS, AND WE gather in their local bar. One woman and I end up comparing social mores of our lands, and finally get around to religion. I tell her I was raised Southern Baptist, but am now more or less a mystical materialist. She clucks in disapproval.

"How can you not believe in God?" she asks me. She tells me that she is a practicing Christian of the Montenegrin Orthodox Church. She asks me why I shudder, and I ask her, emboldened by beer, how she cannot, given the church's role in the war. She claims that the church can't be blamed, that it stayed outside of politics at the time, that perhaps it encouraged values that made people critical of the war. I don't know how to respond, I forget to tell her that the very hand I just kissed at the monastery had also blessed Arkan at his wedding, as one example. I am so surprised by her claim that I cannot think of a response.

"Did you grow up going to church?" I ask her. She laughs. "No, of course not. My parents are communist."

How can she go from being raised communist to embracing the church? I ask her, even more astounded. She doesn't understand the question enough to answer. Someone changes the subject.

Here, with a friend in fatigues in the early morning hours in a small town in Montenegro, I encounter the mystery of our times. After generations of Tito and his dreams of brotherhood and unity has come a generation that looks to the Middle Ages for inspiration. Abdel Gamel Nasser, a close friend of Tito's, represented the same dreams of progress and unity, of better lives and liberation from poverty and oppression, in the Arab world (though, more than Tito, he often relied on oppression to accomplish his claims of liberation.) Now, the closest thing to an opposition in the Arab world talks of reinstating the Caliphate, while much of the Balkans dreams of kings and patriarchs. Foucault, in his last years after a lifetime of brilliant critique of the practice of power through the micro-politics of everyday life, ended by embracing Ayatollah Khomeni, who might have executed Foucault for his homosexuality. For all of modernism's critics, and the damning post-modern critique of universalist humanism, I wonder if this is the best alternative it has to offer. For all our hatred of our old world of shahs and empires, can't we think of anything more interesting than Ayatollahs and Patriarchs? Ancient ethnic hatreds might be nothing but a mythical past, but they could well be our future, if all the alternatives are so successfully sabotaged.

MY BUS GROANS ALONG THE FOOT OF CHALKY SLOPES hanging over the gem-blue sea of Montenegro's coast. Castle-cities hunch, bundled on rock cluster islands, a catapult-throw from shore, connected only by narrow sand-bridges. Time and again, wave after wave of invaders never managed to take and hold this land of Himalayan heights and salt, pounded by the elements. Njegoš, Montenegro's most famous poet, used to display his vigor by hiking into the mountains for lightning storms, and, in the absence of storms, by staring into the sun for long periods. Montenegrins may have claim to being the tallest population on earth, beating out Samoans and the Dinka. "We're tough!" the young woman sitting next to me on the bus explains humbly.

I step off the bus in exquisitely gnarled little Kotor, the kind of fortress town only little kids can imagine. Windy little streets cut between pizzerias and cafes set in looming stone, and, outside the walls, an algae-stuffed moat keeps out the latest invaders. Over the town, a crumbled castle stares down from atop severe mountains. All around the town, the peaks tumble down to the Bay of Kotor, with only this town nestled on its brief level ground.

Dropping off my pack at a local hostel, I flag down a bus for a day-trip to Perast, a small town farther along on the Bay. In the Perast museum, I stare at a bejewelled relic of a saint's hand—right there, a hand in silver with saintly bones and wisps of flesh inside, waving at me just like that. At the local cafe, the proprietor makes me pay for my coffee by taking a picture with him. I meander down to the stony shore and commandeer a boat for a couple dollars.

A sporty young man with not a crease on his brow buzzes me out to sea on his outboard rowboat. His terrier perches at the bow, hale like a little Walt Whitman. In a few minutes, the boat pulls up to *Gospa od Škrpjela*, Our Lady of the Stones, the little man-made island just off Perast's shore. Every year, the local residents—never much more than a thousand—held an annual festival where every citizen dropped a stone or two into the lake at the same spot. Occasionally, a sunken ship would be dragged over to help with the effort. After two hundred years, the pile had grown to an island, and in 1452 local residents built an Orthodox church on it. Today's church is Roman Catholic, built in 1632. The island has grown to 28,000 square feet, stone by stone.

I step down solid old stone steps through the church's entry. Medieval oil paintings hang dustily along the halls as I make my way through the meditative chambers, now turned into galleries. Charms line the walls in stacked shelves, ancient kitsch—a Ganesh from India, coins from China, an African fertility fetish, odd in this Catholic frame. The guide pulls me down through another door into an antechamber. There, as my eyes adjust to details submerged in shadow, I make out a jagged wall roughly tiled with irregular shapes.

"For centuries, sailors from all parts of the world have made pilgrimages to our church to visit Our Lady. Represented on these plates—we have over 2,500, many in silver and in gold— are the many dangers they have survived. They brought them here as their way of showing thankfulness to Our Lady for their safe passage."

Each of the small metal plates is stamped with a unique image of terror and suffering—ships overturned by storm, gangrened legs, pirate attacks, pestilence. With each one, I pause to imagine the sailor meandering from whichever corner of the earth, all the way across the world to this little island, and humbly presenting the Lady with their particular agony, having survived. The priest then must have thanked them, nailed it to the wall, right next to all the others, until after hundreds of years the walls were covered. Quiet histories of tempest-tossed lives finally lived out in an unlikely and unexpected peace, silent, yet narrated exactly and wholly right here for eyes that care to adjust to the shadows.

*P*ART *T*WO:

GREECE, ROMANIA, BULGARIA, ALBANIA

Romani family, Romania.

Agency for Secret Tourism, Timisoara, Romania.

TOOLBOXES AND ROUTINES

MORE AND MORE—A LIFE PHILOSOPHY" READS THE SIGN ON THE CLOTHING STORE. WALKING ACROSS THESSALONIKI'S MAIN SQUARE, I STARE UP AT A MAMMOTH ROTATING HIGH-HEELED SHOE, SOAKED IN BLINKING CHRISTMAS LIGHTS. IT'S BEEN AWHILE SINCE I'VE BEEN IN AN ESTABLISHED CAPITALIST COUNTRY. IT *IS* LIKE THIS, MY MEMORY WASN'T EXAGGERATING. BUT THIS DOESN'T EXACTLY LOOK LIKE THE EUROPEAN UNION IS SUPPOSED TO. THE CARS ARE NEWER MODELS, BUT THE PLATES ARE STILL CROOKED. GENTLY SEVERE FACES RESEMBLE GREECE'S STONY EARTH, CLEARCUT BY THE ANCIENTS UNTIL THE RAINS WASHED ITS EASY FERTILITY INTO THE SEA. ELDERLY WIDOWS IN SQUARED VEILS, OLD MEN IN BERETS ARGUING OVER TEA OR COFFEE—DON'T CALL IT TURKISH—AND YOUNG PEOPLE OBVIOUSLY TOO OLD TO FALL FOR ANYTHING.

Francisco and I lunch on a hill overlooking Corfu behind a lot full of broken, rusty buses. A Roma mother sweeps around her family's Mack-truck home. The elements seem familiar from elsewhere in the Balkans, even some roofless houses and crumbling '60s decor. But somehow their arrangement this time is not quite so jumpy and edgy. This place lacks the quiet panic, the uneasy slow slide, and the fear of some ruinous trap. I experience something I haven't felt since home, an absence, an internal division, an alienation in store signs and shop windows, in the crumpled wrappers napping in the park grass, in the Gyro turning in the stands. Maybe I'm just mad that lunch costs more than a dollar here.

IF IT WEREN'T FOR THE GRAFFITI ON THE OUTSIDE, I would not think this house could be "Mauri Gata," or Black Cat. Otherwise, it seems just like the family homes surrounding it, as it must have been before it was abandoned and then squatted as a community center. On the second of three floors is a cafe with all its tables full of animated discussion. I motion towards an empty chair at one table, and the others at the table insist that I join them. One architecture student quietly explains the different activities based in the three-story house, squatted for three years so far: the Internet-based Independent Media Center, photo lessons with a free darkroom for whoever wants to use it, sign language courses, Greek dance lessons, a bookstore, a record store, a library, and a communal meal every Saturday. Several groups, such as one that organizes anti-war protests, hold their meetings here. I can't imagine how a sleepy little three-story house could host so much activity.

One Austrian woman in the cafe explains how she arrived here. At first, she came to Greece to do environmental research for the EU. Her perspective changed a bit when she visited one "conservation zone" not far from Thessaloniki. Even though the land was officially protected from human interference, she was not particularly disturbed to find rice fields cultivated on it. She worried more about the dump directly upstream from the field: piles of plastic and batteries. Her complaints were filed, and she never heard a response. She later tried to volunteer in Thessaloniki's municipal recycling program, but was met with such vehement refusal when she asked to see the center, that she suspects the only aspects of the program that even exist are the pickup and the funding. "It changed my perspective," she says. "That's why I'm here."

IN ANOTHER DRUNK ARGUMENT, I AM TRYING TO EXPLAIN to my new friends why it's terrible if the US is actually becoming a nation, after avoiding such a curse for more than 200 years. I am surprised that they don't understand me. Perhaps the difference between citizenship and nationality isn't as obvious here as in the neighboring states. My friend tells me that his grandparents were Slavs who these days might call themselves Macedonians, but that he is Greek. His grandparents' culture is to him a curiosity, but nothing like roots. Should I feel sorry about his assimilation? The bloody history of forceful assimilation of Macedonian Slavs by Greeks—generations of coercive depatriation—flashes through my mind. Greece screamed "Macedonia is Greek" and refused to acknowledge Macedonia when it broke away from Yugoslavia in 1991, pressuring the US to put disastrous sanctions on Macedonia, simply for claiming its historical name. Finally the latter agreed to change its name to the utterly unfortunate FYROM (Former Yugoslav Republic of Macedonia.) It's hard to get indignant at my friend for not caring about his own nationality. Yet he doesn't understand that I might be revolted by this process of nationalization in the US. I tell him that nationalism is a big mistake, the mistake of trying to make culture the same shape as a state. I'm still upset with a near stranger for abandoning his grandparents' culture. But how far is such a defense of culture from an aggressive nationalism?

I get more upset when I notice the name brand of his stove is Napalm. Everyone is mystified, until I explain that Americans take brand names very seriously.

IN ATHENS, CHRISTINA TELLS ME ABOUT PRESIDENT Clinton's visit in November 1999. The city took for granted that there would be huge riots, so they set up a riot zone, far from where Clinton would be visiting. The rioters destroyed all the McDonald's restaurants and all the banks in the area, but Clinton's visit through the town proceeded smoothly. "The power of the leftist political parties would have made direct repression difficult," Christina explained. "Probably rebuilding the shops is cheaper than hiring all the police on overtime anyway."

I tell her a story I'd heard from the protests in Prague, in September of 2000. An American liberal journalist had at first been taken aback by the aggressive methods of the Greek Black Bloc. As the protest continued, however, and he understood what the police were doing to protesters, both pacific and confrontational, he requested an interview with some of the Greeks. "In America, we have a saying that to get a job done, you need a lot of different tools in your toolbox," he began. The translator relayed the comment, and they discussed it for several minutes. Finally, one of them made a conclusive comment, to which all nodded in agreement.

"What did he say?" the journalist asked the translator.

"He agreed completely, you need many tools in your toolbox. You must have rags, gasoline, a lighter or matches, and of course the bottle."

Tomislav shows me a video from the Thessaloniki protests. "The European Union summit was happening over there, on the other side of the railcar containers they stacked to block us," he says, pointing to the left of the screen. "Police lined up in their stormtrooper gear here, and here, and all along on the other side too." The containers were stacked ten meters (30 feet) tall along the entrances to the town. Tomislav fast-forwards to a scene in the center of the city. A phalange of broad shoulders capped with balaclava masks runs forward and collides with police blocking a street, framed in a tear-gas cloud. Batons swing down on balaclavas; rocks and bottles fly into the police mob. The cops gradually retreat out of view. Tomislav again advances the tape. Flames lick the trim of a jagged bank window. A line of police lean against a wall, awaiting orders. One black-clad, gas-masked youth paces in front of the camera and tosses a molotov at the police. Two in the line are swallowed in flame until another shoots them with an extinguisher. The police pull themselves up and step forward in loose rank. One tosses a concussion grenade at the camera as an afterthought.

"Everyone looks kind of bored," I offer.

"Yeah, well, it's kind of routine in Greece," says Tomislav.

WALKING PAST ANOTHER STAND SELLING "AMERICAN SNACK" chips, I wonder—is it simple to talk about Greek anti-American sentiment when people so prefer American Snack over Greek

Snack? Even here, where the majority hasn't forgotten the American support for the fascists who dominated the country for years, America is already the great Other of hope, not understood but with its own mysterious logic, a kind of sense that must promise success more than the familiar poverty and dysfunction. Like the omnipresent absurd T-shirts spouting mystery in international English, hope is articulated locally as American Other. Snack as spiritual revelation of the overdetermined failure of global homogeneity.

I NOD AND FLASH A SMILE AS I PASS THE YOUTH IN LONG black sleeves with a chaos-star necklace. He returns a nervous yet warm smile. He is more friendly than I expected from what I take to be my first Greek metalhead. Having no one to pass the time with on the ferry, I finally approach him and his friends, who eye me nervously. Their style is difficult to locate. I ask for a light, and we walk together to the smoking lounge.

"Speak English?" I ask, and the metalhead nods and returns another sweet smile. They sit down in the corner with a dinner of bread, feta, and cigarettes, and insist that I share it with them. We eat together in friendly awkwardness. "So, what music do you listen to?" I ask the metalhead.

"Music?" he asks back. "You know Madonna?"

"Certainly," I assure him.

"Do you like Michael Jackson?"

"Who doesn't like Michael Jackson?" I answer.

He is satisfied. "I like very much Michael Jackson. My friend is a very good dancer, he dances as good as Michael Jackson," he enthuses, pointing at the friend at his side. Then he points at his other friend, who shyly looks up and smiles before looking back down at his dinner. "He also likes Michael Jackson, he is a DJ, much good music." I am duly impressed and give the dancer and the DJ a respectful eyebrow raise. I also return to my dinner, not quite sure what to ask next.

"Greek?" the metalhead asks me.

I shake my head. Is he checking to make sure I don't speak Greek, or can he somehow not tell that I am not from here? "English, French, Spanish, Serbo-Croatian," I tick off on my fingers.

He nods, then returns, "Greek, German, French, Arabic."

"Arabic?" I ask. I did not expect Greek metalheads to speak Arabic. "How did you learn Arabic?" He looks at me, not sure what I am asking. I drop the subject. Dinner finished, the dancer motions towards the deck.

Outside, I realize the metalhead is tentatively translating the loudspeaker's announcements for his friends, who apparently don't speak Greek either. "I am from America. Are you from here?" I ask the metalhead. He responds in a firm whisper: "I am from Lebanon, my friends also."

"From Beirut?" I ask. He nods. "For work?" He looks at me, says flatly: "I have no house in Lebanon anymore, I came here years ago but now my asylum papers are expired. I cannot get new papers here. My friends just came here, but we don't want to stay in Greece. People here are very bad. Do you understand?" he stares in my eyes. I nod, yes, bad people, I can imagine.

After a long silence, I ask, "So, where are you traveling to now?"

"This, why we are here, we were getting out of Greece, but the border guard for Italy did not like our passports. Italy is much better than Greece, yes? You have been to Italy?" I try to assure him that Italy is beautiful, that he will love it when he gets there.

"You know, not all Arabs are Muslims, many like to dance, and drink, and have fun!" the DJ tells me as we walk from the ferry to our bus. Before I can figure out how to respond to that, he continues: "There are too many Arabs in America?" I violently shake my head and tell him, "No, no, not too many!" which seems to hurt his feelings a little. Later I realize he says "too many" to mean "many."

We all sit together in the back row of the bus. The metalhead pats my knee. "Five hundred euros, it's too much. You know how much I am paid at my job? Fifteen dollars every day." For a moment I raise my eyebrows; not bad by Macedonian standards, but then I remember he is not living in Macedonia. "For the passports, we had to work a very long time, and then look. I took mine back to him, very bad job! But he said, 'You paid for passports, I gave you passports.'" The metalhead pulls out his passport and hands it to me. Outside is a very worn Norwegian cover, but inside are folded crisp, thick, untouched pages, without a single country stamp. The obviously Norwegian names sits uncomfortably next to my olive-skinned friend in the photograph. I hand it back, and he is distracted, not smiling anymore. He addresses his friend sitting on my other side, who then hands me his passport with a wide smile. The condition of the cover—French—matches the worn pages inside, which boast a number of country stamps. In the front cover is my teenage friend's picture, and beside his photo the name "Juliette Toulouse," birthdate 38 years ago. I shake my head as I hand it back. He just smiles sweetly and shrugs.

We stare out the window into the night. "I am very unhappy here, Greece is a very bad place," my friend says. "Of course I cannot get into Italy with this passport. People in Greece are not good, money is not good." He looks in my eyes until he is sure I understand. His misery strains through his eyes. "I think I will kill myself if I cannot leave." His voice is cracking. I try to assure him that in time he will make it to Italy, but can't think of any reason he should believe me. He suddenly starts, and looks firmly at me. "Can I ask you a favor? If I only had the proper numbers, if I could only copy the stamps inside, a man I know could make a very good passport. Could I borrow your passport, only for one day?" I look down. "You can come with us to our town. If you want, you can come later. Look for people who look like us." He pauses to think. "Look for people with bad clothes. Ask them where is Said's store. I will be there. Please come soon."

"If I lose my passport, I cannot get another, and I will never be able to leave America," I tell him. "This one is temporary, so the numbers would not be good for you."

He keeps looking at me with hope. "It's OK," he assures me, "they will be good enough."

"No, I'm sorry," I say. "I can't."

"No problem, my friend, I will find something," he says, and pats me on my knee. We look back out the window.

The bus slows, and its lights go on as I awaken. Darkness still fills the window; we are obviously not in any town. The front door opens and three uniformed men climb into the aisle.

"Border police," the metalhead whispers to me.

"But we're nowhere near the border!" I whisper back. He shrugs. I wake the friend on the other side and whisper, "Passport!" He groggily stares, then whispers back as he comes to, "Not passport!" with a shaking finger. The police make their way slowly towards us, yelling and waving papers at every row, until each time the pleading Greek voices cajole the officials into returning their papers. They call in several numbers to the central station before handing them back to their holders. Finally, they reach us. I hand the cop my passport, which he flips through, back to front, over and over. He stops at one page, points at the Yugoslav visa. "Tourist," I shrug. He stares hard at me, then hands me my passport.

The metalhead hands a sheet of paper, hand-typed, with his photograph on it, to the official. The official glances over it then hands it back. The dancer and the DJ do the same. The official checks their photographs with their faces, then returns the papers, bored, and walks off the bus.

"Look, this is the expiration date," says the metalhead, pointing to the corner of his paper. The date is two years past. The bus starts up and accelerates onto the road. The dancer falls asleep with his head on my shoulder as I stare out at the night. When I wake up, they are gone.

CHRISTINA TAKES A BREAK FROM TYPING CAMUS INTO HER website to grab another coffee. "You know, we have skinheads here as well. They're usually very into religion, hyper-Orthodox. Do you know the church owns something like a third of the land in Greece? Some of the skinheads are even pagans, like worshiping Zeus and everything, always saying things about Plato, Solon, Homer. Of course, they would never admit that Achilles was gay."

> "The attitude of the Greeks towards the whole question of ethnicity is perhaps the most retrogressive in the entire Balkan region. It by law denies the existence of any ethnic group other than Greek in its country and is aggressive in combating any efforts by individuals or budding organizations to claim otherwise... Several years ago, the Greek government protested vigorously to the US Embassy because one of its diplomats in Thessaloniki agreed to meet with a political 'dissident' claiming Bulgarian origin and suffering intense discrimination as a result...
> *"Despite relative tranquility, a great deal of voluntary ethnic cleansing continues to go on [within Greece], with ... ethnic groups moving from areas in which they are in the minority to places where they are in the majority. ... Greece's action [in blocking MK from NATO membership] is helping to drive one more wedge between these groups, as well as raising nationalistic tensions in a country—and region—which absolutely needs exactly the opposite if it ever is going to stabilize."*

> — WILLIAM MONTGOMERY, "PLAYING WITH FIRE", 11 MAY 2008, B92.NET

NEXT TO ME ON THE FLOOR OF THE BLACK CAT SQUAT IN Thessaloniki, three punk kids are sleeping. As we wake up, I try to place their accent. German?

"Hebrew." I realized I should have known from the black-and-white checkered scarf around one of their necks. "I wear a *keffiya* to piss off other Israelis," says Rebeka, in perfect English with a thick London accent. She explains that her mother is English, and her father moved to Israel from Zimbabwe. Besides Hebrew and English, she speaks Arabic fluently, which she tells me is an easy language to master. "Maybe if Hebrew is your first fucking language," I tease.

Her friend Itai wears a denim jacket with "21" written huge across the back. That night over drinks, he explains, "It's the number rating you get when you fail the psychiatric and physical tests for the army, the worst rating you can get. People at home get pretty mad when they see my jacket, beat me up. Fuck 'em." I ask Itai about the Israeli officers who refuse to serve in the West Bank, the "Refuseniks," but he's not impressed by them. "If you're against the war, why would you be in the army in the first place, conscription or not?"

They tell me about getting jumped by Nazi skinheads during their first afternoon in Bulgaria. One of them still boasts a purple eye from the encounter. "He just came out of nowhere, just because we're punks, he didn't even know we're Israelis." Their hosts didn't allow them to leave the anarchist office without a large escort of anti-fascist skinheads for the rest of their stay. I take a mental note to save Bulgaria for another trip.

A year later, I read on the Internet site of Anarchists Against the Wall, "On March 12, Itai L. was injured in Hirbata. The [Israeli] army simply fired rubber bullets like crazy. Itai was standing in front and talking to the soldiers by megaphone. At every demonstration we talk to the soldiers by megaphone and tell them that this is a quiet demonstration of Palestinians, Israelis and internationals. While Itai was talking on the megaphone he took a rubber bullet between his nose and his left eye." He spent several months in the hospital recovering.[135]

SIPPING MY *RAKOMELO*—HOT *RAKIJA* WITH HONEY, A CLOVE on the bottom of each glass, lit with a healthy blue flame, traditionally extinguished by hand—I decide that civilization still exists here after all, even if Greece is in the EU. My conclusion is con-

firmed by the proliferation of *kafeneions* full of old people arguing and playing cards, young people arguing and flirting. People
still slap tables and chairs down in the middle of narrow streets
and get down to life's business of the *dialektik*. We are joined by
Dragonslayer, known as such for his job cleaning "dragon" fungus
off trees in a nearby national park.

"I hear you are writing a book on anarchists in the Balkans?"
he asks. Dragonslayer was once an anarchist, and was involved
in the Greek situationist movement in the '70s, until it was
smashed. "The ideology of the anarchists, the cultural borders
with which they go to great care to set themselves apart from
everyone else," says Dragonslayer, "isolates them from everyday
life, which is the only grounds for radical change. If you are
writing a book on the Balkans, you must write about history."

"That's all that anyone talks about when they talk about
the Balkans, as if they don't have a present or future," I say.
"Everyone I meet is tired of talking about tradition. 'Tradition
here is Patriarchy,' my Serbian friend Maja told me, tradition
is the watchword of the nationalists. She told me she doesn't
have an ethnicity, she doesn't want one."

"OK," says Dragonslayer, "but if you are writing about these
anarchists in Romania, in Macedonia, you must know history to
know why they are anarchists. You know about the Bektashi?"
I shake my head. "You know of the Alevi, to which perhaps
one third of Turkey adheres? Bektashi is the dervish, monastic
order of the Alevi. It proclaimed equality of the sexes in the
fourteenth century, and the women still won't wear the veil. It's
an antinomian sect, if you know about antinomianism—the only
real law is that which is revealed through your own heart. They
formed such a massive anti-state movement in the nineteenth
century, even becoming the official religion of the Ottoman
army, that they were outlawed and exiled to the outskirts of the
empire, Albania. Bektashi almost became the state religion of
Albania. It had to go underground when Hoxha made religion
illegal, but they're still around. I think they moved to Detroit.
The anarchists, the revolutionary Marxists, and other anti-state
revolutionaries in Turkey now, they're all Alevi, even if they
don't realize. It's a culture of resistance."

"I read something about them in Turkish novelist Orhan
Pamuk's *The Black Book*.[136] Did you say Detroit?"

"And the Bogomil," he says. "They were brought in the seventh century to Bulgaria, something like an anarcho-communist army, all across northeast Asia Minor, 'Pavlikians' as people called them then. 'Spirit is God and matter is Satan,' which didn't work so well with Jesus as God in the flesh. They smashed all the armies of the Byzantine empire for about three centuries. They even made it as far as southern France, where people called them 'Cathari.'"

"Yeah, yeah, or Patareni," I break in, "the name of the first grindcore punk band, from Zagreb in '81."

"So the Bogomil and the Bektashi were popular here because they were Muslims and Christians at the same time, and at the same time heretical and unique, neither Islamic nor Christian. Then you have the Gnoramraki in Cyprus, the majority of Muslims there, who are actually Christian/Muslim hybrids. Under the British they would go to both churches and mosques, before things were polarized nationalistically."

"How do you know all this, Dragonslayer?"

"I'm a musician, I play with Turkish musicians."

"Do you play Rembetika music?"

"Of course. You know how Rembetika was born? After Kemal Ataturk created Turkey as a nation-state out of the leftovers of the Ottoman Empire, Greece and Turkey decided the best way to legitimate their modern statehood was to exchange Turkey's large 'Greek,' i.e. Christian population, for Greece's 'Turk,' i.e. Muslim population. Forcibly exchange, since most of the people were happy where they were. The Ottoman Empire was too multi-cultural to fit into modern Europe."

"Just like in the '90s. This area, old 'Turkish Europe,' is *still* too multi-cultural for modern Western politics."

"Evidently. Suddenly, Athens had two million homeless and unemployed 'Greeks' off the boat, many of whom didn't speak Greek. Rembetika was born from their culture, a criminal culture, since they didn't have a place in Greek society. All the songs are about prostitution, guns, heroin. The music was declared illegal, but they kept playing it. They even played it on mini-*Bazukis*, so the musician could stick it up his sleeve when the cops came in. You ever heard of Katsaros? He's maybe the best Rembetis. He lived to be 107 years old. Spent his youth visiting expatriate Greeks around Asia. One of his most famous Rembetika songs is about leaving his soul in Arizona."

"Arizona?!"

"Where else?"

"YOU HAVE NO IDEA WHAT IS GOING ON, THERE IS SIMPLY NO way to describe it."

On December 6, 2008, a member of the Special Forces police kills unarmed fifteen-year-old anarchist Alexandros Grigoropoulos in the Eksarhia neighborhood of Athens. Riots erupt in 26 cities around Greece. Within days, 800 high schools and most of the country's universities are occupied by their students, and central Athens has nearly burned to the ground. At one count, twenty-five police stations are simultaneously "under siege by school students." five thousand students march on parliament, chanting, "Shoot us too!" Just as in the days of the military dictatorship, armed fascist thugs work with police, knifing and beating many on the sidestreets, chanting, "Anarchists, sons of whores!" Konstantina Kuneva, "a migrant cleaner and militant union organizer at the Athens Piraeus Electric Railway (ISAP), had sulphuric acid thrown at her face as she was returning home from work. She is still in critical condition."

Soon, despite the repression, huge numbers of workers and residents of all stripes have joined in, notably migrants. Workers occupy the offices of Greece's main labor union, GSEE, and hang a giant anarcho-syndicalist flag from its balcony, calling for an indefinite general strike. The police soon exhaust their entire supply of tear gas—4,600 canisters—and have to wait for new supplies. Town halls in Athens, Thessaloniki, Patras, and other towns are occupied by local residents, who declare social war. Scores of television and radio stations are occupied, including the state television station, students hold up banners reading, "Stop watching—Everyone to the streets!" Greece burns for eighteen long days, then decides to regroup for a longer struggle.

Hundreds of solidarity actions take place around the world. In the midst of the Israeli massacres on Gaza in following weeks, the People's Front for the Liberation of Palestine issues a special call to "the Greek movement" to halt American arms shipments to the Israeli army, routed through Greek ports.

IN THE WORDS OF JOURNALIST URI GORDON IN THE MAINSTREAM Israeli newspaper *Ha'aretz*[137]:

The corporate press has trotted out various theories to explain the cause of the unrest—frustration with a corrupt government, the global financial crisis, and discontent among Greece's youth, who face meager prospects of secure employment or welfare rights—the riots being a blind reaction to objective conditions. But all these explanations are in fact decoys intended to silence and ignore the rebels' own declared motivations...

These are no single-issue protests or vague grievances. This is full-blooded revolutionary anarchism. The mainstream media simply cannot stomach the notion that what is happening in Greece is by now a proactive social revolt against the capitalist system itself and the state institutions that reinforce it. It is time to acknowledge that the Greek anarchist movement has successfully seized the initiative after the killing of one of its own, framing the issues in a way that appeals to a larger—albeit mostly young—public. Few people realize that the Greek anarchist movement is appreciably the largest in the world, in proportion to its country's population. It also enjoys wide social support due to its legacy of resistance to the military dictatorship from 1967 to 1974. Highly confrontational demonstrations are a matter of regularity in Greece. It is practically a bimonthly occurrence for anarchists and police to engage in fiery street battles in Thessaloniki or Athens. The current events are only marked by their breadth and duration, not by their level of militancy. Another rarely appreciated factor is that Greece is a country in which the security apparatus is normally kept on a relatively tight leash. For example, Privacy International's 2007 assessment of leading surveillance societies found Greece to be the only country in the world with "adequate safeguards" against the abuse of government power to spy on its citizenry. The legacy of the dictatorship has created a lasting image of the police as inherently oppressive, even among the middle class...

I SIT DUMB BACK IN THE STATES, TRYING TO REACH MY ZAGREB friend on the streets of Athens. The book is already past its deadline. I beg her to send me word of what is happening, but she can only tell me moments: Lines charging towards the police, molotovs in hand, as Ravel's Bolero pounds through the speakers of the Polytechnic University. A young Roma boy, chatting up a riot cop, then kicking him full-on in the balls. No one can narrate this, least of all someone who is living its reality, not one can explain what it all means, or pretend like it is already an event.

The following are all quotations from a blog named Occupied London, which she and many others on the streets of Athens have been writing for.

Quoting the 6th century Greek poet Pindar:

The nomos, sovereign of all mortals and immortals
Leads with the strongest hand
Doing violent to the most just.

FROM "GIRLS IN REVOLT":

When the cop shouts "hey, you", the subject to which this command is directed and which turns its body in the direction of authority (in the direction of the call of the cop) is innocent by default since it responds to the voice reproaching it as a product of authority. The moment when the subject disobeys this call and defies it, no matter how low-key this moment of disobedience might be (even if it didn't throw a molotov to the cop car but a water bottle) is a moment when authority loses its meaning and becomes something else: a breach that must be repaired. When the manly honour of the fascist-cop is insulted he may even kill in order to protect (as he himself will claim) his kids and his family. Moral order and male sovereignty—or else the most typical form of symbolic and material violence—made possible the assassination of Alexis; they proped the murder, produced its "truth" and made it a reality."

ANONYMOUS:

Urban space, from end to end, is recomposed into a thick burning network of heterotopia: the city is on fire."

FROM THE LOCAL EMPLOYEE'S COMMITTEE, OCCUPYING THE Agios Dimitrios town hall in Athens:

We are in Civil War: With the fascists, the bankers, the state, the media wishing to see an obedient society... The generation of the poor, the unemployed, the partially employed, the homeless, the migrants, the youth, is the generation that will smash every display window and will wake up the obedient citizens from their sleep of the ephemeral American dream.

Goodbye Alexandros, may your blood be the last of an innocent to run."

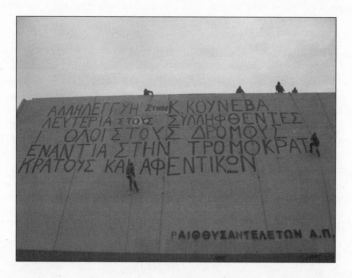

Graffiti at the Aristotle University, Thessaloniki: "Solidarity with K. Kuneva. Freedom to all the arrestees. Everyone to the streets, against the terrorism of the state and the bosses" (Photo from www.OccupiedLondon.org)

ANONYMOUS:

For what is democracy other than a system of discriminations and coercions in the service of property and privacy? And what are its rules, other than rules of negotiation of the right to own—the invisible rules of alienation? Freedom, rights equality, egalitarianism: all these dead ideological masks together cannot cover their mission: the generalisation and preservation of the social as an economic sphere, as a sphere where not only what you have produced but also what you are and what you can do are already alienated. The bourgeois, with a voice trembling from piety, promise: rights, justice, equality. And the revolted hear: repression, exploitation, looting. Democracy is the political system where everyone is equal in front of the guillotine of the spectacle-product. The only problem that concerned democrats, from Cromwell to Montesquieu, is what form of property is sufficient in order for someone to be recognised as a citizen, what kind of rights and obligations guarantee that they will never understand themselves as something beyond a private citizen. Everything else is no more than adjusting details of a regime in the service of capital.

Our despise for democracy does not derive from some sort of idealism but rather, from our very material animosity for a social entity where value and organising are centered around the product and the spectacle. The revolt was by definition also a revolt against property and alienation. Anyone that didn't hide behind the curtains of their privacy, anyone who was out on the streets, knows it only too well: Shops were looted not for computers, clothes or furniture to be resold but for the joy of destructing what alienates us: the spectacle of the product. Anyone who doesn't understand why someone delights in the sight of a destructed product is a merchant or a cop. The fires that warmed the bodies of the revolted in these long December nights were full of the liberated products of our toil, from the disarmed symbols of what used to be an almighty fantasy. We simply took what belonged to us and we threw it to the fire together with all its co-expressions. The grand potlatch of the past few days was also a revolt of desire against the imposed rule of scarcity. A revolt of the gift against the sovereignty of money. A revolt of the anarchy of use value against the democracy of exchange value. A revolt of spontaneous collective freedom against rationalised individual coercion.

ANONYMOUS:

No repressive project and no ideological attack managed or will manage to blackmail the return to normality and to impose social and class pacification. Nothing is the same any more! The surpassing of fear, of isolation and of the dominant social divisions, led thousands of young people, together with women and men of every age, refugees and migrants, workers and jobless to stand together in the streets and behind barricades fighting the tyrants of our life, our dignity and freedom. And this is a reality lighting with its flames the future of revolt, both its intensification and deepening, until the absolute subversion of the world of the bosses.

It is a spirit that is already spreading like fire: Municipal buildings and town halls are being occupied across Athens, and popular assemblies (λαϊκές συνελεύσεις) are being organised in neighbourhoods of both Athens and Thessaloniki. In what turns out to be one of the most positive aspects of the revolt, people are starting to take back their lives: street after street, square after square, neighbourhood after neighbourhood. This is not about a government falling, about some "justice" being paid, about a mere meeting of some demands, a vindication of some sort. The people on the streets demand nothing; they occupy, they organise among themselves, they know that there is no way back to normality, that fighting this very normality is, quite literally, a matter of life and death.

From the students occupying the Athens School of Economics:

Against the supposedly peaceful caricatures of bourgeois media ("violence is unacceptable always, everywhere"), we can only cachinnate: their rule, the rule of gentle spirits and consent, of dialogue and harmony is nothing but a well-calculated pleasure in beastliness: a promised carnage. The democratic regime in its peaceful façade doesn't kill an Alex every day, precisely because it kills thousands of Ahmets, Fatimas, JorJes, Jin Tiaos and Benajirs: because it assassinates systematically, structurally and without remorse the entirety of the third world, that is the global proletariat. It is in this way, through this calm everyday slaughter, that the idea of freedom is born: freedom not as a supposedly panhuman good, nor as a natural right for all, but as the war cry of the damned, as the premise of civil war.

The history of the legal order and the bourgeois class brainwashes us with an image of gradual and stable progress of humanity within which violence stands as a sorry exception stemming from the economically, emotionally and culturally underdeveloped. Yet all of us who have been crushed between school desks, behind offices, in factories, know only too well that history is nothing but a succession of bestial acts installed upon a morbid system of rules. The cardinals of normality weep for the law that was violated from the bullet of the pig Korkoneas (the killer cop). But who doesn't know that the force of the law is merely the force of the powerful? That it is law itself that allows for violence to be exercised on violence? The law is void from end to bitter end; it contains no meaning, no target other than the coded power of imposition.

Anonymous:

Last night, the stage of the national theater was occupied by around 100 people, who held a banner reading, "Everyone to the streets!" A text was passed through the audience, including the phrase, "You've deactivated your cell phones, it's about time you activated your consciousness!" The cast and director refused to continue the play, in solidarity with our struggle. Once hitting the streets, the crowd quickly formed an impromptu demonstration through central Athens. Yesterday, a similar action took place at the Athens concert hall.

From the Athens Haunt of Albanian Migrants:

Now is time for the street to talk: The deafening scream heard is for the 18 years of violence, repression, exploitation and humiliation. These days are ours, too.

These days are for the hundreds of migrants and refugees who were murdered at the borders, in police stations, workplaces. They are for those murdered by cops or "concerned citizens." They are for those murdered for daring to cross the border, working to death, for not bowing their head, or for nothing. They are for Gramos Palusi, Luan Bertelina, Edison Yahai, Tony Onuoha, Abdurahim Edriz, Modaser Mohamed Ashtraf and so many others that we haven't forgotten.

These days are for the everyday police violence that remains unpunished and unanswered. They are for the humiliations at the border and at the migrant detention centres, which continue to date. They are for the crying injustice of the Greek courts, the migrants and refugees unjustly in prison, the justice we are denied. Even now, in the days and nights of the uprising, the migrants pay a heavy toll—what with the attacks of far-righters and cops, with deportations and imprisonment sentences that the courts hand out with Christian love to us infidels.

These days are for the toil and the blood of our parents, for informal labour, for the endless shifts. They are for the deposits and the adhesive stamps, the welfare contributions we paid and will never have recognised. It is for the papers we will be chasing for the rest of our lives like a lottery ticket.

These days are for the price we have to pay simply in order to exist, to breathe. They are for all those times when we crunched our teeth, for the insults we took, the defeats we were charged with. They are for all the times when we didn't react even when having all the reasons in the world to do so. They are for all the times when we did react and we were alone because our deaths and our rage did not fit pre-existing shapes, didn't bring votes in, didn't sell in the prime-time news.

These days belong to all the marginalised, the excluded, the people with the difficult names and the unknown stories. They belong to all those who die every day in the Aegean sea and Evros river, to all those murdered at the border or at a central Athens street; they belong to the Roma in Zefyri, to the drug addicts in Eksarhia. These days belong to the kids of Mesollogiou street, to the unintegrated, the uncontrollable students. Thanks to Alexis, these days belong to us all.

ANONYMOUS:

If something scares us it is the return to normality. For in the destroyed and pillaged streets of our cities of light we see not only the obvious results of our rage, but the possibility of starting to live. We have no longer anything to do than to install ourselves in this possibility transforming it into a living experience: by grounding on the field of everyday life, our creativity, our power to materialise our desires, our power not to contemplate but to construct the real. This is our vital space. All the rest is death.

ANONYMOUS:

Last night, I met a friend of Alexandros' who was sitting close to him when he was assassinated. Standing there silently, listening to him describe the moments of the assassination (for the n-th time I imagine) I couldn't help but think: How many years did this kid grow over these seven days? Listening to him explain exactly how the cop is now attempting to cover up the story, how the ricocheting scenario can't possibly stand... Seeing him argue how we need to change our tactics to take our struggle forward. Joking with us about the incapacity of the indymedia servers to hold the incoming traffic in the first days of the revolt. How many years did he grow? I can't help but think; they took 15 years from Alexandros, but years and years of life were transplanted into all of us who are here now. In these days of revolt, normalilty and normal time have been suspended—finally giving us ample time in which to live and grow. For this reason, as for a million others, there is simply no way back now: time can't move backward, what we have lived cannot be unlived. "Remember this", I heard the old man telling his grandson at the spontaneous mural for Alexandros at the spot of his assassination. "Remember that it is always authority killing the people, it is always the powerful who kill the powerless". The kid will never forget this week, none of us will. This is the longest week of our lives.

THE PLACE BEHIND YOUR EYES

SUNFLOWERS CARPET THE EARTH TO THE HORIZON AS THE TRAIN SHUD-DERS ALONG THE BENT TRACKS. THE ONLY TIME I WAS ON A TRAIN IN BULGARIA BEFORE, DURING THE NATO BOMBING IN 1999, I WAS TOO TRAVEL-WEARY TO GET OFF, AND THE ONLY BULGARIAN I MET WAS AN OLDER SCARF-HEADED PEASANT WOMAN WHO SAT DOWN NEXT TO ME. SHE LAUNCHED INTO LONG A CONVERSATION AND REFUSED TO ACKNOWLEDGE MY "I DON'T UNDERSTANDS." I FINALLY GIVE IN, NODDED MY HEAD, AND SAID, "DA!" TO WHATEVER SHE WAS TELLING ME. AFTER A LONG SERIES OF "DA'S," SHE LOOKED AT ME, APPARENTLY AFTER HAVING OBTAINED MY CONSENT, AND PLUNGED HER WET LIPS ONTO MY NECK. WHEN I GET UP AND SIT DOWN ON THE OTHER SIDE OF THE TRAIN CAR, SHE LOOKS CONFUSED AT MY REACTION, SHRUGS, AND LOOKS OUT THE WINDOW WITH A SMILE. AT HER STATION, SHE WAVES A CHEERFUL GOODBYE.

"SMASH CAPITALISM," AND "STOP RACISM" ARE SPRAY-PAINTED in English, between circle-A anarchy signs on the walls of small-town train stations that we chug through. The man standing next to me, smoking out the window in the train isle, reads my mind as we pass another massive gutted factory complex and offers, "like from war!" Perhaps the Yugoslav army got lost during one of their ventures, and just kept blowing up everything out of habit. I keep having to remind myself that Bulgaria hasn't seen war since WWII, and that what are euphemistically called "post-communist transitional economics" were the shells for this devastation. This stretch of decaying industry strikes me as the most literal meaning of "post-modern." The man smoking good-humoredly explains that he used to travel, working for a shipping company, and once owned two houses, a couple cars, and some land. Now, he says with a mild smile, "I don't have anything. It is a very bad position here," he explains, "all corruption, no work."

In Sofia, I check my bags and wander between the train station and downtown. I purchase another sim-card for my cell phone—my eighth card in the last month over 500 miles, since each country charges 20 times the normal rate to use cards from any of the neighboring countries. By contrast, all of western Europe accepts the same card. But I still don't have any contacts for the anarchists here, so I wander the streets to scan the telephone poles for posters.

A few minutes from the main station, a young cop stands in the middle of the sidewalk before me, preoccupied with some paperwork he is shuffling through. As I near him, we seem bound to collide, so I proffer a friendly "dober dan," or good afternoon, with a nod. He jumps, nearly drops his papers, and practically screams, "Dokumenti! Pasos!" As I dig for my passport, he stares me over nervously, as if I am about to detonate the two of us into a giant fireball. Apparently, people here don't often exchange greetings with police. Unable to trace the origin of my madness in the pages of my passport, he finally allows me to go, still visibly upset by my greeting. At the next intersection, I try not to stare into the one-way mirrors that line the elevated police booth, sullenly glaring down on the street from inside their rusty eyelids.

Farther down, shining new boutiques line both sides of the avenue. I could suddenly be in Paris. Cafes teem with leisurely patrons sipping machine-pressed espressos. Polished storefronts offer a wide selection of sophisticated, if a few decades out of date, fashions. The dome of an ancient orthodox church sits sunken beneath a central traffic circle awash with taxis. Friends in Croatia warned me to only accept rides from one taxi company, but later I was warned that many taxis counterfeit the logo of this one reputable company. In a little bookstore in the subterranean mall adjoining the central church, I pick up an English translation of Bulgaria's most famous novel, Ivan Vazov's "Under the Yoke."

As evening falls, a woman in her early 20's approaches me near the station, with a cute skater boy trailing behind her, and asks if I have a telephone she can use. As soon as the other party answers, she begins crying, as if on cue. I make out that she is saying she is sorry, so sorry, she has never been so sorry, but she really needs the money... she screams her friend's name into the phone, and again, until she is sure that her friend has hung up. "Excuse me, can I use your phone for another call?" Of course. She calls again and her friend hangs up before she can finish a sentence. She calls again and the friend doesn't even pick up. She shrugs and hands me back my phone. "So," she smiles, "What do you do for fun? Do you party? I mean, besides drink," she says, pointing to the plastic bottle in my hand, half-full of water, which she assumes to be rakija. "Do you want to party?" I am bored and lonely after walking in circles all day, but hesitate, as her phrase often carries troublesome connotations the world over. Her boyfriend is cheerfully flipping me the bird and pointing at her, with a look of expectation. She invites him over and introduces him, her boyfriend. I shake his hand, which I notice, a bit late, to be sticky. The couple look like models from the cover of *Thrasher* magazine, if a bit unslept. He hugs me, I hug him back, and he whispers in my ear, "You want to fuck this bitch? She's a real bitch!" I slap my hand on his shoulder and tell him that's his job, and tell them I have to get back to my friend's house.

A few blocks away, my phone rings. The voice on the other end sadly asks repeatedly for the girl, and I attempt to explain in Serbian, perhaps close enough to Bulgarian, that I have left her at the train station but perhaps she is still there. The friend seems to understand, sadly thanks me, and hangs up.

Further down the main street, a woman with striking eyes

and dangerous curves sprouting from her jeans is walking the other direction on the sidewalk, directly in front of me. I veer to the left just as she does, then we both veer to the right, about to collide. Suddenly, she has her arm in mine. "Sex!" she exclaims happily. We trot down the sidewalk. "Sex?" she directs towards me, in a querying tone. I shrug as we keep walking. "Sex!" she yells in demand. Still walking down the sidewalk, I shake my head with an apologetic smile. "Sex..." she pouts. "Zasto?" "Why?" She whines, and I keep walking, unable to attempt a response, other than my friendly smile. She stomps off, pissed.

I finally decide that I am not going to meet a friendly host on the streets of Sofia today, and check into a youth hostel.

ON PAGE 68 OF "UNDER THE YOKE," I READ THE FOLLOWING passage of life in Bulgaria under Ottoman rule:

> "[A]long with all its evils, oppression has one privilege, it makes people merry. Where the arena of political and spiritual activity is closed with lock and key, where the appetite for rapidly acquired wealth has nothing to arouse it, and great ambitions find no scope for development, society expends its energies on petty local and personal intrigues, and seeks for consolation and distraction, which it finds in the small, ordinary, and easy benefits of life. A flask of wine, drunk in the cool shade of the willows by the babbling, crystal-clear river, makes one forget thraldom; a hotchpotch, baked with red tomatoes, fragrant parsley and hot peppers, eaten on the grass under the hanging branches through which you see the blue sky high above, is a kingdom in itself, and if there are fiddlers, it is the height of earthly bliss. Enslaved people have their own philosophy which reconciles them to life. An irremediably ruined man often ends with a bullet in his brain, or in the noose of a rope. A people enslaved, no matter how hopelessly, never commits suicide; it eats, drinks and begets children. It makes merry. Look at the folk-songs in which the people's soul, life and outlook are so strikingly reflected. There, intertwined with the black cares, long chains, dark dungeons and festering wounds, you will be regaled with fat roast lambs, ruby-red wines, burning brandy, merry weddings, winding dances, green forests and dense shades, from which a whole ocean of songs has sprung."

SITTING WITH MY FRIEND CHRIS IN A BUSTLING CAFE SHADOWED by Byzantine columns in the beautiful ancient city of Plovdiv,

I hang up my cell phone again after trying, unsuccessfully, to reach my one anarchist contact in Bulgaria for maybe the two-hundredth time. I am happy to finally be here, I guess, but am somehow not doing my job if I leave Bulgaria without meeting the anarchists here, in the country in the Balkans with the deepest anarchist tradition. Depressed, I open my book.

In Vazov's novel, written 130 years ago, I find mention of Bakunin, the founder of modern anarchism. Two characters debate the form of Bulgaria's liberation, one espousing social struggle and the other national struggle, "on the eve of the Liberation," in a conversation one might still overhear in this very cafe:

"You tell me it is necessary to undertake this struggle," Kandov went on ... , "because its aim is freedom. Freedom? What kind of freedom is it to have a prince again, that is, a little sultan, civil servants to rob us, monks and priests to grow fat on our backs, and an army to drain the very life of the people? Is that your freedom? I wouldn't give a drop of blood from my little finger for it!"

"But listen, Mr. Kandov," Nedkovich answered, "I too respect your principles, but they have no place here. What we need above all is political freedom, that is, to be ourselves the masters of our land and our fate."

Kandov shook his head in dissent.

"But just now you explained things differently to me. You appoint new masters for yourselves who are to replace the old ones. Because you don't want the Sheikh-ul-Islam, you embrace another who bears the name of exarch, that is you change tyrants for despots. You impose chiefs upon the people and destroy every idea of equality; you consecrate the right to exploitation of the weak by the strong, of labour by capital. Give your struggle a more contemporary, more human aim; make it a struggle not only against Turkish oppression, but for the triumph of contemporary principles as well, that is for the destruction of the stupid customs hallowed by age-old prejudices, such as a throne, religion, the right to property, and of the fist, which human folly has raised to the level of inviolable principles. Read Herzen, gentlemen, Bakunin, Lassalle... Rid yourselves of this narrow-minded patriotism and raise the banner of modern reasonable humanity and sober science. Then I'm with you."

"The ideas you express," replied Ognyanov with animation, "merely prove how widely read you are, but they are a deucedly eloquent sign of your ignorance of the Bulgarian question. Under such a banner you'd find yourself alone, the people wouldn't understand it. Observe, Mr. Kandov, that there's only one reasonable and possible aim we can present to them: the breaking of the Turkish yoke."(p. 70)

The irony that anarchism is too "modern" for Bulgaria is more evident than ever now, when a significant percent of the population still votes for a return of the monarchy. Such realism allowed an oppressive and ultimately pro-fascist monarchy to drive out the Turks, then a colonizing Moscow-dominated communism to drive out the fascists, then a merciless "transition" of austerity-measure capitalism to drive out the communists. Will Bulgarians ever stop being so ground down by realistic options? And where the hell are these anarchists?

FINALLY, I GIVE UP, AFTER TWO WEEKS AND SEVERAL HUNDRED unconnected calls to my one anarchist contact in Sofia. Fine, no fucking problem, I'll just write a book about anarchism in the Balkans without saying anything about Bulgaria, the country that—like Spain—would probably have become an anarchist society if Moscow (and the local Fascists) hadn't mowed down the massive indigenous Anarchist movements in and after World War II. My phone buzzes with a text message from Serbia—"If you can't find Magdalena, here's Nikola's number. And none of your Californian post-modern bullshit, our Bulgarian comrades believe in class struggle." Touché. Nikola answers his phone after the first ring.

"We think anarchism is for normal people, so we don't dress like weirdos," Nikola explains. He has just stepped out from a gathering of the local anarchist group, so he can take me to meet everybody right away. As we approach, I am a bit surprised to see them throwing down b-ball skills on an after-hours high-school court, itself lined with Fascist graffiti. I once again appreciate Eastern Europe's breadth of political spectrum. "We also don't have a problem with sports," clarifies Nikola. I begin to feel a revolutionary guilt for being such a nerd, and excuse myself from the game on the basis of my bad shoes.

Nikola points to members of the opposing team, who are apparently members of a local left-communist youth group. "Kronstadt! Kronstadt!" I yell for the anarchists. Nikola whispers that everyone calls the bushy-bearded lead communist player "Che," which he pretends to mind, but is obviously flattered by the comparison.

At the bar after the game, the victorious anarchists fill me in on their movement's proud history. Before World War II, the Anarchist movement was the third most popular in the country, after the Communists and the Bulgarian Land Worker People's Union; it was the third largest Anarchist movement in all of Europe, in one of Europe's smallest countries. Bulgaria's greatest poet, Hristan Botov, was an active anarchist, though history books now describe him as a "national liberationist." Anarchist resistance during WWII waged bloody guerrilla war both with the occupying Nazis, and against the Communist-Bulgarian Fascist coalition. Anarchists were a central part of the Bulgarian resistance to Nazism, which was strong enough that it—unique to all of Europe—refused to deport any of its 48,000 Jews to concentration camps. But despite their long, fierce resistance to Fascism—because of it—Bulgarian Anarchists were arrested and interned in concentration camps by the Communists after the war, 600 in 1948 alone.

"This is the movement we are working to resurrect."

Had Bulgaria entered the Federation of Yugoslavia, and a Balkan Federation independent of Moscow, history might have gone differently. Georgi Dimitrov, the communist leader of Bulgaria after WWII, publicly cooperated with Stalin, while quietly working together with Tito and the Romanian leadership to form an independent Balkan Federation, with Bulgaria to be included in Yugoslavia. Shortly after Tito's break with Stalin, Dimitrov mysteriously died during a diplomatic visit to Russia. He was poisoned. Dimitrov had also made himself unpopular in some quarters by insisting that the people of Blagoevgrad Province—the area Macedonians claim as a third of historic Macedonia called "Pirin Macedonia"—had the right to call themselves Macedonians, and not have Bulgarian identity forced upon them.

Back at the home of my new host Gogo, I look up an article on the history of Bulgarian Anarchism by South African Anarcho-Communist veteran Michael Schmidt. Although anarchism had—as Vazov's book shows—the first large-scale groups formed in 1909–1910. Quoting Grancharoff:

> Anarchism succeeded in becoming a popular movement and it penetrated many layers of society from workers, youth and students to teachers and public servants. The underground illegal activities of the movement continued [despite govern-

ment repression.]' ... [The Federation of Bulgarian Anarcho-Communists] consisted of syndicalist, guerrilla, professional and youth sections which diversified themselves throughout Bulgarian society. During the 1919/1920 transport strike, the anarchists planned to arm the workers, but the strike was betrayed by the leftist political parties and savagely crushed. ... Delegates reported that the working class of Yambol itself, of Kyustendil and Radomir to the west of Sofia, of the central village of Nova Zagora and the southern city of Khaskovo, and of Kilifarevo and Delebets were almost wholly affiliated to the anarchist movement and that great progress was being made in Sofia, the southern city of Plovdiv, the Black Sea port of Burgas, Rusee and other centres. ... [A] group of anarcho-communists from Khaskovo had been organising among the peasant tobacco farms in the district, making use of traditional old rural mutual aid co-operatives called Vlassovden (after the feast-day of Vlas, an old pagan god.) ... 'Vlassovden syndicalism' spread like wildfire and by 1931, the Vlassovden Confederation boasted 130 sections. ... "[I]n Bulgaria's first May Day celebration [in 1931], the police attacked an anarchist student ... meeting and arrested eleven students. The BOSF [Bulgarian Federation of Anarchist Students] demanded an end to clerical control of education and military recruitment on campus, demanding that 'the priests and sergeants major be expelled from schools and universities and taxes abolished. ...

An example of a typical Bulgarian anarchist of this period is found in the police file (compiled later under Soviet occupation) of the miner, farmhand and locomotive fitter Alexander Metodiev Nakov (1919–1962), who came from a poor family in the village of Kosatcha in the department of Pernik. Becoming an anarchist in 1937, Nakov launched an anarcho-syndicalist group in the Machinostroitel factory in Pernik and was later to serve time in both a fascist prison and a Soviet concentration camp. The Stalinist police described him despairingly as 'a fanatical anarchist'—but also a 'fine worker,' with 'a good overall political grounding' who was well-read and an Esperantist. At the outbreak of the Spanish Revolution in 1936, some 30 Bulgarian anarchists including Grigoriev went to fight in the militia. Grigoriev represented the FAKB at the CNT-FAI congress in free Spain in November that year. The revolutionary challenge to fascism finally forced the dispersed anarchist movement to rally again at the FAKB's final pre-war congress, held at Vitosha in August 1936. Despite their many jailings in concentration camps, the anarchists also managed to circulate the mimeographed *Khleb i Svoboda* (Bread and Freedom) during 1936–1939. In 1938, the BKP attempted to appeal to a broader audience, renaming itself the Bulgarian Workers' Party (BRP), until reverting to its Stalinist colours in 1948. Returning to Bulgaria in 1939, Grigoriev was arrested and spent the war years in prison then a concentration camp."

The Anarchist movement, including Anarcho-communists, felt little affinity with state communism. "With a few exceptions, anarchists had not accepted the Soviet Union as being a socialist country. And their argument was cogent: 'In Russia as everywhere else, there is capitalism. It is stupid to think that the latter can exist without being defended by a government [even if in] Russia, this government is referred to as proletarian.' ... The Platform of the Federation of Anarchist Communists of Bulgaria ... repudiated fascism, democracy, the state and capital, and reaffirmed an anarchist communist mass line of the total eradication of private property and the full socialisation of the means of production under working class control ... rejecting the form of the political party as 'sterile and ineffective, unable to respond to the goals and the immediate tasks and to the interests of the workers,' but speaking in favour of 'the true strength of the workers,' 'the economy and their economic organisations. Only there lies the terrain where capitalism can be undermined. Only there lies the true class struggle.' " The Platform also asserted, remarkable for its time, the necessity of women's and youth organizations within this struggle.

First the monarchy, then the Bulgarian fascists, then the Bulgarian communists who allied themselves with the Bulgarian Fascist movement, and finally the post-war Communist Party were absolute in their repression of the anarchist movement. By 1948, "hundreds had been executed and about 1,000 [Federation of Anarchist Communists of Bulgaria] members sent to concentration camps where the torture, ill treatment and starvation of veteran (but non-communist) anti-fascists—some of whom had fought fascism for almost thirty years—was almost routine. Anarchist prisoners were singled out and worked to death, being forced to work 36-hour shifts compared to the 12–16-hour shifts of other inmates. ... As Grancharoff says, 'The dark veil of communism used to entomb anarchism was also the same that buried ... genuine communism and all revolutionary hopes for the emancipation and liberation of the downtrodden.'"

Gogo, reading over my shoulder, nods his head. "We know one

guy who got so frustrated after the war that he yelled at one communist, 'You're not real communists!' For that sentence, they gave him five years in the gulag."

THE DOOR OPENS AND INTO THE APARTMENT WALKS A SKINHEAD. I get tense after my experiences in Croatia, but my host Gogo and his roommate exchange hugs with him, and he introduces himself to me with a broad smile. "You're the American Anarchist! What the hell are you doing in Sofia? I'm Plamen," he says, with a big hug. He walks over to the computer and puts on Bulgarian Romani music. When I tell him I have just been living with Roma in Kosovo, he asks me, "Sar syan?" How are you?

"Mishto, latches! How do you know Romani?" I stutter. Not your typical skinhead, this Plamen.

"I work with a lot Roma at my job, we're good friends so they teach me some."

When Plamen learns that I am a teacher in the US, he gets even more excited. "I have an idea that I have been trying to do about education, maybe you have an idea? Have you heard of Francesc Ferrer i Guardia from Spain? He was also an anarchist, from Spain, and he started this school called the Modern Schools. The idea was teaching in a rational way, without force, and without religion. The government shot him without a trial in 1909, but lots of people started Modern Schools after that. He was the first to have the idea and to apply it, that the education of children has to be gradual, depending on their age and their accomplishments. His ideas are still popular, after a hundred years." I wonder how Plamen is going to surprise me next.

"Here's an article I wrote about my idea, I have one in English, would you like to read it?" As I open up his article, Plamen walks over to the computer to download songs from Bulgaria's official pirated music site.

"Need for knowledge has always accompanied the instinctive and the conscious (of animals and of mankind) worlds. But while for animals it is expressed as awakening of instincts, for humans that need is demonstrated as need for ongoing revival: first, as desire to survive, second, as struggle for a better living, and third, as passion to understand the surrounding world, as passion to extend the inborn potential, either for science or arts.

May God be glorious (I am not atheist, maybe you would

proclaim glory for the Absolute Mind or glory for the Absolute Nothing—it is basically the same thing but again, everyone has his own perception), so may God be glorious for the sparkle of passion for knowledge lights the long expected fire of Prometheus (as a Bulgarian poet says, "You can't extinguish what would not fade") and humans are going out of darkness.

The old authorities—bounding knowledge only for distinct circles (classes) and not letting the impoverished, honest people develop their potential—are still present nowadays. Can we change the situation in favor of the vulnerable and inferior people? Where is the boundary for how much knowledge each person can have and is there such a boundary at all?

As long as our community is not changed, there will be people who gain superior positions and people who are second-rate in society! There will always be circles of people who would believe that knowledge is a privilege only for the ones who can afford to pay a 'certain price'! There will always be people who would be trying to stop the development of science and progress of mankind because of personal or commercial reasons.

At the same time, however, there will always be another side, represented by the people who would be fighting against the unjust forces in the world!!! Let's help them become more and stronger!

Let's provide knowledge for the ones who want to have it but are held back because 'they belong to a lower caste, they don't have the right to know more!'

Let's make an: ANARCHO-UNIVERSITY "Boundless knowledge"

But where could it be done? Internet—a great idea, but can a child in Zaire afford it—No. As a result, we should consider founding Anarcho-Universities in different points in the world (maybe in every anarchic commune or somewhere else, I leave it up to you for now) These universities should be able to co-operate among each other. For the foundation of the Anarcho-Universities, there will be need for 'missionaries' of knowledge in every point in the world...

PS1: ... Well, many people would have to consider the way the Anarcho-University would operate, but time goes by and we have about more than 1000 years to change the world, although each of us doesn't have so much time. But this is really going to happen!

    P.P.2: Fight for it!

    P.P.3: And happy Day of the Alphabet!"

Plamen turns up the computer speakers and passes the plastic beer bottle. Before long, the Romani music has us all jumping up and down on the bed like little kids, strobing Gogo's light switch for disco effect. Sofia dance party.

THE NEXT MORNING, HANGOVERS DRENCHED IN COFFEE, we hike to the group's office for a meeting. The ages of the members sitting around the table is itself a kind of history of Bulgarian anarchism: Aleksandar Makov, aged eighty-seven, and Georgi Konstantine, seventy-two, are both veterans of Bulgaria's heroic pre-WWII anarchist era, and survivors of the communist labor camps. The remainder of the group are high-school students, or in their early 20's. Apparently, the intervening 50 years were not amenable for attracting anarchist activists. As I watch the meeting proceed, the group's dynamic seems a demonstration of anarchist egalitarianism: the veterans pay full attention to the younger members, who in turn address the veterans with openness, at times disagreeing, but still within understated bounds of respect. In some way, the members could all be the same age, just that Aleksandar (whom everyone calls "Dado," or grandpa) and Georgi clearly know what they are talking about on some matters.

I flip though my copy of *Anarkhizmut v Bulgariia* by Doncho Daskalov, fascinated by the pictures, wishing I could read Bulgarian, wishing I knew someone who wanted to translate it. On a search of my local library database, eighty-one books show up for "Anarchism—Bulgaria—History," none of which I can read. Fiddling on the net in the corner of the office, I am trying not to get nervous about interviewing Georgi Konstantine after their meeting is over.

Konstantine spent ten years in a gulag for blowing up a statue of Stalin in the center of Sofia. When he was arrested, one of the police found a picture of Friedrich Schiller, the great German poet, in his pocket, and asked Konstantine, "Who is this man and where does he live?" After his escape from the camp, he lived in exile in Paris until 1989. In 1990, he was one of 300 original members who gathered to restore the Bulgarian Anarchist Federation. Behind him on the shelf of the infoshop rest a long line of books he has written, in Bulgarian with some translated into French; I cannot make out their titles. What the hell am I going to ask him?

Once the meeting wraps up, I sit down confidently across from Konstantine and shake his hand firmly. I regret not having any questions prepared. We start to speak in French, but I quickly get flustered as he gets a little annoyed despite himself. We ask a young woman from the group who speaks perfect English to translate for us, which somehow turns the atmosphere formal. I have just found out that an independent journalist acquaintance of mine back in California was imprisoned that day for refusing to hand over a video to the FBI, of a protest that he had filmed. I spout out my first question without too much thought: "There is a persecution of activists right now where I come from, and I know some people who are maybe going to prison for a long time. After your experience as a political prisoner, do you have any advice to offer them?" The translator stoically translated for him, and he shoots back a word to her, then she translates, "Advice?! What kind of advice?" Both of them look at me uncomfortably for a long moment.

Next question. I mean, is there anything you learned that you can share? Georgi speaks carefully, and the younger member translates: "The only free place in an oppressive society is in prison, because you have nothing to lose." I am not sure how to follow up on that.

Finally, I manage, "How did you get into anarchism?" Georgi waves his hand. "My father, my uncle, all of my friends were anarchists. The whole situation at the time led me to the conclusion that you can't rebel against the system unless you are an anarchist."

Aleksander, who has been smiling in his chair, chimes in. "I wasn't able to rebel against the communists," he mourns. "I was already locked up ten years before they came into power, by the monarchists and the fascists, and then the communists put me in a camp for another five years." He shakes his head, chuckling, and gets up for a tea.

"But why," I ask, "was Bulgaria so influenced by anarchism, and not the other countries in the Balkans?"

One of the younger members chimes in, people complete the sentences, debating facts at times, but it arrives to my ears as a narrative. "There were many preconditions for anarchism here. Slavic social structures were much like Indians in the US, decisions were made in collective meetings, and elders were only consulted when people couldn't decide among themselves. No concept of private property existed until relations with the Byzantines were established. Then, the Knjaz, or prince, became more important, and things changed. But even he was chosen for his position by popular choice, not by birth.

"The second major precondition was our long history of religious heresy," says Konstantine. I wait for someone to smile in mischievous pride, but I realize the topic is as scandalous for them as George Washington is for me. "The Bogomils originated here, of course. They believed that the church and state, as powers of the material world, originated with Satan, not with God as the Czar claimed. After being driven out, they went west, settling along the way, as for example in Bosnia. In France, they formed an anti-State society in the city of Albi, where they were then called Cathari. They thrived from the 10th until the 13th century, when the French army drove them out. During the fourth crusade, Pope Innocent III besieged Albi, and was so threatened by the Cathari that he ordered the whole town massacred. When warned that some Christians resided in Albi as well, he ordered, "Kill everyone and let God sort them out," a saying which you may have heard.

"Even long after the Bogomils left, Bulgarians have had this mentality of heresy. Under the Ottoman Empire, Bulgarians continuously refused to pay taxes. When the sultan passed a law that said Muslims didn't have to pay taxes, everyone started to convert, and the government canceled the law.

"The first anarchist organizations came out of *haidouks*, the mountain bandits. Bakunin himself wrote the manifesto of the biggest group in Bulgaria, the BRCC, which led the revolution against the Turks. Bulgaria was a very closed country, the people who traveled became revolutionaries, as they ran into ideas. Many exiles actually fled into Bulgaria from other countries, and brought their ideas. Many of our greatest, most famous folk songs are anarchist anthems.

"One final reason is that, for many neighboring countries, the 'national question' remained after national liberation, more than in Bulgaria."

"The anarchist influence was so strong at the beginning of the century that the State had many special laws only for anarchists. The *razbonik* law said that everyone the State designated as a *haidouk*—in this context obviously intending anarchists—could be killed after twenty-four hours by anyone—especially by nationalist 'volunteers.' Dmitr Petkof, the prime minister, passed this law in 1908. Later, during WWI, as the movement was criminalized, many anarchists became criminals. At one point, there were 3000 anarchists in direct-action revolutionary groups. Others were in anarcho-syndicats, or anarchist labor unions, but not as many as in Spain or Italy—here, mostly, anarchists practiced 'propaganda by deed.'

"Kiril, the 1st patriarch of the Bulgarian Orthodox Church after the war, was a former anarchist. When he was a priest, he sheltered Jews in his church, and when police entered and asked where the Jews were hiding, he pulled a gun on them, and they left."

I ask Konstantine and the rest of the group if they have faced any repression since the end of communist rule in 1989. "We haven't really faced any repression, but a lot of the rewriting of history that happened under communism has remained. Under communism, anarchists in our history were simply called 'anti-fascists.' We're still not mentioned in the official accounts."

As I'm closing my notebook, Georgi Konstantine stops me. "Oh, when you write about the camps," he says, creasing his brow after a moment, "make sure you call them 'Gulags.'" I promise him I won't forget.

Waiting on the corner for our bus, Nikola, who introduced me to the group, points out one of the group's stickers—"Join the bus strike! Don't punch your ticket! Free transportation for all!" I ask him about the group's other activities. "Besides the newspapers, and our sticker campaigns, we organize marches through the center of town every month. We always get at least a couple hundred people. You know, against the Iraq war—since we are in the 'coalition'. Mottos like, 'Prices are rising up, time for us to rise up!' and 'Politicians are scum, the state lies.' It sounds better in Bulgarian. And there's one, 'Solidarity between people is our weapon against the State.' During our last march, a bunch of elderly women were clapping when we said that one. You understand, this has not happened here in seventy years. If you understand that, you understand the whole situation."

ON THE BUS OUT OF TOWN, I REFLECT, NOT FOR THE FIRST time, that the plenitude of ancient communist cars on the roads proves that they must have been built really well, without the market motive of planned obsolescence. The radio plays American-style pop, rock-opera, and hip-hop such that I have never heard anywhere else. Is it a way to sexify the public sphere with (pseudo-)Americana without having to risk paying royalties someday? I cannot believe the lyrics:

> There's a hole in my soul, you can see it in my face, it's a real big place...

> Well, I don't think you understand the power of my game... She's my girl and I know she wants me.

> Take me to the place behind your eyes, make me melt like ice...

The lyrics sound like the dial-tone of the phone in Kafka's *The Castle*—hollow, infinite, a line with nobody on the other end, ever. English language songs made for export to places, or perhaps within places, where few people speak English. It suddenly occurs to me that the lyrics to these songs may have been written and recorded with the expectation that no one would ever notice them. Just as I doubt anyone here drinks coffee for the taste. Perhaps both date back to the false functionalist aesthetic under imposed communism: if you point out that these wondrous buildings that our triumphant society are constructing for the progress of man are all actually ass-ugly, there goes a decade of your life in a gulag.

I realize that I was correct, back in Trieste, when I guessed that this is no longer in the realm of spectacle. If spectacle is defined as "capital accumulated to the point it becomes image," then these are but bankrupt stand-ins, decoys, for a fulfillment no-one even really expects. As the authors of *Afflicted Powers* suggest in their analysis of Al-Qaida, societies stuck in the first phase of commodity culture undergo a kind of exquisite torture, where meaning is sucked up into things that people can only gaze at through shop windows.[138] The price tags of every meaning-object are always out of their budget. And the frustration and resentment nourished by this semantic tease can erupt into the most volatile expressions. Perhaps Bulgaria will prosper as it becomes integrated in the European Union, and people's material hopes will seem within reach. But if its "development" keeps going in the same direction as it has, what are people going to do?

Sighisoara, Romania.

THE FINEST LOW QUALITY

AND THAT, WHAT IS IT?" I OPEN MY BANJOLIN CASE FOR THE HUNGARIAN BORDER GUARD. HE EYES IT SUSPICIOUSLY; PERHAPS HE SUSPECTS ME OF SMUGGLING HYBRID MANDOLIN-BANJOS FROM HUNGARY INTO ROMANIA. I MOTION AS IF PLAYING, POINTING TO MYSELF. FOR PERFORMANCE, NOT SALE. HE NARROWS HIS EYES STILL MORE. "PLAY IT." I HUMBLY REFUSE, AND HE RAISES HIS VOICE. "PLAY IT!" I WILL NOT BE ALLOWED TO LEAVE HUNGARY AND ENTER ROMANIA UNTIL I HAVE PROVED MY BANJOLIN PROFICIENCY. GRUDGINGLY, I PLUCK OUT "OH SUZANNA," UNTIL HIS CRITICAL EAR IS SATISFIED THAT I PLAY BETTER THAN A SMUGGLER WOULD.

I get off the train to wait for the next, cheaper, local train into Romania. The guard follows me into the station. "This is the end of Europe. That," he says, pointing to Romania, "is Asia." Off the train, his official posture relaxes. I offer him a beer, which he hesitantly refuses. "Here it is very hard to find a good job. I have to feed my wife, she is pregnant and soon we will have our first child," he offers as an apology. After my second beer, I pull out the banjolin and serenade him and the empty station with my favorite bluegrass classics. After the third song or so, the lady in the ticket booth slams open her yellowing window, screams, and slams it shut. "She said to you, 'Shut up, I am trying to sleep,'" translates the border guard matter-of-factly.

As the next train pulls up, the guard and I board separate cars. I hear him scream at someone in the next cabin as their bags hit the floor: my new friend. A conductor comes to sell me a ticket for the same price as the previous train, and as I hand him the money, he refuses to let me pay. "Half price," he insists. I shrug and obey. "No ticket," he clarifies with a whisper, and we shake on it.

"YET THE 1893 CENSUS OF HUNGARIAN GYPSIES FOUND THAT only 3.3 per cent of all Gypsies were still fully nomadic while more than 89 per cent had become entirely settled. Even so, the lingering traces of nomadism were viewed as a menace to civilization. In a report evaluating the findings of the 1893 census a leading ethnologist of the day and academic expert of 'the Gypsy question', Dr Antal Herrmann, described nomadic Gypsies as living as freely as 'wild animals.' He hailed the end of Gypsy nomadism as 'a political as well as a humanitarian duty' that would safeguard society, while the abandonment of a nomadic lifestyle was described by the learned scholar as nothing less than 'the foundation of cultural development,'" he goes on:

> Dr Herrmann's policy recommendations were, to say the least, thorough and far-reaching. Arguing that it may be necessary to 'commit a little cruelty in the name of humanity,' he advocated the founding of educational establishments around the country. These were to be used for the 'internment' and education of the children of any nomadic Gypsies unwilling or unable to send their children to school, in compliance with the law. By invoking the threat of removing their children, opined Dr Her-

rmann, 'it would be possible to have a greater influence on the parents through their children, then vise versa.'[139]

To the parallel with Native Americans of forced deculturalization through boarding schools, and with African Americans of de-industrialization impoverishment, must be added the parallel legacy of slavery. How many Romanians, how many Roma, know or acknowledge that Roma were officially enslaved here for centuries, freed as recently as African Americans? Is it any wonder that fear and resentment and alienation persist—particularly if this legacy has never even been *acknowledged*?[140]

If all of Romania's over two million Roma were as criminal as their reputation, they would have taken over the country by now—the streets would be choked with a million begging children, and the adults would have cashed out the banks. Instead, most do what they can to limit risky interactions with *Gadje* (non-Roma), do what they can to get by and enjoy their generally difficult lives. There are, of course, the musicians, whose music is beloved even as their houses are torched. Of those few others who seek out interactions with *Gadje*, some are motivated by desperation—which doesn't always help the reputation of their people as a whole. (Even then, Roma criminals have also tended to eschew violence, preferring the way of Odysseus.) Does that excuse this "Beware of Gypsies" sign in front of me in the Bucharest train station? Or is this just another wave of excluding and scapegoating the weak, invigorated by post-communist nationalist politicians, Romania's own *Birth of a Nation*—the "Whites Only" sign over the water fountain?

Again, I ask when the train leaves for Timisoara. Though it is the nearest big city, this ticket agent, like the first one, shakes her head—no trains to Timisoara. I thrust my guidebook forward and point to the thick black line between Budapest and Timisoara—the main line east of here. No, she shakes her head, no train. But the person at the information booth told me it leaves at three! She shrugged and called to the person behind me in line.

Yes, yes, Timisoara train, at noon, tickets at the ticket booths, confirmed another person behind the information booth. No trains, no Timisoara, says the next ticket person. The fifth person nods and punches me out a ticket; the train for Timisoara leaves at 1:30, track 6. I nod thanks and pray St. Kristof doesn't betray my good faith.

On the Romanian border, the border offices are guarded by a number of Kalashnikov-wielding official thugs. I abandon any subconscious plans I may have had to take over the Romanian border station. Certainly, no Austrian refugees fleeing through Hungary would sneak their way into Romania today. The security payroll seems not to have shrunk much with Romania's transition into Democracy. One guard goes from room to room, tossing passengers' bags to the ground and thrusting a long metal rod into holes beneath the seats. Another slides a ceiling panel off and his feet deftly disappear into the ceiling. The customs officials gleefully extort a pair of counterfeit Adidas from the elderly scarf-headed woman across from me, one pair over the sliding quota: heroic defenders of the Romanian economy.

At the first stop, many passengers leave the train. "Timisoara?" I shout with a hint of panic out the window. "No Timisoara!" warns one person. "OK!" beams another, pointing at my train. A third points to a different track. The scarf-headed lady in my train compartment motions for me to sit, no problem. "Have faith in what you want to believe," says her wise gesture, "and maybe it will happen, maybe not." I sit back down.

"No Timisoara!" yells the train conductor, indignant as a televangelist. He jabs the map in my guidebook—train north, Timisoara south. I throw my arms up like a junior high drama student. My acting hasn't cowed the conductor; he knows I am a foreign agent sent to bankrupt Romania by taking trains for free. I slap my ticket to Timisoara as proof of the train's treachery. "No Timisoara!" he repeats. He calls down the hall for the train police. Stupidly, I surrender my passport. My scarf-headed friend pleads on my behalf. The three hold court on my fate; perhaps I will be allowed to purchase a ticket to the next station. I accept the verdict. The conductor shows me some official photocopied pages, and shows me his official calculator, which reads, "80." "Dollars," he clarifies. For the price of his ticket to the next stop, I could traverse the entire length of Romania about 30 times, return ticket. I pull out a stack of Romanian bills, in denominations of 500 lei, and offer it to him. He laughs, feigns to wipe his ass with it, and hands it back to me. After protracted negotiations, we settle on $1.50. He pats my back as the police officer hands me my passport. But, he emphasizes, you get off next stop.

Dusk is already falling as I step off in Deva. The train conductor wishes me a good trip with a contented wave. One money exchange is still open, but the opportunities for camping in Deva's cramped streets seem sparse. None of the city's three hotels are as open to bargaining as was the train conductor; all charge Western prices, three times my daily budget. As night falls and Deva's street dogs run out of other people to bark at, I give in and take a room that had somehow escaped Ceacescu's Socialist Realism aesthetic; dignified but unpretentious carved oak predating the ubiquitous concrete of modernist utopia, built before Romania's forests were reserved for export. I drop off my bags and go for an evening walk.

Music leaks through the door of a nineteenth century Austrian building along the main promenade. I peek in the door, walk past the guard, and go up the stairs. A rock band is playing to a large room of well-dressed people seated in plastic chairs, a high-school multi-purpose room filled with the city's bourgeoisie. A middle-aged woman grabs my shoulder and guides me to an empty plastic seat, between a decorated military gentleman and a fur-coated matron. The woman who seats me doesn't believe I don't speak Romanian, that I'm from somewhere else. We stumble through introductions until we realize we both speak French.

"But where are you from? What are you doing in Deva, in Romania?" she whispers, kneeling. Her jaw drops when I say America. "No, you're not. Americans don't know how to speak anything but English. At least the white ones." I assure her that some speak other languages, that sometimes we even have to take them in school. She accepts my explanation with a hint of suspicion. We applaud as the rock group takes a bow and a speaker steps up. "They are all performing the works of Eminescu, our most famous poet. You have heard of him?" I apologize that I haven't. We listen to the speaker's cadences, read passionately, without singsong.

"You're not really a typical American, are you?" she asks.

"I don't know," I manage. She waits for me to think about it. "I mean, I'm kind of tired of America, but most people there still seem excited about it or something. I'm not sure." Hushed by the fur-coated woman, we sneak to the back of the room to continue our whispers.

"Are you a Republican or a Democrat?" she asks.

"I'm an anarchist." She doesn't acknowledge my answer, so I go on. "My friend Leah says, 'I don't need cops or bosses to tell me what to do.' Anarchists would rather figure things out with other people than trust somebody to tell us all what to do. I guess typical Americans trust cops and bosses more than other people, so maybe I'm not a typical American. But typical Americans never think they are, so probably I am."

"Many people here don't like America," she says after thinking a bit. "You know, we had partisans in the hills waiting for the Americans to liberate us from the Russians for many months. They didn't understand America had given us to the Russians with a handshake." I've never heard anyone accuse America of being responsible for the spread of Communist influence before. "And that television show, *Baywatch*, it is really terrible." I agree vehemently.

The last speaker has finished. The woman introduces herself as Mircea. "You know, there are some people from the Mayor's office where I work who would like very much to meet you. Do you have a place to sleep?" I consider lying, but admit I have a place at the hotel. She gives me a glare that says, "typical American." "Well, anyway, will you please meet us for some drinks tonight?" I take her phone number and promise to call after I take a brief shower.

I cannot go straight back to the hotel. Pacing Deva's boulevards, I try to consider my situation through a dense cloud of sleep deprivation and travel fatigue. Was Mircea just being friendly? Was she picking up on me? Do I hope she was? Should I have told someone from the Mayor's office that I believe in the overthrow of government? Judging from the border guards today, I doubt that the infamous secret Securitate police have gone away either. One in four Romanians was employed as an informant at one time under Ceausescu. Is this the group of friends she knew would be interested in my opinions? Do they think I am CIA, here to sow subversion? Or, now that Romania is dependent on IMF loans, does it have a deal with the CIA to report opponents of the neo-liberal capitalist agenda?

After two hours, I return to my hotel room, convinced that Mircea is picking up on me, and that she is also handing me over to the Securitate, who may or may not be in cooperation with the CIA. My only option is to out-drink them, since I did tell her where I was staying. I call up Mircea, who is upset that

I kept her friends waiting.

She gives me directions to the bar. I try to sharpen my wits on my walk there.

"America!" yells one of Mircea's friends gleefully as I approach. I shake hands all the way around the table. "David Hasselhoff!" he yells, to Mircea's chagrin. The man to her left, tall and square shouldered, nods and smiles shyly. "*Unde?*" Where? Resisting the urge to lie, I admit California, and several of the men fall back in their chairs with astonished roars, as if a prodigal son had walked through the door. "America," another says as he runs his thumb over his fingertips, much money, much money. I shrug. "Ey, California, California GIRLS!" yells another, and I give him a high five. I hope the Securitate show up soon.

Mircea's shy boyfriend is driving us to the outskirts of town after we finally crawl from the fourth bar. We are all quiet for some time, relieved to be away from the barhopping enthusiasm of the Mayor's office staff. I am nauseated from hours of hearing America flattered like God. Mircea asks: "How do you know we're not just going to take you somewhere and kill you? I mean, you must be crazy just to get into some stranger's car like this." I tell her I think it is more dangerous to live suspicious of everyone than it is to get into strangers' cars now and then. She translates my answer for her boyfriend. They talk back and forth quietly for a few minutes. "Look, this anarchism is a contradiction," she relays back to me. "You want everyone to think like you, but you don't want to tell anyone how to think. That's a contradiction." I tell her that I think sometimes you can change people's minds without telling them what to think. She translates for her boyfriend again, then shakes her head. Typical American optimist idiot.

We reach our destination and climb the stairs to an abandoned bar, a failed business venture of Mircea's boyfriend. His teenage sister greets me, kissing my cheeks, and introduces herself with firm eye contact. The electricity and water are off, but so is the heating, so the beer is cold. Candles are lit, and we all enjoy each other's company in silence for some minutes, sipping our tall beers and thinking our various thoughts. "You know," begins Mircea's boyfriend in cautious English, "it is my biggest dream in life to move to America. Every month I put my name on the list for the lottery they have at the embassy. For ten years they haven't picked me, but I still have hope."

I speak slowly, trying not to slur my words or my thinking. "I'm not sure you'd like it in America. It feels dead, kind of soulless."

His sister looks up at me and says, "You don't believe that you don't need material things to be happy or something, do you?" Apparently the Baptist missionaries have been here recently.

I tell her I might say that sometimes in California, but never in Romania, and she smiles without breaking her gaze.

"But it's not really like on *Baywatch* or *Dallas*. At least, for most people."

"OK, I know," Mircea's boyfriend says, "but at least in America everyone has enough to eat and a place to live and work, they can have their own lives, not like here." His words bump up against a shelf in my mind, a drunk and exhausted shelf piled high with hours of America-worship. Dish after dish falls crashing to the floor: dishes that say North Philadelphia, West Oakland, East St. Louis, Bridgeport, Watts, Chicago's South Side, San Diego shantytowns, Birmingham, Richmond, Charlotte, Washington D.C., Mississippi, Georgia. And in raised, cursive, gold-plated letters: Detroit. My fist is pounding the table, tears welling in my eyes. Every time I try to catch a dish, three more slide down crashing. My friends glare with amazement but listen intently to my growing hysteria.

I list off the prisons, the murders, the rapes, the bleach poured in dumpsters so that hungry people can't eat out of them, the drug war, my friends locked up for activism, the meat-packers, police beating train-hopping migrant farm workers, the Klan, Prozac and Ritalin, the slavery that never really ended, Vietnam veterans on the street, the fear and racism and genocide and schizophrenic denial marbled through society: the proud colonial heritage that we've yet to outlive.

"Is it really worse than Romania?" Mircea asks me quietly.

I recoil, "No! I mean, I don't know. I don't know anything about Romania, this is my first day here." Her boyfriend isn't listening anymore. When I finally stop talking, he slams the table.

"OK, I don't want to go to America anymore! Are you happy?" He yells at the table, but looks up at me for my reply.

I pause to swallow the lump in my throat. I try to sort through my thoughts first, and then speak. "Look, I guess a lot of people go to America from other countries and like it there, they get good jobs and make enough money to do what they want. Maybe if you're not born there, you can still hold on to your soul. I mean, I guess I know a lot of good people there. I mean, there's like 300 million people, it's a big place." They all stare at me, struggling to decide what to believe. We return to our beers, empty bottles already covering the table. Mircea's boyfriend relaxes somewhat but stares quietly at his beer bottle. His sister, with grave amusement, offers me another beer. Mircea changes the subject.

The next day, I drop a postcard in the mailbox to thank Mircea and her friends again for the evening. "I am sorry," I wrote, "if I said anything stupid last night. My pinching hangover is forcing me to leave town sooner than expected. I promise to visit Deva again soon."

In Sighisoara, I stay in a hostel on the bottom floor of a girl's boarding school. Twice I have lost the key inside the lock while trying to open the massive institutional doors; conspirators from upstairs try to break me out, but only succeed with the help of the headmistress. Chickens run wild out front, teasing us with their freedom. English students shyly practice a phrase or two before skittering away in a fog of giggles; I blush during my entire stay.

Late one night, a gang of five knock on my door and whisper one English word they know: "Cigarettes?" All five stare blankly at me, between giggles, as I try to make conversation in gestures. After our cigarettes are done, they keep staring; I race back into my room in a flustered panic. Bobby, the hostel's 22-year-old patron, is always plotting to bring hordes of tourists to Sighisoara, though deep down I'm not sure it's the best idea.

Bobby's mother asks as she hands me a coffee if I have heard about the miner's strike. I shrug; strikes seem common lately. Do things here function enough for anyone to notice when they stop? But I tell her I always support striking workers. She says she doesn't agree with what they want: they want to go back to the past, but it is too late.

Bobby's mother tells me of the bloody oppression faced here by her family and other Hungarians. Transylvania used to be in Hungary but was given as a prize to Romania after WWI, and the Romanians have been trying to rid it of Hungarians ever since—though far worse since the fall of communism. At least communism denied the existence of ethnicities; the

Demonstrators protest IMF austerity measures, Brasov, Romania.

nationalists try to wipe out anyone who isn't Romanian. Then she asks, "In America, do you have problems with the niggers? In Romania, we have problems with the Gypsies." Shuddering at her Hollywood vocabulary, I say, "I think we white people are the ones who make problems for black people. Usually the people with more power are the ones making problems for those with less, not the other way around. Like here, what you said for Hungarians. Perhaps it is also the same here with the Gypsies?" She shrugs her shoulders.

"In Romania, it is very hard," she tells me. "I have a very good job, I am dean of the boarding school, I make only 60 dollars a month. My utility bills alone are 80 dollars a month, before food, before rent." I ask her to repeat the numbers, but I heard right the first time. How does she survive? She thinks for some time, then laughs. "I have no idea," she says. Is she worried about capitalism's effect on Romania? She takes a napkin and writes "2150." I stare at it and back at her until she explains: "This is the year we will have capitalism in Romania." I guess she means the good parts.

OBLIVIOUS, DAN AND I STROLL INTO THE CENTER OF
Brasov. Near the main promenade, our guidebook leads us to the
very spot where in 1989 Ceausescu's secret police forces gunned
down the populace, including rival police forces that had joined
the revolution. I put my finger in the bullet holes, one by one.
Across the street, a solemn row of martyrs' tombstones divides
the park. I dwell on one, a sculptor in her mid-twenties, next to
a nine-year-old boy. Could it really be true that, however real
the revolution was in Timisoara, it was entirely an artificial
product once it reached here; that the heart of the communist
party set up a few of their own ranks for a fall, then christened
themselves overnight as the new democratic resistance? The
sculptor stares up at me, leaving her latest work unfinished,
but sure in her expression.

A flood of tone fills the streets. Dan and I find ourselves drowning in a vertiginous whirl, mournful, angry, vast. I can't decide
where to focus. Trucks. Wave after wave of industrial transport
looms overhead, a steady polyphonal cacophony. Trucks upon
trucks, blocking the road. Fists leap from windows, heads jut
out to peer behind then ahead. We are laughing, uncontrol-
lably, too loud as we drown in the orchestra of air horns. The
purest sound beats us dumb. Dan is half-shaking his head, just
as astonished.

The public square on the other end of the promenade is filling. We trickle in with the others. A few children bounce balls
back and forth in front of riot tanks. Echoes of angry amplified
voices bounce down narrow side streets. Mostly older people,
pensioners. Determined. Everyone has been here before. From
a balcony facing the front of the crowd, a woman yells with an
authority void of charisma and is heeded. To the left, the flag
of the USSR flies large in someone's hands, with the Romanian
communist party flag. Other hands wave a Romanian flag with
the center cut out, the symbol of the 1989 revolution. I walk
underneath the balcony and stare: here, a miniature coffin
bearing the birth and death dates of one of the martyrs, their
martyr. Beside the coffin, other hands hold up a portrait of
Ceausescu. I snap a photo, and several of the faces then turn
uncomfortable. Damn, how could I forget—bad memories here
with photography. I walk back into the crowd.

On the far end of the promenade, the bodies of those who died
in 1989 to oust Ceausescu. The new leaders caught and executed

him. Two days later, on Christmas night, they broadcast footage on TV of the firing squad gunning him down, to cheers throughout the country. The next year, President Iliescu called in the country's miners to defend the capital, which he claimed was being "overrun with acid-crazed hippies." The miners brutalized scores of students protesting "neo-communist" rule. In 1995, Constantinescu won the election, and the communists finally fell from power. The new president immediately instituted the austerity measures demanded by the IMF. I am beginning to understand, on this end of the promenade, these people holding portraits of Ceausescu alongside those who died fighting him, flying the communist flag and the flag of the overthrow of communism... pensioners without pensions. The miners are flooding into Bucharest again, but this time it is the president they want to kill. He stopped all the trains. Good thing we stayed here in Brasov, I guess, because today the miners are tearing the trains apart as they turn back from the capital. Today, the miners are shouting the same thing that these people are shouting on this promenade: Give us back Ceausescu, give us back the Revolution, give us anything else.

ON OUR WAY OUT OF THE INTERNET CAFE IN BRASOV, THE guy working behind the table asks us where we are from. We get to talking about the state of the world, about life in different countries. He asks us where we are from again. We tell him. With sincere pity in his eyes, he says, "In America, it is very hard to live, isn't it? I have read that Clinton destroyed the welfare system. Your social services there are very bad, aren't they?" Dalia and I sputter and reluctantly agree.

I AM TRYING TO EXPLAIN PUNK ROCK TO THE BANKER sitting on the next barstool. "Sex Pistols? The Clash?" He hasn't heard of any of it. He asks for the pen and notebook. "Smoki," he writes. He is shocked that I've never heard of his favorite band. "Everyone knows Smoki!" Our common vocabulary exhausted, he pulls me out of "Bar No Limits" and speaks patient Romanian to me as we snake through Sighisoara's ancient fortress alleys. We drop into a bar across the street from Dracula's birthplace, but he grabs me after one silent round. With a leer and a masculine pat on my shoulder, he assures me that he knows what I'm looking for. He brings me into a strip club with a few lingering patrons. After some swift words with the bartender, he returns and apologizes. No more dancing tonight, he shrugs. Relieved, I make for the door, but he shakes his head excitedly and pulls me to a table in the corner. As we sit down, the two mafiosi and a Nordic Amazonian at the table stare at us. What in the fuck am I doing here? I demand to myself. The banker introduces me: "American!" I warmly shake the mafioso's hands and we all laugh.

The dancer turns to me and asks in perfect, unaccented English, "What the hell are you doing in Romania?" I admit that I myself don't understand. As the conversation continues, I can't believe she's not a native English speaker, except that no native English speaker would have to dance in a strip club in Sighisoara. She assures me she's learned it from books, and seldom has a chance to practice. I explain to her that some of my friends in the US are dancers, that some of them see the power and pay they get from their job as empowering, though like any other job it has drawbacks.

"How is it, dancing here?" I ask. She shrugs. "I mean, how much do you make in a night?"

"In one night, about a hundred dollars on average," she states flatly: the equivalent of three month's wages at an average job. She doesn't look like she's lying. "But I want to leave here."

Soon, the background changes back into Bar No Limits, with only black lights to see our drinks by. The banker is eagerly humiliating himself before the amused mafiosi. I am attempting to explain my theory of the Punk Rock Rule of Labor to the dancer: the more social mores you break, the more money you make, for less work. At first she understands it as a business offer and stands up defensively, but I hurriedly explain my own work history and she sits back down, amused. After a break in conversation, she repeats, "Yeah, I want to leave here. My boss found me an offer dancing in Japan. He has the visa arranged and everything. I guess I'm leaving in a month."

For the fourth or fifth time tonight, the jukebox starts playing the day's number one Europop hit, by Emilia. "I'm a big, big girl in a big, big world..." I choke on my warning; the dancer's eyes stare phosphorescently through me, surrounded by black-lit platinum. She seems about twice my height, her shoulders fit for the NFL. What can I say?

"Umm," I stammered, "you know that a lot of women here..."

Mr. Vodkabottle.

"Of course I know," she cut me off. "But I know him, this won't be like that." Her eyes stare past me with marble determination.

"I'm a big, big girl in a big, big world, it's not a big, big thing if you leave me. Outside it's now raining and tears are falling from my eyes..."

The banker is too engrossed in the mafioso's discussion to notice me getting up. I give her my address, and she promises to drop me a line from Tokyo.

DALIA AND I ARE STARING OUT THE TRAIN WINDOWS AT THE rusty factories crumbling into the autumn forests. A man sitting a few seats in front of me pulls out a vodka bottle, slugs on it, and passes it to the guy in the seat next to him. I am careful not to make eye contact. The man takes back the bottle and tries to make the guy sitting on the other side of him drink from it; this man refuses. Mr. Vodkabottle starts tugging at him, yelling, insulted. The yelling spreads to those in the surrounding seats. I look away from the fight and back at the trees. Curious,

I look back a few seconds later and all of the men are kissing each other like elderly lovers.

An older, surprisingly sober-looking man in an impeccable pin-stripe suit sits down swiftly across from us and stares straight at me. Behind him, the man who refused the vodka bottle wrestles an accordion out of a case and plays poetic bursts of improvisation, slouching, bored, for long periods in between. I try to stare out the window. Dalia, gently smirking, watches me for a reaction. The man's glare breaks my will. I give him a friendly nod. His hand is on my knee, liquor breath escaping his wild teeth, and his eyes stare at me from every direction. We discourse passion-ately in the Universal Language, significant gestures too packed for any words. Heart—Sky—Pounding Fist On Knee—Both Eyes Open—Stomp Stomp. Kiss on the Cheek.

Mr. Vodkabottle is eavesdropping on our Universal Conversation. He and his friend join in, and soon we are startled to under-stand each other's Serbian. He rides this train three times a week, taking goods across the border to the open market in Pančevo, Serbia, coming back to restock and see his friends. Life of a Salesman, Romanian. I cannot safely refuse the vodka bottle. I stare at the English words on its foil label to buy time between swigs—"Voronskaya Vodca, established 1993," and in raised script—"The Finest Low Quality."

Mr. Vodkabottle will not leave us all alone and vulnerable in the train station. He warns us with drunken persistence about omnipresent thieves. He lapses into Romanian, and I agree with everything. A familiar-looking man, guidebook in hand, approaches and assures us in English that his rooms are famous and reliable and clean, as Mr. Vodkabottle screams something and tugs viciously on the man's shirt. "He is telling you I am a thief," the man translates for me. I thank him and shake Mr. Vodkabottle's hand.

"But this isn't a taxi?" says Dalia as we step up to the man's friend's car. Her backpack knocks the rearview mirror off the neighboring vehicle, and I hurry her inside as the driver walks up and stares bewildered at his missing mirror. She looks at me concerned, and I pat her leg with vodka confidence as the car pulls out. She avenges my condescension with a brutal jab to my leg. The car spins through the little streets of Brasov, the men in the front talking in low Romanian, Dalia and I in the back silently awaiting our fate. The car pulls up to an apartment complex, the same one, it turns out, that I stayed in three years ago.

NEITHER OF THE BANDS HAS SHOWN UP YET, AND THE SHOW was supposed to start two hours ago. The band from Hungary may have been denied visas, explains Mani, and no one knows what happened to the other one. "See them?" Mani points to a group of burly, short-haired guys entering the gate. "Those are the skinheads." After the Gay Pride march in Zagreb, the word carries special meaning for me. I jerk out of my seat. "No, no, don't worry, there aren't that many in Timisoara. Punks are always beating them. I feel kind of sorry for them." Certainly they seem outnumbered here. The ancient underground remains of a fortress are filled with kids waiting for the show to start, and the courtyard around it holds as many more. I open another beer.

Two kids on my other side ask me where I am from. They have been wandering around Romania for some weeks, trying to get to the border with Hungary. "I am sick of life in Bucharest, in Romania." They have no visas for entry into Hungary, or even any passports. How do they plan to get over the border? My friend confides his plan to me with sparkling eyes. "We will cross in the wilderness. When we get near to the border, we will get very, very drunk. If they catch us, of course they will beat us," inadvertently quoting, verbatim, the opening of Samuel Beckett's *Waiting for Godot*. "But we will say, 'Where are we? How did we get here? God, I must be really drunk.' Nothing they will do could be worse than if we don't try." The longer I think about it, the more brilliant the plan seems.

One of their friends had recently gone to camp on the beach along the Black Sea, to clear his mind and get away from it all. The police found and arrested him, took him to the station to run his papers, and then released him, only to arrest him again as soon as he'd got away from the station. After three sleepless days of arrest, booking, release, and rearrest, he grabbed a knife and cut himself and several police. A judge sentenced him to seventeen years in a mental asylum. "This is why we are leaving here," my friend explains.

Emma and I go to buy beer from a neighboring kiosk after moshing around to the local two-piece that has replaced the bands that never showed up. As we reach the beer kiosk, a big short-haired guy steps messily in front of us. "You know why my country is better than your country?" I tell him I can think of several reasons. "Because it's Romania!" he slurs. Emma tries to step around him but he stumbles in front of her. I yell that I started playing violin because of Romanian music. He steps forward. His friend runs up between us and says, "You should go, he is a Nazi." Emma tugs at my sleeve, but I insist. "Romanian music is the best music!" I yell at him. He nods angrily. "You should go!" his friend says, and the big guy pushes him out of the way. "I am Romanian!" he says as he steps into my face. "Hey, do you know any poems by Mihai Eminescu?" I ask him. "Not in English," he growls, bumping into me. "No, no, just in Romanian, I would love to hear one, just for the sounds." He straightens himself, lifts his arms, and valiantly spews forth measured verses for several long minutes. We stand respect-fully attentive. As he finishes and stares at us, we thank him, shake his hand, and go back into the show without any beer.

Later, we talk to Darko from Vojvodina, who lives here to be with his Romanian girlfriend Roxie. Darko studies to be a veteri-narian; Roxie studies psychology, and asks me, "Can you imagine being a psychiatrist *here*?" Darko's bulk is reassuring, though no fights have broken out yet. He explains that Timisoara under communism was the most diverse city in Romania, with many students from across Africa, and from Iraq, Iran, Turkey, and other Middle Eastern countries. Romania, like Yugoslavia, invited internationals to strengthen diplomatic ties, in the original com-munist ideal of international solidarity. Many of the students lived in Timisoara after college, though most have now moved back. The poetry-reciting Nazi walks past and exchanges a greeting with Darko in Serbian. Seeing my surprise, Darko explains that the guy is an ethnic Serb, though he's lived here all his life.

Darko, Roxie, Emma, Frank and I end up at the Mad Professor Augustus's house after the concert. Augustus flops his mass of curls about as he bashes out Depeche Mode classics on the piano. We mumble semi-forgotten lyrics through drink and exhaus-tion. Finally he crawls toward the couch. Frank asks Augustus what he's doing his Ph.D. thesis on. "Well, mathematicians have already found the formulas for translating objects between two spaces of any finite number of dimensions, even if the number of dimensions is undefined. I think I'm the first to find a formula for transformations across spaces of infinite number of dimensions.

I think I've got it, just a few more weeks." Augustus's slurred pronunciation seems to translate his perfect mathematical English into the appropriate dimension of the evening.

Augustus's friend Octavio, a geologist, is explaining the future to me. "The plates might shift considerably for the next few hundred years, and of course as water covers much of the land mass, people are going to have to move around a lot, and then you have the climate shifts. But don't worry, in a few hundred years, maybe a millennium, things will settle down to normal." I make a note to remember the geologist's time line next time I start to worry about things.

THE NEXT DAY, AUGUSTUS TAKES US ON A WALKING TOUR of Timisoara. "That's still there from the failed revolution of 1848," he says, pointing up at a cannonball stuck in the side of an Austro-Hungarian fresco. As we walk onto the Piazza Victoria, the city's giant open pedestrian boulevard, he tells us about the events of December, 1989.

"It began when some students on a tram started yelling that they couldn't take it anymore. Years of fear, starvation, freezing... Ceausescu claimed he was just doing it to pay off our IMF loans, but at the same time he was building the People's Palace, the second largest building in the world after the Pentagon, out of gold, pink marble, whatever he felt like. You can't imagine how ugly it is. So the students came here, onto the main square, and word got out. Soon the square was full.

"I was in my village, and my parents refused to let me leave. I told them this was the one time in my life to speak out, to live history, but they were too worried for me. I went on hunger strike until they realized I would die at home if not at the protests. So finally, I took a train into town and came here."

I tell Augustus that I read in some books that sixty people died, while others claim 10,000.

"No one knows how many. People rushed to the church doors—the same church that talks about them now as the 'holy martyrs'—but the church locked them out. Police killed maybe 1,000 at the time, it's hard to say. At least that many have been dug up from mass graves in the last few years. But many more died from 'migrating bullet syndrome.'"

None of us has heard of this disease before, so Augustus explains. "Many, many people were injured when the police were shooting, so thousands were carried to the hospital, or got into the ambulances that pulled up here. The ambulances never went to the hospital. We took one man directly to the hospital for a bullet in his leg; when we went to visit him the next day, the bullet had 'migrated' to his head. Many died like that, perhaps three or four thousand more. I don't think anyone will ever know how many."

Augustus takes us on a long detour after our walk down the main square, pointing out historical spots along the way. After half an hour of walking down small side streets, he stops at a kiosk to buy cigarettes. Then we turn back towards the center. "This is the only place you can buy these cigarettes, the ones everyone used to smoke before '89. Everyone keeps acting like history started ten years ago, so I guess I smoke them to preserve some kind of continuity." He offers each of us one from the pack.

As we pull into Sighisoara at dusk, our first sight of Transylvania is a living cloud of bats, chirping and stretching and thrusting like an airborne vampiric amoeba. This is how we know we are safe, in beautiful Gothic little Timisoara, safer than home by far, safer than the cities falling into Third World urban turmoil. Staying with the punks, whom the secret police blame for all of Romania's problems, but who spend their time swapping homemade cassettes of raucous hope and raising money to feed the glue-sniffing starvelings that the city lets die. Like the Roma, their lives are so vulnerable and fragile that a mystique of magical malignancy is their only defense against complete oblivion. The banshee's howl has grown deeper and shriller, and as reassuring as a heartbeat.

"Hey, hey, you speak English?" The kids run across the park to our bench. "Your friend is looking for you, she saw you earlier but couldn't catch up. She told us to look for you. You know, your friend, Catherine?" My heart thumps; there are several Catherines I would love to see, but I didn't figure any of them could be in Europe, let alone Sighisoara. "Don't go!" the kids shout and take off.

Before we decide what to do, a young woman runs up with the kids, her smile visible a block away. We have never seen her before in our lives. She grabs our hands as we stutter. "Hello, friends, it's so good to meet you! I never get to speak English

Kids with riot cop transports,
Brasov, Romania.

here—people here don't have much education. I can't believe that you're here! I can tell you are such good people, you have to meet my friends, they are good people like you, and it's my birthday! So you must let me take you to the cafe, you can't say no..." We are already swooping out of the park, Catherine tugging us like a comet's tail.

Dan and I can't exchange more than bemused shrugs before she seats us, hostages to her cheer. I struggle to focus on my coffee as I pour the sugar. Her eyes are utterly immediate; somehow not entirely present, but unavoidable. My "don't talk to strangers" upbringing and traveler's skepticism can find no footing around her; she is already impossible to mistrust, much. "I am so sad my husband cannot be here, I think also you would love my children, two little gypsies, like me, imagine them not coming with me on my birthday. Where are you from?" She pauses, but Dan and I are too stunned by her barrage of white teeth and gymnastic intonation to contribute much.

"You are Americans? Then you are Baptists! I knew you were good people, like us, you have to meet my friends, they are all good Baptists too, I am sure you will love them, maybe also I can get my husband and children to come and meet you, they will be very excited, although I am so sorry that they don't speak English yet. They will never let me teach them, but I will make sure they learn before they are grown. My children I mean, my husband won't learn anything, but I love him so much anyway. So we will meet in the bar for my birthday in one hour after I go now and see if my children are OK?" and she has run out the door.

Dan and I nurse our coffees and reflect. The invitation is a little questionable. Whatever Catherine's motives for taking us to the bar for her birthday, she'd had them before meeting us. We don't know anything about her friends, except that they, like us Americans, are good Baptists. And we've been deceived into her company by her little accomplices. But her presence, though incomprehensible, is evidently harmless. Perhaps she really just wants to practice her hypersonic English a little more, for her birthday.

Catherine and three friends are already waiting for us; she regrets that her husband and children couldn't come. Tony smiles huge and warm in his leather jacket like a square-jawed, mafioso member of the Ramones. Dan fidgets. The first round of beer appears.

Alcohol relaxes Catherine's pace a little. She tells us of her job at an orphanage in the next town over. "I am very glad to have such a good job, but it is so sad to see the little children. They have such sad lives, really bad conditions because the orphanage has so little money. There is so little money here. They are always hungry, or sick, or cold, and there is no space for them, they have no parents, nobody loves them, I try to but there are so many I would never have time if tried to love every one. But still I try, sometimes it's difficult but I try. And also I have my own children, I love them so much. I am so glad they are OK, that I can give them a good life." Catherine's friends sit guard and stare away, bored with all the English.

"Many people here will do anything for money. I am so glad I have the job at the orphanage. Many girls are—I'm sorry if it is a bad word—prostitutes?—because they are greedy and want money. Don't you think that's wrong?" Dan is clearly uncomfortable. I try to explain that some of my friends are prostitutes, that sometimes it's sad, but not really wrong. She waits for an answer. I tell her it's sad when people have to have sex to make money, and she seems satisfied.

Dan tells me I'm on my own, that he can't drink anymore and is going back to the hostel. Catherine is a little offended, but excitedly suggests we try a different place. Would I like to go to a gypsy bar? I shrug, sure, if it's OK. "Of course it's OK, you are my friend!" she says. I pay for the drinks. As we walk, I tell Catherine that I'm not a Baptist. She looks at me, surprised. "Why not?" I tell her I'm an atheist, and that where I come from, some Baptists shoot doctors and blow up hospitals where women get abortions. She is quiet for a minute, then says, "If I lived there, I wouldn't be a Baptist either."

The Roma bar, Cafe Bar Jennifer, is hidden behind an unmarked door in a residential alley. The four of us shuffle in and find an empty table. Catherine introduces me to some of her family: her grandmother, two aunts, and a younger female cousin. One of her aunts barely winces a smile before looking away; the other, glowing with dignity, tells me *buna ziwa* with disdain. Her cousin, whose face is furrowed by acid burns, smiles shyly. A boy in his early teens sits alone at the next table, motionless and miserable, with a nearly empty bottle and shot glass. His shoulders sag blankly with relentless habitual forgetting: even sweet memories slip into terrible ones until none of them are worth messing with. I can't understand how the alcohol is making it up into anyone's mouth. A two-piece plays with severe apathy on Casio and electric guitar.

"My aunt wants to know why you came to Romania," Catherine says as the birthday bottle of cherry liquor arrives. I try to steady my thoughts by staring at the table.

"There's this French movie about gypsy music called *Latcho Drom*. When I saw the part from Romania, it was so beautiful, I felt like I had to come here."

Catherine impatiently waves me away. "There's no movies about gypsy music. You must be thinking of something else, you would never hear about this in America."

I look up at her and say firmly, "No, really, I'm sure, I've read all about it and everything. Gypsy music, from Romania." She stares long at me, struggling to believe what I've said, then translates for Tony and her aunts in a rush. They all stare at me dumbfounded, I smile back and nod. With a unanimous roar, the three of them embrace me laughing, shaking their heads, still suspecting me of mocking them. We toast with such drunken violence that our glasses nearly shatter.

"Come on, do you like to dance?" yells Catherine as she gets up and grabs my hands. Horrified, I refuse and clutch my chair. "Come on!" She drags me into the middle of the room. Every last patron stares in disbelief and naked disgust. Catherine won't let me go. I give in, alternating between punk moshing and a terrible imitation of her subtle moves. She grabs my hands and tries to demonstrate how to dance through my wrists. Her grandmother looks away. I resort to the Chubby Checker, and the band looks distantly curious. She is laughing at me and having fun. Before she can grab me for a slow dance, I dive back into my chair.

"Shon, I have an important question. My best friend is in the hospital to have a baby." I congratulate her, but she doesn't smile. "She needs a special operation, because the baby won't come. How do you say? A Cesarean. We are supposed to have free care, but the doctor will never do it unless we give him 150 dollars. I know it is a lot, but I think you are a person with a good heart. Tomorrow, you should come visit my town. I have many cassettes of Gypsy music I would like to play for you, and it would be my honor to prepare you a meal with my family. Maybe while you are there, we could visit her?"

In slurred syllables, I tell Catherine how when Karl Marx

said, "Workers of the world, unite!" he meant Roma and punks. She stares through me. Tony and the aunts talk among themselves, tired. Catherine asks about my family, and I tell her how in America, my friends are like my family. My grandmother raised me after my mother died, but with my friends I have a large extended family, with the same ups and downs. She sits up. "Your mother is dead?" I nod back, shrug. In a suddenly strange, flat, sober voice, she demands, "Why didn't you tell me this before?"

"Before what?" I ask, feeling sick, as she runs out the door. Her aunts jump up after her.

After ten minutes, they return, Catherine in a glassy-eyed panic. "I just received horrible news. My baby, she was in a car accident. I have to go now to see if she is OK, but I don't have a car. I hate to ask you this, I can pay you back tomorrow, but could you give me any money for a taxi?"

"It's three in the morning, Catherine."

"I know, but my baby was in a terrible accident!" I pull out my wallet and give her my last four dollars in Romanian money, and she jumps in a car and drives away. Tony puts his arm around my shoulder, pulling me back towards the bar. I stop. "No money!" I shout at him. He shrugs incomprehension. "No money!" I shout and show him the insides of my empty wallet. He laughs and motions for us to return to the bar. "No money!" I shout and start walking away. He pats my shoulder, waves goodbye, and goes back into the bar.

The next day, my tortuous hangover and Dan's impatient skepticism make my decision. When I call Catherine to tell her I cannot come, that I must leave today, the elderly voice at the number she gave me only says, "Eh? Eh? Eh?"

THREE STREET KIDS ARE STARING UP AT THE CAMERA, which in turn is staring at the Local Political Figure. The rest of us have climbed aboard the bus, but the Political Figure has one last sound bite to offer the viewing audience before leaving: something about youth, the future, pulling together to make it work. The television crew is catching a shot as we climb aboard the bus. We all wave to the crew and the street kids who still haven't figured out what's going on.

I stand packed in with some of the Young Friends of Nature, the organizers of the event. As the bus bounces out of town, swerving around horse-drawn carts and frequent breakdowns on the shoulderless highway, all the heads nod together in mesmeric beat: old men in tweed bowlers, scarf-headed matrons, college students, toddlers on their parents' laps. A few conversations can be heard over the grinding engine, but most of us are enjoying the moment, pacing ourselves for the drive, quietly relishing the shiatsu of jabbing strangers' elbows.

The bus pulls over on the washboard village road and spills its contents. Two girls from Young Friends of Nature rush into the monastery's courtyard and raise their eyebrows significantly; they are the first women ever through its gates in its centuries-old history. The long drive has melted the ice, and strangers start conversing. A teenage boy grabs my arm and pulls me into a one-room plaster building; an ancient icon glares down at us from behind his fresco. We drag our bags from the bus into the monks' quarters. Over dinner, I tell one friend that spices were all prohibited in a Buddhist monastery I visited; I was glad that Romanian Orthodoxy had no such rule. A monk nods and passes a jar of pickled Serrano peppers.

Over morning tea, the Political Figure hears that one of us is American. He excitedly grabs my hand and ceremoniously introduces himself. My aversion to authority figures might seem like nationalistic condescension, so I return his flattery. "What is your religion?" he asks immediately. "Atheist" might seem rude in such surroundings, so I say, "Taoist," and he briefly searches my face for mockery. He lectures me in broken English on Romania's problems, on the importance of youth, of the future, of pulling together to make it work, with a disarming directness that wins my earnest agreement.

In the field, we are all equal. The whole scene is a glorious cliché from some communist schoolbook. One of my friends from Young Friends of Nature even jokes about being back in the Young Pioneers. This time, however, everyone is here by choice. I grab another yard-long twig from the bundle.

"So, you just plant this in the ground and it makes a tree?" I ask the high-school girl digging next to me.

She laughs. "You know, in Romania, trees are really important. In some places, when a child is born, you still plant a tree. The two grow up together, like one being. If you want to propose marriage, you have to ask the tree too." I prop up the twig in the hole with a few dirt clods, and it falls to the side. "If someone dies at sea, they bury the tree instead."

I'm amazed that such unchristian practices persist. "Oh yeah," shrugs Elena, "we've got all sorts of stuff like that. Everybody casts spells on each other. People in the countryside still hunt vampires: just stick a virgin boy on a pony outside a cemetery, and when the pony stops, that's the vampire's grave."

We start on another row without talking. The shovel rubs a blister on my travel-soft hands. The sun heats our dusty faces. Elena looks up as she stabs the dirt and hops on her shovel. "Why are Americans so dumb? I mean, you guys have all these great libraries, books are cheaper for you than for us, and everybody has the Internet for free. But nobody knows any poems, or knows where Romania is on a map. I think I know more Shakespeare than most Americans do. At least the ones I meet on chat boards."

In Timisoara and Bucharest, kiosks sell translations of Immanuel Kant and Rabelais next to socks and cigarettes. Books in foreign languages, even ancient Greek and Latin, are almost as common as pulp romances.

I pull back on the shovel and tear up the packed ground. A half-earthworm shrivels into its trauma-clod. "Maybe if you have power, you don't need culture," I say. She passes me a shoot and waits for me to finish. "I mean, the Cold War made schools care more about science than literature and arts. In the '80s, right-wing people in churches got control of a lot of school boards, and they probably don't like social science. Like if you look at a map, you might see Vietnam and ask your teacher the wrong question. But I don't know, we have a lot of denial and guilt in our society, so maybe people don't want to know about the world, or even about our own history."

"You know who is our George Washington in Romania? Dracula!" she laughs. "We call him Vlad Dracul, and Vlad the Impaler is his son. He saved Romania from the Turks by impaling 20,000 prisoners of war along a road the Turks were taking to attack his castle, and they turned back after about the first 10,000. He was a little crazy, but I don't think he was a vampire."

My blister pops, my sweat runs down the handle to the hand-forged shovel blade. A shepherd in a raw fleece coat strides up to us and stares, shaking the hand of the Political Figure as he puts down his shovel. The flock behind him prunes the weeds and bleats lazy complaints.

That night, after another meal of spicy navy bean soup with the monks, we are invited to participate in the nightly services. I stick a tape recorder in my pocket and press record before going through the door. As I edge along the back wall, a hospitable stranger grabs me and pushes me forward. Friendly hands pass me along until I drop to the floor in front of the tiny room, surrounded by prostrating monks. Lit by a few candles, the black-clad, bearded brothers take turns intoning the Greek scriptures in a mumbled staccato: the faster they get through the nightly reading, the longer they'll have for whatever monks do in their free time. The tape rolls on, its mechanical buzz barely audible above the rustling habits and whispered prayers. For 45 minutes, no one makes a noise loud enough to mask a click from my pocket; when the tape thumps to the end of the reel, I cough to squeeze the "stop" button. Asshole.

The next day, Iliana introduces herself as my translator. I pass her a branch to stick in the dirt. She interrogates me with warm formality. "In America, is everyone really as materialistic as they say?"

I have to think about it. "A lot of people are just trying to get by, not as many as in Romania but still a lot. Some crazy people live for their ideas instead of money, like some Christian fanatics, or my friends," who for brevity I call "punks."

"What do punks do?" she asks. I tell her about collective houses, concerts in basements, riding trains that are supposed to only be for cargo. We travel a lot, most of us drink too much, we read and talk about what a better world would be like, we go to protests.... Some people show children in poor neighborhoods how to fix bicycles. She doesn't say anything. We shovel in silence as fecund as the turned dirt.

Someone waves us away from our digging towards a flock of sheep over the hill. The shepherd, playing lazily on his wooden flute, doesn't seem to notice as we sit in the grass around him. Sun pours over us for a very long time. He finally hands the flute to someone and laughs at their squeaks. When he takes it to play again, I pull out my tape recorder and ask if I can record him. "Why?" translates a friend. I tell him the music is very beautiful. The puzzled shepherd creases his forehead.

"Don't you have better music in America?"

"No," I tell him.

With dirt ground in our skin from another long day of digging, we pull ourselves onto the bus. Iliana moves over to make room on her seat. My head rests on her denimed shoulder as the engine's grind lulls me to sleep. I wake up a few times to the sound of tired singing. The song rolls with stoic cheer over the beats of the potholed highway.

As Timisoara surrounds us, Iliana and I straighten in our seats. After the quiet hours through the dark countryside, she suddenly remembers a question. "Do all punks work the earth?" I tell her many would like to, but most of us don't ever get out of the cities. She asks me about life in the city; I tell her it is similar to here, although people there spend much less time sitting together, drinking coffee or beer, they live more quickly and don't take so much time to reflect. Iliana thinks over my description, then comments, "Maybe you can have progress and prosperity, or you can have humanity." I think over her words, then tell her I hope you can have both, but I can't think of any evidence that it's possible. The bus pulls into the city center. We step off, shake hands and say goodbye.

A CONDUCTOR ON THE TIMISOARA TO SIGHISOARA TRAIN sees us smoking in the non-smoking compartment we have to ourselves, steps in, and closes the door. He makes a smoking, then a no-no gesture, with a big smile. I smile back and shudder a bit, and we all brace ourselves. He throws us a long, long stare. "Tickets?" I falsely offer, and sternly he shakes his head. No. He points to my orange drink, and I hand it to him. He takes a big gulp. Then he grabs our garlic bagel chips bag, throwing it down in mock indignation when he sees that it is empty. He returns a big smile, the universal "that will do" sign, and leaves.

A few minutes later, Emma spots him in a compartment farther down the train, sitting across from a discontent mother, whose napping little girl has her feet on the seat. He is munching on somebody's animal crackers.

DALIA'S FACE LOOKS CONFUSED AS SHE CLINKS DOWN THE domino bone. She pauses, reaches inside her mouth, and pulls out a curved chunk of glass. Her fingertip is bloody from a slice in her palette. We stare at the shard for some long moments until Dalia picks up her beer bottle and fits the shard to its missing lip. She pushes it aside, a bit shaken, and we continue playing.

Romanian baba posing, Sighisoara, Romania.

At the next table, four American men are comparing consumer research on their favorite wines. My ears perk up, a bit annoyed, but curious, as I've never before overheard English in Sighisoara. I figure they are global carpetbaggers as their conversation shifts to the exciting new markets opening up in Nigeria and Zimbabwe. Still, their conversation isn't so banal, for businessmen. They converse about African political developments gleaned from *The Economist*. One of them hears Dalia and I speaking quiet English and asks where we're from.

Three of them are visiting the fourth, who lives in Bucharest. "What kind of business you got there?" I ask. He shrugs. "No business. I just live there." I'm impressed—the only other Americans I've even heard of around here are Baptist missionaries, or vacationing NATO personnel. He tells me about traveling through small towns in Bosnia recently, around Sarajevo. His curiosity moves me.

One of his friends pokes him and jests, "Man, tell 'em why you're really here!"

He smiles, shrugs shyly, and admits, "The women here are very beautiful." He blushes. "And you can get away with anything." His friends grab him. We shake hands and make a date for the bar.

Over dinner, the phrase returns to my head. "That was weird," agrees Dalia. What did he mean? The pork turns rancid on its bed of corn grits and sour cream. A physical impression, strong as memory, starts to loop in my head: I am twisting a broken beer bottle into his face. People here can't do anything to him; he's an American. After dinner, I rush to the bar to find its doors locked. I stand for a long time under its unlit sign.

A group walks up behind us and asks in English if we know any bars that are open. We start to talk to them, and lead them to Cafe Bar Jennifer. In the display window, a guitar with no strings rests lonely on a bed of rocks. The wooden walls inside boast nudie Samantha Fox posters and one sado-masochistic bondage poster with a Yoko Ono lookalike. The bar is covered with flavored hard liquor bottles—plum, cherry, pear—with single-serving bottlecaps. Six little wooden tables huddle together under the low, ancient ceiling. Old men nod off and snore at them, and shady characters return huge, honest smiles if you risk smiling at them first. Dalia points out plastic strands hanging along the ceiling and comments, "Romania is the world capital for strings of unlit Christmas lights." The radio plays a techno remix of "Take Me Home, Country Roads." My frustrated bloodlust begins to subside as a new friend hands me a mug of Jennifer's best.

All four of my new friends, sitting around the table, are in the Israeli Defense Forces. They are on vacation, twenty people all together, driving jeeps across the Romanian countryside with a guide for a week. They've already visited several Roma villages and a leper colony on the Black Sea. Tomorrow morning, they are leaving for Bucharest. Have I seen the orphanages here? Terrible, terrible. Not as bad as Albania, where they were closed because people were only adopting kids to sell their organs on the black market, but still. We shake our heads. They promise to send me the photos when they get home.

Alcohol dissolves my tact, and a loose bit of frustration floats to the surface. "How about that Ariel Sharon?"

The young woman across from me shakes her head. "He is as bad as your George Bush. A real war criminal. He is reducing our country to shambles, like Bush is to America." His friend jumps up, and we all smile for his picture. The stereo blasts Black Sabbath's "War Pigs":

> Generals gather in their masses, just like witches at black masses. Evil minds that plot destruction, sorcerers of death's construction... Politicians hide themselves away, they only started the war. Why should they go out to fight? They leave that role to the poor.

"We are stuck in a cycle of violence and fear," her friend continues. "The Army humiliates everyone in the Occupied Territories, makes their lives impossible with the curfews and checkpoints, shoots the children. Then, the Palestinians' resentment grows into hatred, with suicide bombings and talk of driving us into the sea. Which Sharon then says is the reason for the occupation, to control their terrorism."

"But if the occupation creates suicide bombings instead of preventing them, why not stop it?" I ask him. Someone goes for another pitcher, someone else changes the subject. One guy says, "You know, in America, your news does not tell the truth. The CNN, for instance, is controlled by Palestinians." I tell him I was unaware of this, that I find it surprising. However, if I am brainwashed, I guess I wouldn't be able to tell anyway. We lift our drinks—*la chayem*—to life. The cassette player is now blasting country-western versions of international communist partisan anthems—"Arise, ye workers of the world," with dobro and fiddle solos. By now drunken, I raise my fist and shout *"Partisani!"* to the bartender, who shakes his head sternly.

"Do you know anything about the soldiers in the Israeli army who are refusing to serve in the Occupied Territories?" I ask.

They laugh. One of them, who has only been speaking in Hebrew to his friend, says, "I am a Refusenik." He has only spent a month in jail so far, but is awaiting his trial. He tells me more than 500 soldiers have signed the letter, refusing to fight in what they call "the War of the Settlements."

The guy sitting next to Dalia shrugs, "I wish I could be a Refusenik, but I just work for the Army on a computer in Tel Aviv." The woman across from me has been in a number of peace groups, but is too frustrated to work with them anymore.

"The day before I left for this trip, I saw a Refusenik speak in Philadelphia," I interject. "Someone asked him if anyone in Israel still dreamed of a united, multi-ethnic Palestinian state, such as both the PLO and the Israeli Left demanded in the '70s. His answer was, 'Nobody talks about that anymore. When I think of a united Palestine, I don't think of Belgium, I think of Yugoslavia.' For forty years, Yugoslavia was considered a shining example of social reconciliation and diversity. That's the tragedy, globally, this forgone cynicism about social potential, like it's automatic, like we're not the ones who create history."

My tired companions agree vaguely to my ranting. They excuse themselves; they have an early morning. We exchange embraces.

The next night in Brasov, in a private hostel Dalia and I are sharing with two others, I am informed by an east German tourist that I am brainwashed. In America, the news is controlled by the Jews. The Japanese pilot agrees. I shrug my shoulders; I tell them I was unaware of this, that I even find it surprising. However, if I am brainwashed, I guess I wouldn't be able to tell anyway.

BALKANISM IS A GAME DREAMED IN THE MIND OF a fevered God, a God laid down with brain fever—fragmented, uncomfortable, with a relentless mathematical logic of absurdity and correspondence. Yet also just a place, with real people, living the reification of this mad idea. The laughing fury of the Goddess who drinks coffee to go to sleep, and of a God who can't exist, God's absence proven by beauty, of Balkan. Why every kid I stay with here seems to have Kropotkin's famous quote hanging on one of their walls: "Anarchy is the mother of order."

Balkan is my own madness and desire, a mad desire for dizzying movement and heretical juxtaposition and exchange, imagined and expressed imperfectly in the terms of life everywhere, but here invoked each moment into reification, yet pre-existing, really, like in the 1913 Belgrade postcard of the dog riding the bicycle past an accident, proving my madness and desire in the world; a stranger's face imagined in a dream, then seen in the street, laughing and yelling with no one, her madness the same madness you thought your own, alone.

In Balkan, the social sphere achieves a biological complexity—so infinitely complex as to be indeterminate, yet a more perfectly functioning order for it. Where else could have survived all of this? When will the rest of the world catch up and conceive with a political order that allows this social order to exist?

AFTER A LONG DAY OF BUSES, BORDERS, TRAINS, AND TAXIS, we step into a villa house on the outskirts of Timisoara. Our bags find the few corners not already filled with the bags of other visitors. Everyone hugs each other, kissing each other's cheeks. What does it matter that we've never met? Beer, bread, and some sort of tube-cheese are passed around. We melt into our seats: Home. Everyone asks each other where they are from, what the scene is like there.

"Who lives here? This place is amazing!" Emma asks. Elena explains that her family has moved to Georgia to work: Atlanta, not the one next to Russia. She stayed behind to look after their villa. Her grandmother lives here too; she was supposed to go with the rest of the family, but hid out in her neighbor's house until their plane had left. She had no interest in America, or in leaving her chickens and plants. That day, grandma had approached Elena, curious about all of the arriving punkers, and asked, "Who are these people? Are they family?" Elena assured her they were good people, something like family. The villa housed not only the two of them and Elena's visitors, but also Romania's only anarchist bookstore and library.

Some of the kids tell us about their activist group. The group formed after a split within the ecology group I'd gone tree-planting with, because some of the group felt compromised by reliance on NGO funds. They also insisted that ecological concerns, however immediate and massive within devastated Romania, could not be separated from social struggles. Within a few days, they put on Romania's first ever Food Not Bombs, giving away free food in the park, mostly to street kids.

"Where did they get the food?" I asked.

"We can't scavenge it or get donations like you do in America, since scavenging is, well, mainstream here," explains Mani. "We had to buy it this time. But we'll figure out something."

At first their actions met with surprising success. When they blocked the streets with a march called "Towards Car-Free Cities," the mayor agreed it was a good idea, closed the streets for them, and donated paint so they could paint murals on the tram cars. Local street kids joined in, and everyone painted their vision of a better world, however sloppily. When they were involved with Young Friends of Nature, the NGO I planted trees with, the authorities did not seem to mind their presence. But recently, the secret police took notice. They authored a series of articles for the country's tabloids about the anarchist threat. Mani leaves for a moment and returns with a newspaper.

"It says here we are Satanists. And down here, it says we all practice bestiality and necrophilia. And you know, fanzines?" We all nod—in America, we usually just call them zines. "Well, they almost got this right. It says here that anarchists make home-made magazines, except it then says the fanzines are child pornography, sold on street corners in order to buy hashish."[141]

I tell Mani that in my last visit to Romania, one local activist told me he was an anarchist when in Western Europe, but in Romania there was no point, since they didn't have enough of a state to fight against. Mani laughs grimly. "We have plenty of state." Most letters and packages arrive at their bookstore and homes already opened; Mani shows us one which had arrived the day before from England, totally empty. Recently the police combed an entire train station, questioning every young man, just because one of the punks mentioned on his mobile phone that he was arriving there with copies of a political zine.

"The police even tell us they have our phones tapped," says a cheery punker girl. She explains that there's not much other opposition in Romania to blame for all the country's problems. In a nation which recently had more hidden microphones than people, the police must be pinched for internal enemies.

Mani and Elena wander off, and I sit down with a table of kids I haven't yet met. We clink our bottles as we make introductions. "What do you say in America for this?" one asks. Hmm. Cheers? A toast? We don't really do that kind of thing as much in America. Another asks if America has many punk bands, besides NOFX. I cringe and assure him that there are many better examples, next time I will bring tapes.

Suddenly, I remember a question I always wanted to ask a Romanian. Under Ceausescu, thousands of families were forced to move from their village homes to the city. When they arrived, they realized they could not possibly accommodate all of the cats, dogs, and children they'd brought along, and turned them out onto the streets. The children were left to starve and prostitute themselves. The dogs bred into giant, roving bands until the

Nesa, friend of dogs, Timisoara, Romania.

police killed most of them off. My guidebook, however, claims that wild dogs are still a danger, and that travelers should always carry rocks in their pockets. I ask my new friends, "Do you carry rocks in your pockets to keep away the wild dogs?"

I receive a tableful of long, cold stares. Finally, one boy says, "Why do you want to hurt the dogs?"

I stammer, "No, not to hurt them, just to scare them away, like maybe a stick or something."

Another says firmly, "Do not scare the dogs."

My friend, who has been translating, looks up at me from beneath her silver-dusted eyelids. "We are the friends of dogs."

FRANK, EMMA, AND I SIT IN BAR RAMOS: SMALL, A little dangerous-feeling. I think I recognize a guy at the next table from seeing him earlier working on his car, which was turned on its side for easier access. He gets up several times to flirt with the bartender. He then sits back down and begins talking to us. "Music?" We agree, music is good, both in general and also particularly the Smoki on the cassette player. He indicates that he plays music, guitar. He is ecstatic that we also play. "Good music. Very beautiful. From heart." He stretches our limited common language with passion and gesture.

He brings us to another bar, one with only three tables, and describes his life—though from Sighisoara, he lives as a professional musician in Germany. He lives well, playing only four hours every day in a bar. He reveals that he has a girlfriend here and also in Germany, to which we raise our eyebrows. I tell him about the open non-monogamy of many of our friends, and he excitedly agrees that such honesty is the best way, but no one here would understand. As we finish our drinks, he grabs our hands and tells us we must now let him play music for us, with his friend, who is a very good person. It is 3 a.m.

Before we can convince him to let his very good friend sleep, we are walking into her living room. In the few minutes we've been waiting outside, she has roused herself as if it were afternoon. Her long platinum hair streams behind her as she seats us, offers us pillows for our backs, introduces us to the kitten. The single-room home has no bathroom, and the demitasses she offers for the beer we've brought are the only hint of a kitchen. On the wall perches a giant teddy bear. She embraces us one by one and passes around a plate of sugar cubes which we gladly accept. None of us can take our eyes off her; though perhaps in her forties, she makes us feel old. Her attention is too flattering and sincere to be embarrassing.

Another friend emerges from the bed. He appears, just waking, in a tie underneath his zip-up snowflake-pattern sweater, a gray beret still on his head. As the woman introduces him, she explains that he is from a village, and that he reads more than anyone on earth, with which the guitarist emphatically agrees; the man humbly acknowledges our looks. His eyes, surrounded by elderly wrinkles, burn like those of a prophet. His fingers clutch a Bible. He starts speaking in rapid Romanian through his wild, signifying smile. As he speaks, the platinum-haired woman explains that the man is "opinionated." We sense he is imparting to us an important mission.

The woman and the guitarist ask what kind of music we would like to hear. What traditional Romanian music do they know? The guitar fluidly trickles an introduction before strumming accompaniment. She carves out Romanian words in marble-solid voice, with ivy vibrato. Overcome by their music, it takes me a moment to reflect that the melody is familiar, though I don't fully recognize it. Between fits of shouting, the old man from the village writes long lines of essential knowledge in Frank's notebook. The next song, also in Romanian, sounds more American than Romanian. The kitten chases a sugar cube around our feet. The three of us sit totally still, entranced by her voice and the serpentine guitar.

"Songs for Jesus," she clarifies with a knowing look.

As they start another song, the old prophetic man from the village slaps Frank's knee, jabs his Bible demonstratively, and explains some esoteric nuance from a phrase in the notebook. Frank stares back with massive attention, nodding intently, not understanding a single word. I work out a few phrases, repeating them to him to make sure:

"People in Afghanistan are crazy."

"French people possess the English people."

"NATO is a satanic institution." We all loudly agree to the last statement. He emphatically repeats "neo-communism" with violent pointing. Between songs, the woman tries to help. "He says after years of thought about who is to blame for the evil in the world, he understands that it is the French."

"Are they the neo-communists, or the current president of Romania, or does he mean NATO?" I ask. He interrupts—yes, exactly, neo-communism! I open his Bible to John 1:1, "In the beginning was the Word," and roar it out in guesswork Romanian. He jabs the Bible. Everyone agrees.

They start playing "The Rivers of Babylon," and I join in. They hand me the guitar, and after I play them my two favorite Balkan folk songs, they remember Roma songs they'd long forgotten. All our feet are stomping along. The prophetic old man makes another point before returning to the notebook. More songs are recalled. We visitors are almost unconscious with fatigue. Our hosts, completely alert, get us to stay for a final rendition of "Hey Jude." Through tears of gratitude, we thank each of them over and over. We sing "Hey Jude" all the way home.

Bunkers, Albania.

Passing on the Curves

Don't be so racist. Albania is fine, it's just like any place else."

I set my coffee down. "Aaron, I know people are racist about Albanians. Like Vladan Djordjević, the Serbian foreign minister who swore in 1913 that all Albanians have tails.[142] I'm not afraid of the tails. It's just, I haven't even heard of one visitor who's been there in the last few years without almost getting killed. The head of the World Bank got fucking car-jacked. I mean, kudos to the guy who did it, but still, it says something."

"Whatever," says Aaron with a light Australian accent, waving me off. "Everywhere you go people are racist against Albanians. That NGO idiot we read on the net was pissing her pants just because people hang teddy bears from empty buildings to keep away bad spirits. You're going to listen to someone who's afraid of teddy bears?"

"Yeah, Aaron, she also got mugged by a little kid with a big knife. The guidebook says there's as many Kalashnikovs as people. Enver Hoxha broke with the USSR for being too reformist, and it hasn't got much better since. Albania is the world center for trafficking women, kids and drugs. I mean, I understand, I would attack tourists too if I was stuck there, but I don't want to volunteer for the position."

Branka orders another coffee for herself and does her best to ignore us.

Aaron goes on. "What about the castles? Aren't you curious what Tirana is like? What about the bunkers?"

The bunkers.

"Whatever, Shon, we're going, come if you want or don't. I'm tired of hearing your racist shit."

SEVEN HUNDRED AND FIFTY THOUSAND BUNKERS, CONCRETE mushrooms three-quarters submerged, a country of quaint paranoid gazebos. Most are like encased walk-in closets. Some, buried in the sides of the omnipresent peaks, could fill an entire mountain, to judge by their entrances. Sixty bunkers per square mile, on average. One bunker for every four people. "One person, one soldier" was a staple motto of Hoxhaism; men had to serve for four years. What's a soldier without a Kalashnikov and a bunker to fire it from?

THE MACEDONIAN BUS LEAVES US A HALF-MILE FROM the border checkpoint. The story Francisco told me comes to mind, when, in the mid-'80s, one of his friends approached the Albanian border on a bicycle trip through Greece. "Might as well stop by, just for five minutes, so I can say I've been to another country." The cyclist approached the border station and the guard.

"Umm, I was wondering..."

"NO!" shouts the guard.

"No, but I just want to..." The guard cocked his rifle and pointed it at the cyclist's head. The cyclist went back down the road.

We walk to the border station. I stare at a large pit beside the road with the word "Quarantine" painted along its side. Branka is nervous. She was supposed to obtain a visa in her home country before coming to the border. When she went to the embassy in Zagreb, they asked her what business she was conducting in Albania. "No, no business, I just want to see it."

"But what company is sending you to Albania?"

"No... look, what do you do when someone just wants to go to Albania as a tourist?"

The officials discussed it between themselves for a moment, then told her, "We have never before heard this request."

In a few minutes, the border guards have politely written out visas for all of us, charging each of us only one quarter of the listed official rate. We walk down a narrow road along the lake, passed occasionally by cars or mopeds. Donkeys graze in the shade of crumbling bunkers. People swimming in the lake stare at us as we near the first town; sunbathers arrange themselves around rusty rebar on submerged bunkers. One bunker is covered in pink and blue polka dots, another sports a silly clown face. First one, then another moped stops with offers we can't understand. An old woman herds turkeys across the road.

AS WE ENTER THE TOWN, EVERYONE TURNS AND STARES. Perhaps Aaron's braids, Branka's waist-length dreadlocks and my green afro are not common sights around here. I risk a smile at a passing teen, and his hard glare jumps to a wide, warm welcome. Within a giant, bustling park, the words "Nestle 100% Club" are spray-painted across the front of a cafe. Satellite dishes hang from every apartment window. A tanker truck with a hose, a chair, and a painted board serves as the town's gas station.

In a variety of pronunciations, we begin to ask everyone we pass where the bus station is. "Bus? Autobus? Tirana? Station?" No one understands, so we resort to charades—rolling tires, steering wheel, big box on wheels with people inside. Each person stares blankly. "Pus?" with a friendly shrug. Some people nod encouragingly, with confused stares. We later learn that in Albania, people shake their heads "yes" and nod their heads "no." One man notices that we are sweating in our backpacks; he darts into a souvlaki restaurant to get us water. We thank him profusely, but my vegan travel-mates force me to drink the entire souvlaki-smeared water bottle. Finally, a man from a cafe stops a passing van and assures us as he throws our bags in the back, "Tirana, Tirana, two Euro."

AS TIRANA'S HOTEL FOR INTERNATIONAL BUSINESS AND diplomatic personnel is outside of our budget, a local tourist agency advises us to walk along the sidewalk on a certain block of the main avenue to find a hostel. When we arrive at the block, a small mob surrounds us, shouting out offers to carry our packs. I rush through, disoriented.

"Why are you being so racist? This is what we were looking for!" says Aaron.

"I just don't like high pressure sales," I say, but agree. We ask the first man to approach us to show us his rooms. He proudly leads us down a street as the other vendors shout in angry disappointment after us.

The man leads us into a convenience store in a corner of a large concrete block, shakes the proprietor's hand with some short discussion, and leaves. The proprietor of the store takes us into an adjacent room with three beds. In one of the beds a half-dressed young man sits up, whom the proprietor starts shouting at. "No, no, just looking, don't leave," we say, but the man is already getting dressed. "OK, OK, no problem, I am police officer," the half-dressed man tells us in English as he pulls on his uniform. "I must go work now anyway." The proprietor changes the sheets and watches us as we argue in whispers.

"Yeah, but it's not our fault he made the cop leave!" whispers Branka.

"What about when the cop gets off work?" I wonder.

Aaron moans, "We don't know anything about this guy!" We take the room.

As I stand in line with more plastic liter bottles of beer, I notice an Enver Hoxha video displayed proudly on the television. "Hoxha!" says the proprietor, slapping his heart. He eyes the bottles suspiciously but has the business sense not to discourage our habits. He offers me a cigarette which I gladly accept, then hands me a lighter with the Albanian flag across it. "Souvenir," he nods.

Later, the proprietor motions for us to follow him. He opens a door at the back of the store and leads us into a shaded courtyard with a walkway through his garden. We walk through the garden to the courtyard's back wall. Within the wall, a little stream drips from an unadorned ceramic jug into a fountain below. On the back of the fountain, the letters "E.H." sit embedded in stone. We coo admiringly.

Our host sits us at a table in the courtyard and brings us soda. "Moment," he says and disappears. A few minutes later, a handsome young man with a square jaw and kind eyes walks out and introduces himself as Ardian. "My father says you are staying here?" he asks in good English. Ardian sits with us and his father joins us. "My father is a communist, you know. In those days, there were no parasites like now. Everyone worked. And there weren't any drugs here then."

"Are there many drugs now?" asks Aaron.

"Yes, many."

"Heroin?" I ask.

Ardian shakes his head solemnly. "Not just heroin. Also marijuana." I decide not to ask Ardian more about it in front of his father.

"My father says that under Hoxha, he only worked six, maybe eight hours a day, and had one day a week off. Now he must work everyday from six in the morning until eleven at night.

"You know what happened here in 1997? The democratic president Berisha told everyone to put their money into new businesses, to help with the transition to capitalism. If you put in money one month, in three or four months you would have twice as much money," he said. "But in '97, eight of the main companies fled the country, taking all the money. People here lost everything, 80 percent of their life savings. Everybody got so mad that they took guns from the army and police and attacked government buildings, police stations, factories, everything. Now Berisha is president again."[143]

Ardian's father gets up to close the store. Ardian excuses himself, but offers to take us on a tour of Tirana with another friend the next night. Overjoyed, we accept immediately.

THE STREET BUSTLES WITH TRAFFIC. SOMETHING ABOUT the cars seems strange, but I cannot place what. The standard communist car models—Skoda from Czechoslovakia, Lada from USSR, even the Yugo—are not to be seen. Many of the cars are older Mercedes, but it dawns on me that as many are recent models. A shiny black Toyota SUV passes us on the right. I eye the country sticker on its bumper: "D" for Germany. Half the cars around us are late model Mercedes, glossy black, with country stickers from Germany, Italy, Holland, France. After a few seconds thought, I calculate that an average Albanian would have to save their earnings for half a century to buy a Mercedes. I ask Ardian in his sub-compact how people can get such cars. "They are stolen in Europe and then people can buy them here for very little money. The CEO of Mercedes came to Albania and said he was very impressed. He saw the latest model here before it was even released in Germany."

This park, says Ardian, used to be covered in office buildings a few years ago. For a long time it was a park, then in '94 they covered it with large office buildings. But in '96 they tore them all down, so now it's a park again.

We park the car across from Enver Hoxha's house. It looks more like a high school than a home: Hoxha's commitment to transcendent bureaucracy revealed. Men with Kalashnikovs still guard the entrances. "No one was allowed in this neighborhood under Hoxha. It was very surprising for us to finally see these buildings, we never knew how big they were." Fatmir tells us that under the streets we are walking on, tunnels connect Hoxha's house with every state building.

Directly behind Hoxha's house sits an open McDonald's, empty of customers. As we enter its courtyard, I realize the decor is not quite right. Beneath the golden arches, the universal orange-red-yellow includes green as well. The formica tables are forest green instead of red. Behind the counter, with its single polyester-clad employee, shelves of gleaming liquor bottles sit in place of heat lamps. "Do you know this bar?" asks Fatmir. "Oh, you thought... No, there is no McDonald's in Albania." I look up again at the sign and read, "McMarriot's." "I know a better bar, for normal people," says Fatmir. We continue walking.

WE PULL UP SEATS AT THE FOOT OF A GIANT CONCRETE pyramid and order a round of Tirana's local beer. On one side, George Michael croons global classics with English subtitles over our heads from a giant screen—has karaoke caught on here, where the first movie theater just opened two years ago?—while a slide show of refugees in flight plays on a screen on our other side. After a taste, I tell Fatmir and Ardian that the Tirana-made beer is better quality than normal American, and he shrugs humbly.

"I'm surprised there's so many women on the streets, like, cruising," says Aaron offhandedly. "They're not dressed like I expected for a traditional country, miniskirts and halter-tops."

"Women here are not very free," says Ardian.

"Is it worse for women here than in, say, south Italy?" I ask.

Fatmir stares at me a second, surprised. "Much worse," he finally answers. "Many families, conservative ones, make their daughters return to the house always at 6 p.m. How do you say, curfew?"

"Is abortion legal?"

"Yes, but if the family of an unmarried girl finds out she is pregnant, she must marry. If the boy doesn't marry her, he is killed by her family, maybe 99 percent of them. Also, if you are going out with a girl and you meet her family, or they find out somehow, you must get engaged in maybe three months, no more. It is very difficult to have a relationship here," Ardian sighs. "My girlfriend and I are together three years, but still we have to hide."

"Is divorce difficult?"

"No, it is legal and not so difficult. But maybe because of the family, it is difficult to marry again."

"So, now that religion is legal again, is everyone Muslim?"

Fatmir sips his beer before answering. "Maybe two thirds of people are Muslims, like us. The rest are Catholic, or Orthodox. But people here don't make a big deal out of it."

I remember a famous quotation from a hundred years ago, "The religion of Albania is Albanianism," but decide not to ask about it. "How many people practice Ramadan?"

"Maybe half, sometimes. My grandmother was religious. Under Hoxha, when she would go to people's houses during Ramadan, she would stick a candy in her mouth, so they would not think she was fasting, but she would not really eat it. If people thought you were religious you might disappear."

"Were there bars during Hoxha?"

"Bars? During Hoxha, every block in the city had one person who watched everyone else." I describe "neighborhood watch" in my suburb growing up, and Ardian agrees it is similar. "Under Hoxha, if any neighborhood watch in the city noticed you were going anywhere besides work or school, they would report it, and the next day your neighborhood watch would go to your house for an explanation.

"People were afraid even to talk. You couldn't even mention to your best friend if you wanted to leave the country, somehow people would find out and you'd be in trouble. You were afraid even your own brother might be a spy."

"Damn," I said. "It's even worse than Romania. In Romania, people only thought their best friend might be a spy, but not their brother."

"One in three people spied for the secret police under Hoxha."

We order another round.

"That's fucking crazy."

"No, Hoxha wasn't crazy, he was very smart. He was one of the richest people in the world. For example, he was selling energy to Europe the whole time, making a lot of money. Everyone in the country had to work eight hours a day, six days a week. In the '80s the average wage was four dollars a month. What happened to the rest?

"But now, my father—he told you how much he has to work. Under Hoxha, housing was provided by the government, food was very cheap, and one could sometimes get a government voucher for a trip to the beach. Now, the average wage is $150 dollars a month, and nothing is provided. One third of the country doesn't have enough for their basic needs—housing, or enough to eat. Many people, like my father, wish it was like before."

"I heard that in the late '80s, a survey was taken here, asking people which was the richest country in the world. Something like 95 percent of people said that it was Albania."

"Yes, although maybe some people were afraid to say what they knew. But the only thing we heard about the rest of the world was how poor they were, how everyone was jealous and wanted to conquer Albania. The news said, 'In America, 6,000 people don't even have jobs.' People here thought, '6,000 people! Everyone I know has a job! Those poor Americans!'"

I interrupt. "When she was in Slovenia, my friend Dalia said she couldn't believe how beautiful and calm it was, since all the images she'd ever seen from ex-Yugoslavia were of refugees fleeing burning villages. My friends in Serbia asked me how American workers can go years without a vacation when everyone gets two months paid vacation every year in France. Even in Serbia workers would never give up their vacations. I wonder if it's the same thing, keeping your population feeling lucky."

Across the street from the bar stand the two largest buildings in Albania, a pair of looming office towers. Office workers sift through the doors of one, covered with shining glass panels, while its skeletal twin hosts only birds. Was it burnt out in the conflicts five years ago? I ask Ardian. "No, no, the construction was halted after September 11, 2001," he clarifies, "the government said because the project didn't have a permit. But the real reason was that the government no longer wanted to accept money from

Osama Bin Laden's "twin towers", Tirana, Albania.

Osama Bin Laden, who was funding the construction. It wasn't good anymore for Albania's relations with the US."

Before we can decide how to react, our hosts laugh as they tell us of one of Osama's visits to Tirana. One time, a waiter at the bar we're sitting in, "Bar Cafe America," begged the passing entrepreneur to take a picture with him. The photo, showing waiter and investor arm in arm in front of Bar Cafe America, sold to a western newspaper for $50,000. I wonder to myself if Albania's non-military participation in the Iraq war "coalition" could be an apology to the US for Tirana's architectural irony.

FATMIR HAS TAKEN THE DAY OFF WORK TO DRIVE US TO Kruje. His gracious conversation doesn't hesitate as he skids through the incomprehensibility of Tirana traffic. Mopeds zip diagonally through traffic in all directions. Fatmir dives into oncoming traffic on the left to avoid incessant potholes and stopped police cars. Oncoming vehicles dive past on the right as quickly as on the left. An old man on a bicycle in traditional Muslim dress, his wife straddling the back, rides toward us on the road's thin shoulder. Pedestrians cross without seeming to notice the cars roaring past them. Sheep and cows wander through the flow. A young kid perches like a bird on a concrete meridian in the middle of it all, lost in thought.

As the traffic thins outside the city, Fatmir points out buildings shattered by artillery in the 1997 fighting. Big, brick-ragged pock-marks and shrapnel holes decorate many walls. Buildings under construction straddle ancient abandoned villages, outnumbering finished houses many times over. They are draped in teddy bear, kitty cat, and Alf doll scarecrows. Flags of hot pink, lime green, purple, yellow and clear plastic fly proudly from the houses. Unlike in Kosov@, hardly an Albanian flag is to be seen. In a gas station beside the road, old men sip their coffees and observe us driving past. Remnants of Socialist Realism mosaics portraying heroic proletariat and revolutionary mottoes line the road here and there, a few still intact.

As Fatmir's car struggles up the steep road into Kruje, kids on roller-skate scooters rocket past us on both sides, hurling down the narrow, windy, shoulderless mountain road without brakes. In the distance, I glimpse the gigantic Elbasan power plant, now abandoned, which Chairman Mao built for Albania during their brief friendship. When asked later why he cut ties with Hoxha, Mao said, "If every man in China stood up at the same time and urinated, it would sink Albania."

Fatmir parks at the base of the old fortress. We hike up alongside its crumbling walls. I pause and close my eyes, trying to return the stones to their past glory. "At night, if the air is clean, you can see the lights from Italy," says Fatmir. Lizards dart through the untended grass. The entire world stretches out below.

Inside the museum, I learn that Skanderbeg, Albania's greatest national hero, earned his glory in this very fortress, by beating back a Turkish invasion in the fifteenth century. Albania was overtaken anyway soon after his death. I remember that Jarmir in Prizren told me that many young Kosovars in some areas study Turkish; I silently ask a brass statue of Skanderbeg if he approves, but he keeps his silence. Poems in Skanderbeg's honor cover the walls in metal letters, and one room proudly displays several shelves of books on Skanderbeg published in various languages. Fatmir points up at one metal relief hanging from a tall wall, and explains, "This museum hasn't changed very much since old times." Hoxha presented himself as the heir to the anti-imperialist tradition of Skanderbeg, and the museum seems to boast the best materials and artistry of anything I've seen here yet.

Pausing by a plaster bust with Lek Dukagjini written underneath, Fatmir asks if we recognize the name. We shake our heads. Fatmir translates the entry below. Lek was the author of Albania's blood feud laws. If one's family honor is injured, atonement in the form of male blood from the offending clan must be paid. Unfortunately, this blood must then be avenged as well. Women in the family are immune from direct vengeance, and thus take over the man's role in providing for the family, while he stays home. Perhaps this is the origin of the ongoing transgender tradition in northern Albania, I reflect, which Western academians describe as "Women Who Become Men."

"Did Hoxha outlaw blood feuds?" I ask. Fatmir nods his head an emphatic "no."

"They were far too popular for him to change. Still, they are very popular, many blood feuds are still going, especially in the north. Some have being going thousands of years." At least Lek's laws don't depend on a central power. Perhaps this is why they are still so popular.

On the way out of Kruje, we pass the local butcher. A gang of young kids are helping the butcher tear a cow apart in front of his store. Down the hill, an oncoming white Mercedes spins out across the road as we come around a tight corner. Fatmir turns quick and brakes a foot or two away from collision. Behind the wheel sits a boy of perhaps ten years old, his father laughing beside him in the passenger seat. We thank Fatmir again for his driving.

As I walk past the shop counter on my way to visit Ardian, his father shouts with aggressive cheer, "Communism! Enver Hoxha! Vladimir Lenin! Joseph Stalin!" giving a sporty thumbs-up. Stalin is too much, I can't agree this time with a cheery shrug.

"Bunkers?" I stop and ask him. "Bunkers good?"

He gazes straight back at me from his chair behind the counter. "Bunkers," he says, weighing the air with his left hand. Then, gesturing with his right, "Korea. Vietnam. Indonesia. Chile. Afghanistan. Iraq."

"Bunkers! Bunkers good!" I say, with a grin and a thumbs-up.

IN TIRANA, WHEN WE ASK OUR FRIENDS AND TRAVEL
agents about going to Shkodra in the north, they all have the
same reaction. "Don't go to the north. Bad idea. There's nothing
to see in the north." They shake their heads when we tell them
we are going anyway. "One day, Shkodra. One day." Some have
relatives in the north, but none have visited them since 1997.
After the armories were raided and the police and government
buildings were destroyed, government returned to Tirana after
a week. It took some time for it to regain control of the south.
Even with the aid of Greek and Italian military forces, the entire
northern half of the country still remains out of its grasp.

My travelmates persist—what about the Shkodra castle? Or
am I so racist that I think Albanians are dangerous there? Even
Albanians are racist against Albanians, I guess, thinking of our
Tirana friends' words—"one day." There is certainly tension
between the Tosks in the south and the Ghegs in the north, but
our friends in Tirana view the distinction itself as racist. They
seem to have other reasons for avoiding the north. Not relishing the prospect of traveling alone back to Macedonia, I try and
fail to convince Branka and Aaron to turn around. Maybe I can
impress people at parties, I dimly console myself, by bragging
about how adventurous I am, if we don't get killed.

On the train, Branka and Aaron play a very loud game of Yahtzee.
I laugh along with their ridiculous reciprocal jibes and bantering,
as a distraction from the stark staring eyes of everyone else in
the cabin. After some time, the train slows to a crawl. Outside,
many buildings have shrapnel marks and gaping, brick-ragged
holes. Many are missing windows or are completely burnt out.
Factories stretching to the horizon sit skeletal, power plants
blackened with silent soot. The train stops at a series of ruined
train stations. Buff skinny old men harvest with scythes at
the foot of dry, rocky hills between towns. Tough trees cover
the land. A mine in the distance seems to be working, but no
cars or trucks are around to carry the load.

As we step off into Shkodra, a taxi driver shouts with a thrilled
look, "Hello! Hello!" as he rubs his thumb across his fingertips —
Money! Money! We walk past him. After a cup of coffee in a
cafe where I again fail to talk Branka and Aaron into turning
around, we walk into the abandoned center. A giant sign at the
main intersection shows a bewildered trollish figure trying to
squeeze through an arched doorway with the word "Europe"

written across the top. The Kalashnikov on his back is stuck in the door. I can guess what the Albanian words across the bottom are advising.

On nearly every block "Berbar" signs hang from little metal shacks, closed like everything else. We pass a monument that seems to honor the anti-communist resistance, from 1300 A.D. to the present. Old, peeling wheat-pasted signs put up long ago by some thrill-seeker NGO sternly advise, "Stop trafficking women and children" in Albanian and English. I wonder when I'll see another bank. If ever. We are all running low on cash—I'm living on money borrowed from my travelmates since my bank automatically froze my account. Apparently my bank, too, is unfamiliar with the idea of Albanian tourism, and assumed any withdrawals in Albania must be fraudulent.

We start walking to the outskirts of town to visit what might be Europe's oldest castle. Oddly colored boxes selling sparse groceries give way to thinning shantytown, scattered around car shells. Nearly everyone stares as we pass. One group of boys trails behind us at a polite distance, laughing and waving. I smile and wave back. A couple of them keep shouting something, pointing at Branka, waving. I shrug. A middle-aged man peddles his bicycle up to us and rides two feet from me without saying a word. He stares so much at the split in Branka's skirt that I'm surprised he doesn't fall from his bike. We walk out of town, and he pedals alongside us. Branka doesn't flinch.

"HELLO!" I finally yell at him, and he flashes me a friendly nod before returning his eyes to Branka's legs.

"I guess people aren't so used to visitors here," says Aaron.

The sign "Stop trafficking women and children" flashes through my head. Branka keeps walking. When we arrive at the castle, the man waves goodbye and pedals away.

The castle's walls are as thick as most houses are tall, and so well preserved that I expect some grandma to stick a surprised head out of a window as I pass. Waist-deep weeds devour the stoic stones. Bats rustle in echoing wells, open under my feet. A young man in a sweater asks graciously, "Have you heard the story of this wall?" In order to bless the castle when it was being built, he explains, the king demanded that a fair young woman be built into the castle's walls. The woman cried and cried, but only because she could not face the thought of leaving her two nursing babes to starve. The architects offered to leave one of her breasts exposed through the wall, and the mother was satisfied.

"This, right here, is where she is. People say on some nights, when it rains, you can see milk flow from the stones. I'm not saying I believe it, but some people do."

"How old is this castle?" asks Branka.

The young man shrugs. "Three, four thousand years? Longer than people have been counting. And people lived in it until World War I, or even after. That's why it still looks like new."

"Do you live in Shkoder?"

"I go to university in Tirana, but I come back to Shkoder often, this is where I am from."

"How is it here?"

"You know," he shrugs, "it's OK I guess." After some minutes, we exchange warm goodbyes and set off back to town.

Once the mid-day siesta is over, people appear on the streets and a few store fronts open. We visit the largest mosque in the Balkans, bizarrely shiny and soda-can characterless in its asymmetrical surroundings. Aaron walks into the central tourist hotel, a brownish five-floor Socialist Realism monstrosity. A few minutes later he walks out, chuckling darkly and shaking his head. "I can't explain, but they were asking a lot of questions. The keys for every single room were hanging on their hooks." We look around more and check into a friendly, spotless little hostel, with candles and matches on the table in case of blackout.

Around dinnertime, the streets come alive. Sitting in a crowded outdoor bar sipping beer, we watch teenagers cruise the strip flirting. Old folks on benches watch us. In "May 1 Pizzeria" across from us, a plastic play-land castle crawls with kids amid outdoor candle-lit seating where well-dressed adults dine in luxury. The evening prayer-call bounces down the street, mixing with euro-techno blasting from the cafes. "Stateless pizza. A little anarchist utopia," I say.

"Not quite," says Branka. "Fine beer, though."

We stuff ourselves on gourmet pizza and drink until 2 a.m. The bars are still going as we stumble to bed.

ARDIAN EXPLAINED TO US IN TIRANA THAT IN ALBANIA people shake their heads back-and-forth to mean "yes," and nod up-and-down to say "no." I was very confused there when I walked into a busy restaurant and asked for food, and the waiter shook his head. Buses would stop in the road for us as we vehemently shook our heads for them to keep going, shouting, "No!" which sounds like *"po,"* the word for "yes." But this morning in Shkodra, I wonder if people here do the opposite. As we ask around the various mini-vans which are heading to Kukes, near Kosov@, people somehow related to each van grab us and pull us over to theirs, but with little concern about our desired destination. "Kukes?" Nod. Or shake? Doesn't the placard in the window say, "Tirana?" We climb into the nearest van asking every client, "Kukes?" and stay as they don't push us out.

The driver insists that I ride shotgun in the small Italian school bus. Ardian told us that Hoxha had built every road, even those in the plains, intentionally knotted with curves. Any straight roads could be used as a runway by invading Russians, or Americans. Even this tiny road, cut into the side of massive steep Tibetan mountains, seems intentionally treacherous. Rocky slopes mottled with green stretch straight down. The tires clamor over the surface of one-third tar, two-thirds dirt, worse than just dirt. Rather than slowing for each of the infinite number of curves, the driver skids across both lanes, flipping the car alarm on and off in place of a horn. Rusted dams sit useless mid-river far below.

A man sitting behind me, who lives in Greece but is visiting home, repeats the phrase that everyone tells me—Albania has no culture. An "Albaturist" brand van passes us on the right, the letters "E I LOVE YOU E" pasted across the back window. Impossibly discordant Albanian folk music screeches out of the treble-scream speakers from a ridiculously warped cassette. It is ecstatic and instantaneous, but bizarrely meandering. Out the window we pass a boy gathering wild lavender, his face blank and pure as an icon. I think Albania has a lot of culture, I tell the man beside me.

For seven hours the driver spins over lumps of dirty tar with just enough caution to keep us upright, yelling and laughing to his friend in back the whole way. He slaps my leg and shouts a running translation of the cassette to me into Italian, not that I understand Italian any more than Albanian.

As we arrive in Kukes, our driver claims that we agreed on 15 euros each, not 15 total. He has changed the figures on the paper we wrote our agreement on earlier. Or had we just misunderstood? The driver indignantly accuses us of thievery. A crowd gathers tightly around, eyeing us. Even if we misunderstood and he is an honest man, we don't have enough money. He starts to grab Aaron as Branka screams at him. I sit on the corner, cold with fear and resignation. A black SUV pulls up, and three big guys, dressed in neat black pants and button-up shirts with rolled up sleeves and dark sunglasses, emerge to suss us out. Branka yells indignantly and throws fifteen euros toward the guy so he has to run after them, long enough for us to jog away.

As we walk into town center, car after minivan after pedestrian comes up and tries to force us to come with them. They all know which town we want to get to. One kid, who speaks good English, walks up and says sincerely, "Hello, where do you need to go? I have a car, I can take you." I pause. "Look, I want to help. I'm not a bad guy," he pleads. I look at his car. On top is a small boat. Under the boat, in the car, are three big guys staring like sharks.

We walk quickly until we find a cafe, with a nice local guy who speaks German and clearly knows nothing about our situation. He brings us to the minivan station, for Kukes has neither buses nor trains nor taxis, but before he can ask a price, he is accosted by a group of ten or so men from earlier, who grab him and reprimand him fiercely. He shrugs his shoulders and translates, "Must pay 50 euros to border," and sadly jogs away. No one cares that we don't have it, that the town has no bank, has probably never seen an ATM or credit card. We slip into a cafe and sit away from the windows.

Police, people from the first stop, and strangers walk up and down the street looking around, I assume for the foreigner thieves. We order a morbid round of coffees. This is a very bad situation, we agree. Honor is a big deal here, blood feuds can last centuries. At least our families aren't here. "What happens when night falls?" asks Branka. We order a second round and try to ask our waiter if he has a car, but he doesn't understand. A man approaches to translate, though he seems to know less English than our waiter. I suspect him of being friends with the driver, but I realize that I suspect everyone in this town of the same. Finally, he and Branka begin to speak Italian. Watch out, there are many bad people here, he tells us. He lives now in Milan with his family, he says, and is back here only to visit relatives. He and Branka talk about Milan and his family for an hour. Finally, he asks us what we are doing here. He offers to help. "I have a friend here with a car, he will drive you to Kosova, please, as I friend, I want to help you." He pays our coffee bill, and we walk out on the street.

The first passing car honks, pulls over, and summons our new friend. They talk for a couple minutes. "This is my friend! He will take you to Kosova," our new pal tells us. Odd that the first car on the street was, coincidentally, his friend. But then, if he kills us, it's no worse than being here when night falls. We get in. He circles around town, and I expect him to pull into an alley where the driver and his extended family await.

"Do you trust me? You are not scared?" our driver eagerly asks again and again. We stop at his house so he can grab his passport. "I show you my passport, so you can trust me. No problem!" We smile back.

We are almost out of town, and still haven't met the van driver from earlier, or his extended family. Out of town, on the freeway, and we still haven't been pulled off the road to be killed. We cross the border, our passports checked by a Bangladeshi UN soldier. Stretching our backs and grabbing our bags, we thank our heroic driver heartily for getting us there alive. Warmly we shake each others' hands. We pull out the five euros clearly agreed on earlier as payment for the three of us, for the hour drive. "What is this?" he asks mystified. "This is nothing!" We call him a traitor, scoundrel, throw five more euros into the deal, and leave without shaking hands. I forget my Alternative Tentacles sweatshirt in his car, so I assume someone in Kukes is touting the height of punk fashion to this very day.

Later, retelling the incident to a friend, I turn to Aaron and say, "Aaron, you have to admit that was fucked."

Aaron says, "Whatever, you can get mugged in London, too."

I say, "Mugged? Aaron, you were as scared as I was, you totally thought we were going to get killed!"

Aaron yells, "What do you expect? It's fucking ALBANIA!" I stare back at him, but before I can laugh, he corrects himself. "But anyway, it's just like any place else."

SARANDE, IN THE SOUTH, BORDERING GREECE, LOOKS identical to Marcus Hook, Maryland, only without the refineries and mills. Same smell of port exhaust, same cranes, same narrow cracked streets stained with resentful stares. The main bars of both towns play the same mix of global pop/rock, fluorescents glaring off yellow plastic-varnished bars, sports on the mute TVs. In Sarande, the decor reminds Francisco of Soviet tourist bars; painted concrete walls and a giant wall hanging of a beach scene fail to distract from the room's bunkerliness. In my one day in Sarande, I survey the town and find one noteworthy column, a strange mix of Turkish and Byzantine construction about four feet tall, sticking out unannounced from the beach. I went to Marcus Hook because my friend was curious about the post-industrial factory town, and we left quickly. I have come to Sarande because everyone I have met in Albania said I had to go, that it was a very, very beautiful place, the most beautiful in all of Albania.

TRYING NOT TO HYPERVENTILATE AS OUR MINIBUS SKIDS down the dirt twists of a mountain road, I stare at the label on my bottled water:

> Tepelene
> Analyzed for all parameters.
> Suffled how it gush from the source of the woods of Tepelena.

"How is this possible?" I ask Francisco.

He points out the window. "Is that an oil refinery?" Through the smog, we both stare at an industrial structure the size of a small gas station, a flame shooting from its smokestack. Oil pumps populate the hills around it like rusty dinosaurs. After some minutes I realize they are barely moving—the first working industry I've seen in this country. The air smells of oil, and concrete riverbanks along murky streams are black. "I think in old cultures, like here, people learn how futile it is to enforce order. It's a process, social fermentation, a chaotic maturity. But I mean, that's a different thing than the poverty and disorder. You can't really blame them for suffering the pressures and impositions of immature civilizations that haven't figured it out yet."

"Suffling. Applied Pataphysics," I whisper to myself. Francisco looks down the mountain.

ON MY SECOND VISIT TO TIRANA, ARDIAN ASKS ME HOW the city seems now.

"How do you mean?" I ask.

"I mean, has it changed much?" he says.

Vacationland, Sarande, Albania.

"But it's only been three months," I say.

"Remember those?" He points to a massive line of rubble along the river, ten feet high and twice as wide. "Remember the restaurant we went to when we met, and the night we went to the different bars? That was them. They were built with no permits. Probably the builders knew that they would soon be torn down, and built them so they'd be repaid for them." Their rebar and concrete ruins spill into the length of the river.

We walk down the main street of the commercial district, beside the massive cable clearly marked "High Tension Power Line" which runs through its center. Buildings loom in absurd pastels and day-glo colors: salmon pink, lime green, highlighter yellow. Ardian explains that under Hoxha, buildings were only gray, so the first use of international aid funds was to paint Tirana with democratic colors. We enter a chic bar with mirrors for walls and order a round. I stare at the pack of cigarettes

Ardian is smoking:

> These superb cigarettes have been skilfully created for the
> discerning clientele who have come to expect the legendary
> perfection of the House of Cartier. Cartier Vandome PEARL-
> TIPPED. les must(r) de Cartier.

Francisco says he's read that statistically, Albanians consume
something like 80 packs of cigarettes a day, per man, woman,
and child, if smuggling is included. Ardian shakes his head.
"Many bad people."

I ask Ardian how people in Albania feel about Macedonians.
He says that after what happened in Kosov@, most Albanians
don't like Slavs. I remember a friend of Agim's in Prizren making an awkward joke when Agim mentioned that Branka was
Croatian, from which Agim defended her. Does Ardian think the
fighting over the border in Macedonia will flare up again?

"Well," he says, "it's a problem to break away from Macedonia,
since Albanians are not a majority."

I change the subject. I heard that there were bad floods since
I was here before?

"Terrible, maybe one quarter of the city was underwater.
Billions of dollars of damage."

"Was it from bad rains?"

"No, it was not natural causes."

"What?" I figure I have misunderstood.

"The story is that this man was working at the dam upstream
from Tirana. While he was working one day, he left the dam
running to go get a beer at the neighborhood bar. After a couple
drinks, he got up to leave. 'That will be one dollar,' the bartender
told him. 'What? Don't you know who I am? I am an important
man!' said the man. 'I don't care who you are, I have to pay my
rent!' said the bartender. The man paid, but slammed the door
when he left. Then he walked back to the dam and opened the
dam gates.

"This is typical Albanian mentality," Ardian says. "People
here have no culture."

"You know the German word *schaudenfreude*?" asks Francisco.
"It means it doesn't matter how bad you are doing, as long as
your neighbor is doing worse."

Formerly glamorous bar strip, Tirana, Albania.

"Yes, that is it," says Ardian. "Oh, and when the opposition party criticized the mayor about the flood, his response was to say on television, 'Fuck you.'"

FRANCISCO AND I COLLAPSE ONTO OUR BEDS IN THE hostel and turn on the TV. The news shows photos and Albanian headlines. Summaries of the day's events in English appear at the bottom of the screen just long enough for me to write them down:

> The Italian citizen owned a rented bar
> The Italian had seven different identities
> Serbs low turnout excluded them from governing
> Durres police block five luxurious vehicles
> International competition for the center of Tirana city

Police: Man killed with the adze
Koci personalizes catharsis movement
Budget 2003 to include even the emergencies
National Theater presented a consummated play
Minister of Culture—three books are published every day
Arton Lane says demolitions in the sea coast to start now
Lame says for next tourist season to find no unlicensed
buildings
Italian injured in a bar while drinking

"Albanian news leaves you with less information than what you started with," says Francisco.

Over a soundtrack of Terence Trent D'Arby and Stevie Wonder, the news moves on to a long list of the day's accidental deaths, murders and suicides. The total seems high for a country of only three million people.

Blast in a stone pit, two people die
Two brothers tried to take stones from the pit
The blast came as a result of hidden weapons
43-year-old man hangs himself due to depression
Xhoana celebrates her son's ninth birthday
Congress of Radicals; Balkan to enter EU soon
The bar owner injures the shoplifter
Salzman: There was no progress in Laws and Economy

We watch coverage of a bomb blast in front of the Parliament building in Macedonia, which seemed peaceful when we were there two days ago. "This is a sad place," says Francisco.

The news ends suddenly with a scene of crashing waves before a sunset. A voice-over in English blurts out, "On today's show, we're going to the hot beaches of Puerto Escondido, Mexico. Stay tuned to the surf channel for some hot surfing!"

I FIND REDEMPTION IN MOULIN PUB AS THE DISCO FLOOR swings. Sliding hips of Albanian traditional dance meet with jaunty hands of global techno. The Bee Gees and West African Dzembe and Sting techno remixes, the sometimes empty dance floor that seems too Albanian, but sometimes full of women dancing. Technically, Ardian, Francisco and I shouldn't be here, since like all of the fancier bars in Tirana, boys aren't allowed without a date. Ardian explained to the bouncer that we're American, so that compensated for not being with women.

Francisco asks if it's socially acceptable for girls to dance with girls. Ardian says, "They are from small villages and away from their parents"—a rare opportunity to cut loose and have fun without being watched, without dealing with boys. Finally.

ALBANIA SEEMS TO BE AN INTENSE COLLECTION OF KNICK-knacks, a miscellany of singularities. The more I see, the less connection things have to each other. Is this what Fatmir meant when he said that they have no culture? Have extreme pressures in so many opposing directions shattered cultural coherence? Tirana makes me doubt that cultural integrity exists anywhere. Cultural consistency, a bland predictability, is only a lack of imagination, accumulated habit to which people finally surrender with pride. I can't see any signs of habit here. Certainly, everyone must have hidden in habit during Hoxha, itself a set of totally new habits of cultural revolution, and perhaps with Hoxhaism's fall some kind of antithetical "democratic" habit may have tried to establish itself. But after 1997, then 1998, when all financial ties to any past, near or distant, were severed, when everyone turned on each other in fear with 750,000 looted Kalashnikovs, when the north and south hid from each other in mutual defensive dread that prevented war, what of even the newest habits could survive? The oldest habits have endured, as has the blood feud law, "the law of the people" that no government has dared to discourage. Yet unlike other parts of the Balkans, actions cannot mask themselves as tradition. Are the police in front of this cafe as I write this leering at people and randomly stopping cars, even searching under the hood, out of a tradition of authoritarianism? They seem as if they have just awakened to find themselves in police clothes, with police guns, in a police van, and have no idea what they are supposed to be doing to be police-like. Yet, unlike in Hungary, where the language was equally incomprehensible to me, I have trouble believing that people understand a word of what each other is saying, that they aren't all just bluffing. But like this limping street dog beside me whose trust I am trying to win, a bright yellow plastic "A12" tag clamped through his ear, everyone here is an expert in making a home in incomprehensible chaos, in threats barreling towards you from any direction, in guessing the intent behind randomness with a confidence equal to certainty. The empty pretense of order takes the place of any pattern, in chaos, comfortably with a childlike smile.

Like the driving: utter chaos, in horrific conditions, but with a calm and total attention that replaces any system of rules. In Romania, at least a surrealist method of alchemy, transforming despair into humor, has endured. Here, nothing but a well practiced confidence in absolutely spontaneous response has found a place to survive.

Is it possible that these people, the oldest surviving "people" of Europe, can have so few evident roots? Is this dog snarling at a Fiat's license plate because it has learned this gesture from dog ages past, or because it has just found its teeth? Has this miraculously tough yet vulnerable people survived conquest after conquest by their very anonymity, their inflexible perfection of adaption? Perhaps this very incomprehensibility is a disproof of assimilation, some proof of an absolute past. These Europeans, as they pretend to see the lights of Italy across the Adriatic, live too immediately to fit into Europe. And these Muslims, 70 percent of the population, are far too familiar with intoning *Inshallah*—if Allah wills—between every other word to ever belong to the idolatry of a fictional past that threatens to unify the Middle East. They embody and live modernism as no modernist could have ever wished upon anyone, unless perhaps Trotsky sadistically envisioned these cops stopping every car on the street, this absurd abundance of bombed-out homes, this street-sweeping Roma woman, the bad traffic, the proliferation of Kalashnikovs and wheelbarrows, this spin of dizziness and nausea that is the evidence of real Permanent Revolution.

NOTES

FOREWORD

As the author of this book is in the most literal sense an amateur and not a professional, I lack the means to seriously dispute the following authors' scholarship. Nor would I wish to dismiss the valuable insights they offer within their areas of expertise. This list also makes no claim to be any sort of exhaustive bibliography on the subject. Instead, by pointing out the limitations imposed by some authors' approaches, I hope to suggest a certain critical perspective, shared by very many people across the Balkans and severely underrepresented in Western discourses, through which readers might approach their works.

1. Rebecca West, *Black Lamb and Grey Falcon: A Journey Through Yugoslavia* (New York: Penguin, 1995).
2. Maria Todorova, *Imagining the Balkans* (New York: Oxford University Press, 1997), p. 4.
3. Robert D. Kaplan, *Balkan Ghosts: A Journey Through History* (New York: St. Martin's Press). Quoted in:Laura Silber and Allan Little, *Yugoslavia: Death of a Nation* (New York: TV Books, dist. Penguin Books, 1996), p. 287. "Another key moment in a shift of US policy was when President Clinton and his wife Hillary read parts of *Balkan Ghosts*, by Robert Kaplan, which describes the violent past of the region. For some reason the book had an enormous impact on Clinton, convincing him that the inhabitants of the Balkans were doomed to violence."
4. Elie Wiesel, foreword to Rezak Hukanovic et al., *The Tenth Circle of Hell: A Memoir of Life in the Death Camps of Bosnia* (New York: Basic Books, 1996).
5. Alexandra Stiglmayer, ed., *Mass Rape: The War Against Women in Bosnia-Herzegovina* (Lincoln: University of Nebraska Press, 1994): Ruth Seifert, "War and Rape: A Preliminary Analysis," p. 59; Catherine

MacKinnon, "Rape, Genocide, and Women's Human Rights," p. 192.

6.   Mestrovic, *The Balkanization of the West: The Confluence of Postmodernism and Postcommunism* (London and New York: Routledge, 1994), p. 1-27.

7.   Michael Parenti, *To Kill A Nation: The Attack on Yugoslavia* (London and New York: Verso, 2000). With the exception of page 6, in which he notes that "the Serbs [have admitted] that atrocities were committed by their paramilitaries...." Besides attributing one voice to all "the Serbs," this severe understatement implicitly denies the complicity of Milošević and much of Serbia proper. Parenti's consistent refusal to implicate Milošević, as some kind of Great Defender of Socialism, in any of the unfolding of the conflict(s) might, in this instance, be compared to a refusal to admit US responsibility for acts of the Israeli state. Like Ronald Reagan insisting that Israel withdraw the settlements from the Occupied Territories, Milošević publicly chastised Radovan Karadžić, leader of the Bosnian Serbs, and attempted to present himself as a moderate. And like Reagan with Israel, Milošević consistently funded the extremist factions which he sometimes decried in public. Parenti's dismissal of systematic rape by Serb forces in Bosnia will be addressed later.

8.   Kate Hudson, *Breaking the South Slav Dream: The Rise and Fall of Yugoslavia* (London and Serling: Pluto Press, 2003), p. 74.

9.   Diana Johnstone, *Fool's Crusade: Yugoslavia, NATO and Western Delusions* (New York: Monthly Review Press, 2002), p. 18.

10. The area has long been known to Serbs as Kosovo and to Albanians as Kosova; this book chooses the slightly unweildy solution of Kosov@ in its designation.

11. Jasminka Udovicki and James Ridgeway, eds., *Burn This House: The Making and Unmaking of Yugoslavia* (Durham: Duke University Press, 2000).

12. Dubravka Ugresic, *The Culture of Lies* (University Park: Pennsylvania State University Press, 1998).

13. Catherine Samary, *Yugoslavia Dismembered* (New York: Monthly Review Press, 1995).

14. Franke Wilmer, *The Social Construction of Man, the State, and War: Identity, Conflict, and Violence in the Former Yugoslavia* (New York: Routledge, 2002).

INTRODUCTION

15. My notion of traveling and reading as a pervert, of getting fucked up, is articulated in academic terms in the following passage by Frances Trix, linguistic anthropologist and Bektashi Sufi, in her study of Bektashi linguistics: "[Paul] Ricoeur's understanding of the power of a text is particularly stimulating. He sees this power as the potential to disclose a world. Therefore, 'To understand is not to project oneself into the text; it is to receive an enlarged self from the apprehension

of proposed worlds which are the genuine object of interpretation.' ...
Instead of speaking of 'enlarged self,' however, Bektashis and other
Sufis speak of 'loss of self,' of 'death before dying.' These expressions
reflect partly the precariousness of trusting into the Unknown, as
well as the reframing that can ensue."

Frances Trix, *Spiritual Discourse* (Philadelphia, University of
Pennsylvania Press, 1993), p. 22.

Samuel P. Huntington, *The Clash of Civilizations and the Remaking of
World Order* (New York: Simon & Schuster, 1998).

16. Protests in Kosov@ in 1981 for increased cultural autonomy within
Yugoslavia contained what could be seen as nationalist demands as
well. To what extent any of them aimed to break with Yugoslavia, and
the connection any of them had to claims of national independence in
World War II and in the nineteenth century, remain highly contested
topics beyond the scope of this book. I do argue that the economic
crisis of the 1980s, the end of the Cold War, the manipulations of the
inherited centralized state/media apparatus, the maneuverings of
profiteers, and other very modern phenomena have been too important to permit attributing traditional cultural distance or conflicting
land claims as central causes of the recent war/s—let alone the racist
silliness of "exploding ancient ethnic hatreds."

17. Alija Izetbegović, *Islam Between East and West* (Plainfield: American
Trust Publications, 1985).

18. Howard Clark, *Civil Resistance in Kosovo* (London and Sterling: Pluto
Press, 2000).

19. The following glossary is taken from this important book that details
the current situation of the 200,000 refugees expelled by the victorious Albanian forces with NATO assistance:

Voice of Roma and Paul Polansky, *The Current Plight of the Kosovo
Roma* (Sebastopol: Voice of Roma, 2002), p. ii. Available at: www.
voiceofroma.com

Roma—plural noun, the Romani people as a whole
Rom—singular noun, a Romani person, man, or husband
Romni—singular noun, a Romani woman, or wife
Romani—adjective, as in "Romani culture"
Romane—noun, the language of the Roma

20. Richard Holbrooke, *To End a War.* New York: Modern Library, 1999.
See also BBC, *The Death of Yugoslavia* (1995), part 6.

PRELUDE: TRIESTE, ITALY

21. Guy Debord, trans. Ken Knabb, Society of the Spectacle (London:
Rebel Press, 2005). Available at: www.bopsecrets.org.

SLOVENIA

22. Slovenia joined the European Union on May 1, 2004.

23. Eddie Yuen, Daniel Burton-Rose, and George Katsiaficas, eds., *Confronting Capitalism* (New York: Soft Skull Press, 2004): Shon Meckfessel, "Standing Challenges to Capitalism in the Balkans," pp. 266–269.

24. Michael Hardt and Antonio Negri, *Empire* (Cambridge: Harvard University Press, 2001).

25. Max Weber, *The Protestant Ethic and the Spirit of Capitalism* (New York: Charles Scribner's Sons, 1958).

26. Ugrešić, cited in Wilmer, p. 128.

27. A commonly accepted figure, though often contested (in both directions) due to the difficultly in gathering information in war-time conditions.

28. Wilmer, p. 47.

29. Greg Palast, *The Best Democracy Money Can Buy: An Investigative Reporter Exposes the Truth About Globalization, Corporate Cons, and High-Finance Fraudsters* (New York: Plume Books, 2004).

30. Ramet, S.P. (1993), "Slovenia's Road to Democracy," *Europe-Asia Studies*, 45(5): p. 878.

31. Jan Morris, *Trieste and the Meaning of Nowhere.* (Cambridge, MA: Da Capo Press, 2002.) p. 18.

CROATIA

32. Dubravka Žarkov, *The Body of War.* (Durham and London: Duke University Press, 2007.) p. 124.

33. Žarkov, p. 92.

34. Quoted by Mark Mazower, *The Balkans*, Modern Library, New York, 2000, p. 45.

35. "Name-brand lives" from conversation with Niko Martinez, my cousin.

36. V. P. Gagnon Jr. *The Myth of Ethnic War: Serbia and Croatia in the 1990s.* (Ithica and London: Cornell University Press, 2004.) p. 8.

37. Gagnon, p. 21

38. Palast, pp. 132–33.

39. Gagnon, p. 150. Also BBC (1995), *The Death of Yugoslavia*. Part 3 for interview with Reihl-Kir's widow.

40. Gagnon, p. 152

41. Laura Silber and Allan Little, *Yugoslavia: Death of a Nation.* (New York: Penguin, 1997). Cited in Wilmer, p. 193. See also BBC (1995), *The Death of Yugoslavia*, part 4.

42. Gagnon, p. 148.

43. Gagnon, p. 140.

44. Gagnon, pp. 155–56.

45. Gagnon, pp. 171–173. For the use of force against protesters, footnote 106.

46. R. Jeffrey Smith, "Croats Find Treasury Plundered," *Washington Post*, June 13, 2000.

47. Ibid.

48. Ibid.

49. Final report of the United Nations Commission of Experts established pursuant to Security Council Resolution 780 (1992) Annex III.A "Special Forces," Section B. Available at www.ess.uwe.ac.uk/comexpert/ANX/III-A.htm#II.B Cited in Wilmer, p. 196, ftnotes 40, 49 (p. 297–298).

50. Carolyn Nordstrom, *Shadows of War: Violence, Power, and International Profiteering in the Twenty-First Century* (Berkeley: University of California Press, 2004) pp. 31–34.

51. Kuzmanic & Truger, eds., *Yugoslavia War* (Ljubljana: Peace Institute Ljubljana, 1993): Miroslav Stanojevic, "Regulation of Industrial Relations in Post-selfmanagement Society." Referred to in *Confronting Capitalism*, Meckfessel, p. 267: "One essay published in Ljubljana even argues that the war was made only by those sectors of society that were not reorganized by self-management: military, police, politicians, and peasants in rural isolation."

52. Sabrina Ramet, *Balkan Babel: The Disintegration of Yugoslavia from the Death of Tito to Ethnic War*. Second edition. (Boulder: Westview Press, 1996.) p. 12–13.

53. Ramsey Clark, Sean Gervasi, Sara Flounders, et al., NATO in the Balkans: Voices of Opposition (New York: International Action Center, 1998). Quotation from Appendix:
The Foreign Operations, Export Financing, and Related Programs Appropriations Act, 1991, Public Law 101-513, appropriated funds for the fiscal year ending September 30, 1991. Below is the paragraph relating to Yugoslavia: Sec. 599A. Six months after the date of enactment of this Act, (1) none of the funds appropriated or otherwise made available pursuant to this Act shall be obligated or expended to provide any direct assistance to the Federal Republic of Yugoslavia, and (2) the Secretary of the Treasury shall instruct the United States Executive Director of each international financial institution to use the voice and vote of the United States to oppose any assistance of the respective institutions to the Federal Republic of Yugoslavia: Provided, That this section shall not apply to assistance intended to support democratic parties or movements, emergency or humanitarian assistance, or the furtherance of human rights: Provided further, That this section shall not apply if all six of the individual Republics of the Federal Republic of Yugoslavia have held free and fair multiparty elections and are not engaged in a pattern of systematic gross violations of human rights: Provided further,That notwithstanding the failure of the individual Republics of the Socialist Federal Republic of Yugoslavia to have held free and fair multiparty elections within six months of the enactment of this Act, this section shall not apply if the Secretary of State certifies that the Socialist Federal Republic of

Yugoslavia is making significant strides toward complying with the obligations of the Helsinki Accords and is encouraging any Republic which has not held free and fair multiparty elections to do so.

54. Ramet, Chap. 1. Also Gagnon, p. 106.

55. Stiglmayer: Seifert, p. 59.

56. Parenti has been one of the most tenacious and widely-read critics within the US of imperialistic designs in the Balkans, and his *To Kill A Nation* is for some matters a valuable antidote to the official line. However, like much of the authoritarian left, he adopted an aggressive the-enemy-of-my-enemy-is-my-friend approach to the regime in Belgrade, made worse by his conviction that Milošević stood as a paragon of Socialism after the collapse of the Soviet bloc. He repeatedly speaks of "Serbs" without regard to intra-ethnic political differences, parroting the same ethnicism as those he critiques for demonizing Serbs.

Particularly upsetting is his denial of widespread rapes by Serb forces during the war in Bosnia.

Given the nature and circumstances of the crime, exact numbers have been difficult to establish; however, large bodies of first-hand testimony have been documented by independent groups such as Amnesty International, who Parenti cites elsewhere to (correctly) implicate Croatian and Bosnian forces.

In his essay "The Media and Their Atrocities" in the anthology *You Are Being Lied To* (Russ Kick, ed., New York: The Disinformation Company Ltd, 2001, pp. 51–55), Parenti executes a sleight-of-hand in order to defend his chosen people. Parenti begins by denying that sufficient numbers of Serbian soldiers were present in Bosnia to carry out a rape-campaign of the alleged scale, as they were "involved in desperate military engagements." Besides dishonestly contrasting rape with "military engagements," this argument is belied by the speed with which Serb forces conquered land early in the war. He goes on to quote one dissident opinion within Helsinki Watch—without citing their name or his source—as claiming that all stories of mass-rape originated with the governments of Bosnia and Croatia.

In the next paragraph, without completing his argument concerning the events in Bosnia, Parenti then moves quickly on to the events in Kosovo, and the propaganda campaign carried out to legitimate NATO intervention. He quotes one official from Organization for Security and Cooperation in Europe as saying that dozens, not masses, of rapes occurred by Serbian forces in Kosovo, "and not many dozens." Parenti then refers again to Bosnia in the last sentence of the same chapter to refer to the conviction of a Bosnian Croat officer for failing to stop his troops from raping Bosnian women in 1993.

In the third and final paragraph concerning mass-rape allegations, Parenti concludes, "A few-dozen rapes is a few-dozen too many. But can it serve as one of the justifications for a massive war?" Following on the inconclusive paragraph concerning Bosnia, and the paragraph addressing Kosovo but ending with a reference to Bosnia, the ambiguous antecedent of this summary gives the strong impression—particularly to a reader unfamiliar with the area—that a "few-dozen" rapes occurred in the conflicts in Bosnia and Kosovo taken together. Parenti has managed to reduce tens of thousands to a "few-dozen." The author then wraps up his argument in one idiotically opportunistic phrase, stunning in its lack of perspective: "If Mr. Clinton wanted to stop rapes... he might be able to alert us to how women are sexually mistreated on Capitol Hill and in the White House itself" (p. 52).

Later in the article, Parenti writes: "A spokesman for the UN High Commissioner for Refugees talked of mass rapes and what sounded like hundreds of killings in three villages, but when [journalist Audrey] Gillan pressed him for more precise information, he reduced it drastically to five or six teenage rape victims" (p. 53). Not only had the commissioner exaggerated the numbers, he'd forgotten to mention that the victims were teenagers. Which, Parenti's syntax bizarrely seems to imply, makes the matter not so serious.

In his book *To Kill A Nation*, Parenti again hastily, if not viciously, dismisses essential evidence in order to establish his case:

> The handful of rape-produced births that actually came to light seemed to contradict the image of mass-rape pregnancies reported by Muslim authorities and Western journalists. An Agence France-Presse news item reported that in Sarajevo, "Bosnian investigators have learned of just one case of a woman who gave birth to a child after being raped."

The article cited by Parenti is dated March 1993, less than a year into the war in Bosnia, itself assumably quoting a report published even earlier. Allowing for the term generally associated with pregnancy, the low figure is hardly surprising. In addition, belligerent Serb forces were not within Sarajevo but on the hills surrounding it, and thus—uniquely in all of Bosnia—were not in close enough proximity to rape.

Independent researcher Indira Kajosevic in her balanced essay "Understanding War Rape: Bosnia 1992," gives a more honest account on the topic of rape-pregnancies:

> Dr. Shana Swiss of the Women's Commission of Physicians for Human Rights who followed up the UN Reporter's investigation found a 119 cases of pregnant rape victims in a small sample of six hospitals in Croatia, Serbia and Bosnia. Based on the assumption that 1% of acts of unprotected sexual intercourse result in pregnancy, the identification of 119 pregnancies therefore represents some 11,900 cases of rape [my emphasis—S.M. See http://orlando.women.it/cyberarchive/files/kajosevic.htm].

For Parenti, the Cold War never ended, and the entire Yugoslav tragedy is explained as Capitalist Hegemony conspiring against the triumph of Communism:

> Why were the Serbs targeted? They were the largest and most influential nationality in the former Yugoslavia, with a proportionately higher percentage of Communist party membership than other nationalities.... Morever, in the 1989 US-imposed elections, Serbs and Montenegrins supported the former Communists over the US-backed "democrats" in their respective republics. No wonder the Serbs were targeted as the enemy [*To Kill A Nation*, pp. 81–82].

57. Alfred Jarry, *Selected Works of Alfred Jarry* (New York: Grove Press, 1965), p. 192.
58. Arthur Miller, *Einstein Picasso: Space, Time, and the Beauty That Causes Havoc* (New York: Basic Books, 2001), p. 31.
59. Gagnon, p. 21.

BOSNIA-HERZEGOVINA

60. Another estimate, perhaps or perhaps not weighted for political ends.
61. Dedijer, Vladimir. *The Yugoslav Auschwitz and the Vatican* (Buffalo: Prometheus Books), 1992.
62. BBC, *Death of Yugoslavia*. Part 4.
63. Gagnon, p. 7–8.
64. Al-Husayn ibn Mansur Hallaj, *The Tawasin: The Great Sufic Text on the Unity of Reality* (Riyadh: Islamic Book Foundation, 1978).
65. Alparslan Acikgenc, *Being and Existence in Sadra and Heidegger: A Comparative Ontology* (Kuala Lumpur: International Institute of Islamic Thought and Civilization, 1993).
66. Farid al-Din Attar, *The Conference of Birds* (New York: Penguin Classics, 1984).
67. John Kingsley Birge, *The Bektashi Order of Dervishes* (London: Luzac Oriental, 1994).
68. Massimo Introvigne, *Mary Poppins Goes to Hell: Pamela Travers, Gurdjieff, and the Rhetoric of Fundamentalism* (Center for Studies on New Religions, 1996). See: www.cesnur.org/testi/marypoppins.htm
69. Antony Barnett and Solomon Hughes, "International Police in Bosnia Face Prostitution Claims," July 29, 2001, *The Observer*. See: observer.guardian.co.uk
70. *The Martyrs of Bosnia*, Azzam Publications, 2006. See video.google.com.
71. Josip Novakovich, *Plum Brandy: Croatian Journeys* (Buffalo: White Pine Press, 2002).
72. Svetlana Broz, *Good People in an Evil Time* (New York: Other Press, 2004). p. 249. Absolutely essential. Broz, as an eminent cardiologist

and Tito's granddaughter, was able to gain the confidence of people who might otherwise have been reluctant to share their stories. After gathering hundreds of testimonies over the course of the war, an anonymous 'burgler' broke into her home in Belgrade and destroyed her entire archives, which obviously were a threat to the claims of the Serbian regime. Broz resumed her work, gathered hundreds more testimonies, and finally published her remarkable book in 2002. She has since permanently relocated to Sarajevo. See www.svetlanabroz. org

73. Broz, p. 97.
74. Gregor Belusic, "Bosnian With Patina" (liner notes): www.kud-fp.si/pregnanc/presss.htm Dertum contact: www.kud-fp.si/pregnanc/dertumm.htm.
75. Dzevad Karahasan, *Sarajevo: Exodus of a City* (New York: Kodansha America, 1994).
76. Huntington.
77. Ramet, p. 156–157.
78. Meša Selimović. *The Fortress* (Evanston: Northwestern University Press, 1999), pp. 148-150.
79. Selimović, p. 155.
80. *Calling the Ghosts*. Directed by Mandy Jacobson and Karmen Jelincic. New York: Bowery Productions/Women Make Movies (dist), 1996.
81. Catherine MacKinnon, "Turning Rape into Pornography: Postmodern Genocide." *Ms.* (July–August): 24–30. Critique from Zartov, 181.
82. Ramet, p. 248. On Brigadier General Jovan Divjak, see his wiki page or various youtube interviews.

Serbia

83. Prince Bishop of Montenegro Petar II, *The Mountain Wreath of P.P. Nyegosh: Prince-Bishop of Montenegro, 1830–1951* (Westport: Greenwood Press, 1970), p. 98.
84. Shon Meckfessel, "Standing Challenges to Capitalism in the Balkans," in *Confronting Capitalism*, pp. 270–271.
85. Eric Gordy, *The Culture of Power in Serbia* (University Park: Pennsylvania State University Press, 1999).
86. Hannah Arendt, *Eichmann in Jerusalem: A Report on the Banality of Evil* (New York: Penguin Books, 1994).
87. Gagnon, p. 2.
88. Ibid.
89. Gagnon, pp. 101–103.
90. Gagnon, p. 110.
91. Ramet, p. 201.

Romania

92. Wilmer, p. 147. "Stipe Šuvar, former president of the Communist Party of Yugoslavia, estimated that by June 1995 somewhere around

700,000 people eligible for military service had left—300,000 from Serbia, 100,000 from Croatia, and 300,000 from Bosnia—because they did not want to fight in the war." Wilmer cites Independent Belgrade Radio B92, June 11, 1995.

ALBANIA

93. Ramet, p. 205.
94. Susan Woodword, *Balkan Tragedy* (Washington DC: Brookings Institution, 1995), p. 49. Quoted in Hudson, p. 59.
95. Hudson, pp. 58–62.

MACEDONIA

96. Georgi Khadziev, *Down with the Sultan, Long Live the Balkan Federation!* See: www.savanne.ch/tusovka/en/will-firth/bulgaria.htm.
97. Basil Davidson, *Black Man's Burden: Africa and the Curse of the Nation-State* (Three Rivers: Three Rivers Press, 1993).
98. István Pogány, *The Roma Café: Human Rights & the Plight of the Romani People*, (London: Pluto Press, 2004). p. 97.

KOSOV@

99. Noel Malcolm, *Kosovo: A Short History*, (New York: New York University Press, 1998.) p. 56.
100. Sebastian Junger, *Fire* (New York: Perennial, 2002).
101. Scott Anderson, "Dispatches From a Dead War," *Harper's Magazine*, February, 1999.
102. Melissa Eddy, "Kosovan Girl 'Killed by US Soldier,'" *The Guardian*, January 18, 2000. See: www.guardian.co.uk.
103. Joe Vialls' article is available at: www.vialls.com/transpositions/pedophile1.html.
104. "What hope of a settlement for Cyprus?," *The Economist*, May 15, 2003.
105. Iain King and Whit Mason, *Peace at Any Price: How the World Failed Kosovo* (Ithica: Cornell University Press, 2006.) p. x.
106. www.state.gov/www/regions/eur/ksvo_rambouillet_text.html.
107. Tim Judah, *Kosovo: War and Revenge. Second Edition.* (New Haven and London: Yale University Press, 2000). p. 210.
108. Interview with Boris Johnson. *The Daily Telegraph*, June 28, 1999. (As cited on wikipedia entry for Rambouillet Agreement.).
109. Voice of Roma. *The Current Plight of the Kosovo Roma* (Sebastopol: Voice of Roma, 2002), p. ii. Available from voiceofroma.com. Roma have steadily continued to leave in the meantime.
110. According to BBC, the bombing cost NATO approximately £30 billion (news.bbc.co.uk/2/hi/europe/476134.stm). For a pre-war per capita GDP estimated at under $400, see www.seerecon.org/kosovo/cinfo.htm. Kosovo's pre-war population was approximately 2.2 million.

Estimate based on a rather weak dollar at the time of writing.

111. Ibid.

112. www.cia.gov/library/publications/the-world-factbook/geos/kv.html

113. King & Mason, p. 243.

114. King & Mason, p. 228.

115. King & Mason, p. 229.

116. King & Mason, p. 185.

117. "Under Workers' Control." *The Economist*, Nov. 9, 2002.

118. In both cases, workers watched the amazing film *The Take* by Avi Lewis and Naomi Klein, on the Argentine occupations. See e.g. freedom-fight.net (click English) for Zrenjanin, or socialismandliberation.org/mag/index.php?aid=629 for the occupation of the TDZ factory in Zagreb.

119. King & Mason, p. 186. Unfortunately the authors give little detail on these experiments, other than that the "result was simply confusion."

120. 4,000 fled, more than 700 homes destroyed. King & Mason, p. 5.

121. John Mueller (2000). "The Banality of 'Ethnic War.'" *International Security*, 25 (1): 42–70.

122. King & Mason, p. 40 and Judah, p. 128.

123. King & Mason, p. 42.

124. King & Mason, p. 143.

125. King & Mason, p. 145.

126. King & Mason, p. 57.

127. Ibid.

128. King & Mason, p. 149.

129. Stella L. Jatras, "'Greater Albania' is no model." Letters, *Washington Times*, Sunday, June 22, 2008.

130. Directed by Klaartje Quirijns. London: Eyes Wide Films, 2005.

131. King & Mason, p. xii.

132. King & Mason, p. 211.

133. Directed by Isa Qosja. Pristina: Kosovo Film, 2005.

134. King & Mason, p. 222–3.

GREECE

135. See www.awalls.org.

136. Orhan Pamuk, *The Black Book* (Fort Washington: Harvest Books, 1996).

137. www.haaretz.com/hasen/spages/1050296.html.

BULGARIA

138. Retort. *Afflicted Powers: Capital and Spectacle in a New Age of War.* (London: Verso, 2005). Chapt. 6.

139. Pogany, p. 31.

140. Ian Hancock, *We are the Romani People*. (Hertfordshire: University of

Hertfordshire Press, 2002).

141. A Romanian anarchist newsletter, including less-than accurate police analysis, is available at: www.alter.most.org.pl/fa/alter-ee/2002/alter-ee%20AACTIV-IST%20NEWSLETTER%202.htm or search for "aactivi-ist newsletter #2".

ALBANIA

142. Stephanie Schwandner-Sievers and Bernd Jurgen Fischer, eds., *Albanian Identities: Myth and History* (Bloomington: Indiana University Press, 2002) p. 103.

143. For more, see Meckfessel, pp. 271–273.

Index

Shon Meckfessel grew up in Sacramento, California. He has resided in and traveled throughout North America, Eastern and Western Europe, and the Middle East. He has spent three years in the Balkans, over eleven different trips (and counting). Previous publications include an essay in *Confronting Capitalism: Dispatches from a Global Movement* (Soft Skull Press, 2004) and a number of articles in literary and political periodicals. He first visited the Balkan peninsula in 1999, and was just feeling at home when NATO began bombing it; upon returning to the US, he found that many who opposed the bombing supported the same nationalist dictatorships that were brutalizing his newfound friends. Attempts to address that situation resulted in *Suffled How It Gush*. He currently resides in Seattle, working as an English as a Second Language instructor, and is pursuing a PhD at the University of Washington in Language and Rhetoric.

SUPPORT AK PRESS!

AK Press is a worker-run collective that publishes and distributes radical books, visual/audio media, and other material. We're small: a dozen people who work long hours for short money, because we believe in what we do. We're anarchists, which is reflected both in the books we publish and the way we organize our business: without bosses.

Currently, we publish about twenty new titles per year. We'd like to publish even more. Whenever our collective meets to discuss future publishing plans, we find ourselves wrestling with a list of hundreds of projects. Unfortunately, money is tight, while the need for our books is greater than ever.

The Friends of AK Press is a direct way you can help. Friends pay a minimum of $25 per month (of course we have no objections to larger sums), for a minimum three month period. The money goes directly into our publishing funds. In return, Friends automatically receive (for the duration of their memberships) one free copy of every new AK Press title as they appear. Friends also get a 20% discount on everything featured in the AK Press Distribution catalog and on our web site—thousands of titles from the hundreds of publishers we work with. We also have a program where groups or individuals can sponsor a whole book. Please contact us for details.

To become a Friend, go to www.akpress.org.